Compliance
and
Your Business

Compliance and Your Business

Frances Martin
(lead writer)
Neill Birss
David Chowdhury
Martin Craig
Jenny Davies
Sarah Johnson
Rebekah Palmer
Fiona Rotherham

Legal contributors

MinterEllisonRuddWatts
LAWYERS

Principal Sponsor

Tailored Financial Solutions

COMPLIANCE AND YOUR BUSINESS

NOTICE OF DISCLAIMER: This publication is intended to provide accurate and adequate information pertaining to the subject matters contained herein within the limitations of the size of this publication. Nevertheless it has been written, edited and published and is made available to all persons and entities strictly on the basis that its authors, editors, contributors and publishers fully exclude any and all liability by any or all of them in any way to any person or entity for damages or losses in respect of or arising out of the use or any reliance in part or full, by such person or entity or by any other person or entity, upon any of the contents of this publication for any purpose.

Published by
Brookers Ltd
Level 1 Guardian Trust House
15 Willeston St
PO Box 43
Wellington

© Brookers Ltd 2004

All rights reserved.
No part of this publication shall be adapted, modified, reproduced, copied, or transmitted in any form or by any means including written, electronic, mechanical, reprographic, photocopying, or recording means.

Furthermore, this publication shall not be stored in whole, part, adapted or modified form, in or for any retrieval system of any nature without the written permission of the copyright owner.

Applications for authorisation of a reserved right of the copyright owner shall be made in writing to the publisher.

WARNING: The doing of any unauthorised act in relation to a copyright work may result in both a civil claim for damages and criminal prosecution.

ISBN 0-86472-465-9

Cover design: Base2, Wellington, New Zealand
Cover photography: Spec Tec Images
Typeset by scopedesign
Printed by Printlink, Wellington, New Zealand

Contents

Foreword		vii
Writers		viii
Legal Contributors		ix
Introduction		xi
CHAPTER 1	Employment	1
CHAPTER 2	Health and Safety	67
CHAPTER 3	Privacy	119
CHAPTER 4	Tax	141
CHAPTER 5	Property	183
CHAPTER 6	Environment	203
CHAPTER 7	Marketing and Sales	231
CHAPTER 8	Corporate Governance	259
CHAPTER 9	Contracts	279
Index		299

Foreword

As a leading commercial law firm, Minter Ellison Rudd Watts has a wealth of experience advising New Zealand businesses on legal compliance. We have enjoyed working with Brookers and the writing team led by Frances Martin in the development of this business-focused resource.

With over 7,000 Acts and Regulations in force in New Zealand, the task of identifying and staying up to date with the law is daunting, especially for small- and medium- sized businesses.

Compliance and your Business has been written specifically for the owners and managers of small- to medium- sized New Zealand businesses to assist them to identify their principal legal obligations and take steps to comply with the law.

Compliance and your Business is a highly practical resource. The law is outlined in plain English and extensively illustrated with case studies. Guidelines, tips, and tools provide a framework for businesses to use in managing their compliance with the law.

We have undertaken a full review of this book to ensure that the content correctly states the law at the date of compilation and are confident that you will find it useful in managing your business.

Robert Falvey
Minter Ellison Rudd Watts

Writers

Frances Martin (Lead Writer)
Frances Martin is a communications consultant who specialises in the areas of business and finance. She has a Bachelor of Business Administration from Victoria University and spent 12 years working as a business reporter/editor. Her former employers include the *National Business Review*, *the Dominion*, and *Dow Jones Newswires*, London. Since 2000 she has worked on a broad range of communications projects for public and private sector clients. She lives in Wellington.

Neill Birss
Neill Birss is a freelance journalist in Christchurch, specialising in business and technology subjects. He was formerly business editor of *The Press*.

David Chowdhury
Dave Chowdhury is an experienced writer and editor with a background in journalism, publishing, and communications. He specialises in researching, writing and editing material for clients in the conservation, resource management, environment, tourism and outdoor recreation fields. He lives in Wellington.

Martin Craig
Martin Craig operates communications and research agency Splash Communications. He was editor of *New Zealand Retail* magazine from 1988 to 2002, and was also contributing editor to the *'Retail Science'* series of retail advice articles now published as *What's in Store* – A practical handbook for retailers.

Jenny Davies
Jenny Davies has worked in radio for 15 years as a reporter, sub-editor and producer, before teaching journalism at Wellington Polytechnic and Massey University. She now works for an internet news service, and as a freelance writer and editor.

Sarah Johnson
Sarah Johnson practised law in New Zealand and the UK before completing a MPhil in publishing at Stirling University, Scotland. She lives in Raglan with her family, working freelance as a writer and editor.

Rebekah Palmer
Rebekah Palmer is a freelance writer and editor based in Wellington. A former print journalist, her first novel was published by Penguin Books in August 2001 and a second is due in 2004.

Fiona Rotherham
Fiona is a mother of three and has been a journalist since 1981, starting off in radio and then switching to business and print journalism in one hit – with stints at *National Business Review*, the *Independent*, and the *New Zealand Herald* before moving on to magazine writing. She gained experience in property covering that round at both *NBR* and the *Independent*.

Legal Contributors

We would like to thank the following people from Minter Ellison Rudd Watts for providing their expertise and ensuring that the information provided is legally correct.

Employment and Health and Safety
Karen Spackman (Partner), Christie Malthus (Solicitor), Anna Moodie (Solicitor), Guido Ballara (Solicitor).

Privacy
Anna Rawlings (Solicitor), Ed McIsaac (Solicitor), Jen Vella (Solicitor).

Tax
Bruce Bernacchi (Partner), Alison Berry (Solicitor) and Amanda Somers (Solicitor).

Property
Jocelyn Martin (Senior Associate), Paul O'Neil (Solicitor).

Environment
Jason Welsh (Senior Associate), Karen Price (Partner), Chris Simmons (Solicitor).

Marketing & Sales
Anna Rawlings (Solicitor), Melanie Tollemache (Senior Associate), Anthony Hosking (Senior Associate).

Corporate Governance
Cathy Quin (Partner), Alisha Uren (Solicitor).

Contracts
Graeme Crombie (Senior Associate), JD Hall (Solicitor), Nick Hodson (Partner).

Overall Review
Robert Falvey (Partner).

Introduction

This book has been designed to assist you, a business owner or manager, to deal with the legal compliance obligations that affect your business.

Compliance and your Business was produced in response to focus group research conducted with small-to-medium sized New Zealand businesses. The research indicated a strong need for a practical guide to assist businesses identify their legal obligations and take steps to comply with the law.

We understand that as a business owner you need to focus as much of your time as possible on developing your business. By using this book to identify and deal with the compliance issues specific to your business, you will be able to spend less time 'cutting through the red tape' and more time on business growth.

Compliance and your Business has nine key topics – Employment, Health and Safety, Privacy, Tax, Property, Environment, Marketing and Sales, Corporate Governance and Contracts. Read each topic for a plain English overview of the law or refer to the practical guidelines, tips and tools when a specific compliance issues arises.

BusinessWise website

In addition to the book you will be able to access the BusinessWise website for additional up-to-date information on the law as it relates to your business.

Website registration

Registering to use the *www.businesswise.co.nz* website is easy. On the inside front cover of this book is a registration code. Enter this code when you first visit the BusinessWise website to receive your free password by email.

Use your BusinessWise website password to access a wealth of up-to-date information and tools. These include:

- self-diagnosis tools – check your compliance 'health' and learn how to take steps to reduce your risk
- news – regular features written to keep you abreast of changes in New Zealand law
- articles, case studies and checklists
- further information on topics covered in the book
- email alerts on significant changes to the law.

We hope that this book and website are useful to you in identifying and addressing your legal obligations and and that it will ultimately contribute to your business success.

Brookers Ltd

EMPLOYMENT

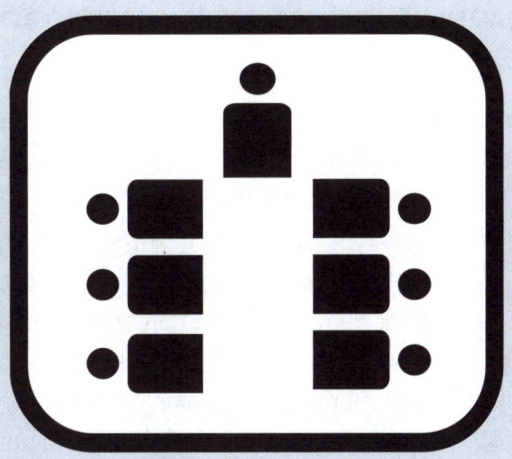

There are two reasons why every employer needs to comply with their employment obligations – and both of them have to do with the financial consequences.

The first is that complying with the principles that underpin employment law – that is treating employees fairly and acting in good faith – usually makes good business sense, and should lead to a stable and productive workplace.

The second is that failure to comply can result in stiff financial penalties as well as claims for damages, compensation, and legal costs from aggrieved employees.

COMPLIANCE AND YOUR BUSINESS

Every employer – big and small – must comply with employment law obligations

Employment law can seem complicated. There are employment agreements, statutes such as the Employment Relations Act 2000 and the Parental Leave and Employment Protection Act 1987, and various decisions of the courts relating to cases against employers.

As an employer, you are expected to know about your employment law obligations, even if you run a small business with only one part-time staff member.

Your first and most obvious obligation is to comply with the employment agreements between you and your employees. Breaching these agreements, like breaching any contract, can result in financial consequences for your business. You can be sued for damages as with an ordinary commercial contract. You can also be ordered to pay a penalty by the Employment Relations Authority or the Employment Court for breaching an employment agreement. These penalties can be up to $5,000 for individuals and $10,000 for companies.

The second main obligation is to comply with the relevant statutes. The most important statute in employment relationships is the Employment Relations Act 2000. This Act sets out the basis for the relationship between you and your employees, and the procedures that apply when things go wrong. There are also various other statutes that apply, such as the Holidays Act 2003, the Parental Leave and Employment Protection Act 1987, the Minimum Wage Act 1983, the Privacy Act 1993, and the Human Rights Act 1993. Other legislation covering health and safety and tax is dealt with in other chapters of this book.

The third main obligation is to comply with the various principles set down by the Court of Appeal, Employment Court, and Employment Relations Authority. In many instances these relate to the processes you must follow to ensure fair and reasonable treatment of your employees.

Complying with your employment obligations can be difficult, but is much easier if you know the basics of the law behind what you are doing and understand the key principles. The information in this chapter will help get you started.

Hiring staff

There are three key statutes you must keep in mind when hiring staff:
- the Employment Relations Act contains rules on negotiating and drafting employment agreements
- the Human Rights Act prohibits discrimination in employment
- the Privacy and Human Rights Acts affect the type of information you can seek from job candidates.

EMPLOYMENT

Advertising for staff

Job advertisements must comply with the Human Rights Act. Generally speaking, it is illegal to discriminate on the grounds of:

- sex (including pregnancy and childbirth)
- marital or family status
- religious or ethical belief (ie. not having a religion)
- colour, race or ethnic or national origins (including nationality or citizenship)
- disability
- age
- political opinion
- employment status
- sexual orientation.

Even using job descriptions like 'office girl', 'tea lady' or 'foreman' can breach the Act.

The Dos and Don'ts of job ads

Here's an example of a job ad that might breach the Human Rights Act and one that wouldn't

	No	Yes
Title	Book Salesman wanted	Book Salesperson wanted
Description	Single man aged 20-30	Must be able to travel away from home for extended periods
Conditions	Must be healthy and Christian	Must be enthusiastic and able to carry heavy boxes

The Act does include some exemptions. For example, you can mention characteristics like age and gender or religion if they are genuinely required for the job.

Job application forms and interviewing

During this process your desire to find out as much as you can about an employee will be limited by the employee's rights under the Human Rights and Privacy Acts. However, the law also gives you rights should you later find out an employee lied about their credentials during the hiring process or omitted important information. It is important that you understand how and when you can use these rights.

To avoid creating an impression that you are seeking information that is discriminatory, take care with the wording of your questions. Keep the questions relevant to the job, and the candidate's ability to do the job. If you need information, such as an employee's age or marital status for a legitimate purpose (eg the EEO policy or the employee superannuation scheme), in most cases you

3

COMPLIANCE AND YOUR BUSINESS

will be able to defer asking these questions until you have actually offered the employee the position.

A brief guide to the Human Rights Act

The Human Rights Act prohibits discrimination on the grounds of:
- sex (including pregnancy)
- marital or family status
- religious or ethical beliefs (not having a religion)
- colour, race or ethnic or national origins (including nationality or citizenship)
- disability
- age
- political opinion
- employment status
- sexual orientation.

It is illegal to discriminate on these grounds:
- when you place a job advertisement
- when you hire a candidate
- in the terms and conditions you offer employees, including the salary you offer
- in the way you treat employees, including providing training and promotion opportunities
- when you are dismissing staff or making them redundant
- by requiring a person to resign or retire.

Exemptions:
Summarised below are some of the exemptions from the Act most relevant to small and medium businesses. In some circumstances, you can discriminate on the grounds of:

How to question candidates
You may:
- Discuss the precise working requirements and whether the applicant can meet them, eg essential weekend work, 3 weeks' holiday to be taken over Christmas (if the company has an annual close-down), and work requiring lifting/being on feet for a long time or wearing protective headgear.
- However, if the applicant has a religious practice that will conflict with the job requirements, you have a duty to reasonably accommodate them.
- Ask whether they are legally entitled to work in New Zealand.
- Ask whether they are able to work overtime or travel frequently for business, but only if these are requirements of the job.
- Ask questions like:
  – This job involves 7 hours of typing a day. Is there anything that might prevent you from being able to do this?
  – Ask for the names of any of their relatives who are already employed by your company.

EMPLOYMENT

- Religion – where religious beliefs require a particular sex or religion for the employment position (eg a priest).
- Sex – for work in another country and to comply with the laws and customs of that country, for the sake of authenticity (for eg if an acting role requires a woman), if there are issues to do with privacy or for counselling, or where sleeping accommodation is provided as part of the job and a person of one gender cannot be reasonably accommodated and so on.
- Disability – if doing the work might put the candidate or others at unreasonable risk of harm.
- Age – an employment agreement may provide for lower wages to be paid to a employee if the employee has not reached a particular age (which must be less than 20 years) or for authenticity or safety reasons.

In some cases, you may also be able to choose not to employ a person if they rely on aids and special services which you can't reasonably be expected to supply. Restrictions can also be imposed if a potential employee is related to or in a relationship with another employee, and one would report to the other or there would be a risk of collusion between the employees that could be detrimental to your business.

Positive measures genuinely taken to help people who frequently face discrimination are not against the law.

Don't ask:
- How old they are or their date of birth. Even for bar work it is more appropriate to say 'legally you need to be over 18 to sell alcohol. Are you over 18?'
- About their:
  - religious denomination
  - religious affiliations
  - church
  - parish
  - pastor
  - the religious holidays that they observe.
- State something like 'This is a Catholic organisation' or 'This is a Jewish organisation' unless an exemption applies.
- Ask about their:
  - complexion
  - skin colour
  - accent
  - lineage
  - ancestry
  - national origin
  - descent
  - parentage
  - nationality
  - nationality of family, eg parents or spouse
  - first language.
- Ask questions like:
  - Are you married?
  - Where does your spouse work?
  - What was your maiden name?
  - What is your father's surname?

COMPLIANCE AND YOUR BUSINESS

Preferential treatment is also allowed for women who are pregnant or people who have responsibilities to care for children or relatives.

Penalties for breaching the Act

These depend on the circumstances but can include damages and pecuniary loss. Damages can range from hundreds, to tens of thousands of dollars.

Sexual or racial harassment

It is against the law for your employees to be subjected to sexual or racial harassment. This requirement applies to:

- You personally. For example, you can't use racial slurs or suggest sexual activity to an employee, implying they'll get preferential or detrimental treatment depending on how they respond.
- You as the employer. You can be liable if you don't protect an employee from repeated or serious harassment from other employees or clients. You need to take appropriate and timely action if complaints of sexual or racial harassment are raised.

- Ask questions like:
    - Do you have children?
    - How old are your children?
    - Are you planning on having any (more) children?
    - Are you pregnant? (Even if it is obvious that she is).
- Ask questions like:
    - Do you have a disability?
    - Have you ever been treated for any diseases?
- Ask about their political affiliations.
- Ask questions about:
    - The applicant's birthplace; or
    - The birthplace of the applicant's parents, spouse, or other relatives.
- Ask questions like:
    - Are you a New Zealand citizen?
    - Where were you born?
    - Do you intend to apply for citizenship?
- Ask questions about the names, addresses, ages, number, or any other information concerning the applicant's children or other relatives not employed by the organisation.
- Ask what clubs, societies, lodges, or associations the applicant belongs to.

EMPLOYMENT

> ## Case study
>
> ### The dangers of discrimination
>
> A 41-year-old man applied for a job as a trainee manager at the Courtenay Place Race Place, an agency of the TAB, through the New Zealand Employment Service. The Employment Service officer handling the vacancy rang the Race Place while the man was present. He only heard part of the conversation, but it was clear he wouldn't be offered an interview after a question was asked about his age. The man complained to the Human Rights Commission, alleging discrimination on the grounds of age. The Race Place claimed it had wanted to employ someone who could be paid youth rates and that this was the reason for not interviewing him. The Tribunal hearing the case found that youth rates hadn't even been discussed prior to the complaint being raised. The Tribunal upheld the complaint. It ordered Race Place to pay $3,000, and the TAB to pay $2,000 in damages because it was also defined as an employer under the Act. The TAB appealed to the High Court, arguing that it did not have any control over the Race Place's breach. The High Court sent the matter back to the Tribunal for further consideration. It is unclear whether this means the TAB's damages have been overturned or reduced. However, the High Court confirmed that the damages awarded against the Race Place were reasonable.

Privacy issues in hiring

The Privacy Act 1993 contains important rules about the way you can collect and use information about job candidates. This is covered in more detail in the chapter on privacy, but below is a brief summary of what you must do to comply:

- Only collect relevant information, check its accuracy, and store it securely.
- Gather all information about the candidate from the candidate directly, unless he or she agrees to you approaching someone else.
- Get the candidate's written permission before you conduct pre-employment reference checks.
- If asked, you must give the candidate access to any personal information you hold about them and allow them to correct any mistakes. Evaluative material confidentially supplied by referees need not be passed on.

Employers can't use information gathered during a job application for purposes other than those connected with the employment of that person. You are also obliged to eventually destroy information that's not needed. But it's worth keeping records on unsuccessful applicants for at least a year. Those records will be essential to defend any allegations of discrimination levelled against you.

COMPLIANCE AND YOUR BUSINESS

Making a job offer

Don't simply ring the candidate and tell them they've got the job. If you do this, and they accept the offer, a verbal employment agreement has been created and your employment relationship will commence. If you later try to withdraw the offer, (eg because you and your new employee can't agree on a salary), the employee can raise a personal grievance claim against you over their 'dismissal'.

A safer approach is to ring the candidate and say you will be offering them the job, and they will receive that offer in writing. If the candidate is interested, you can then send a written offer, along with a proposed employment agreement that explains all the terms and conditions of their employment.

Misrepresentation

In some circumstances you may have the right to fire a staff member who lied or supplied incorrect information when they were being hired. Employers have this right under the Contractual Remedies Act 1979. That Act says that if you make it known that the existence of certain information is essential to you choosing to employ a certain person and you later find that the employee had misrepresented that information, the agreement can be cancelled in some circumstances. This is also the case if the information substantially reduces the benefit you otherwise would have received out of the employment relationship (eg the employee says they have extensive experience in a certain area, but they actually have none).

Job applicants do not need to provide information unless you ask for it. You cannot usually dismiss an employee simply because you think that he or she should have told you something that you failed to ask him or her about.

You may be able to increase your level of protection by asking applicants to sign a declaration such as: 'I declare that all information I have provided (employer's name) is accurate, complete, and correct, and I have not provided any false information or omitted any information which would affect the decision to employ me.'

Normally you are not entitled to require an employee to provide information that is not relevant. The Employment Court has ruled that an employee who failed to disclose that she had cancer was not guilty of misrepresentation, despite a pre-employment form asking if she had any medical problems. The Court held that the question was too wide and its relevance to her job wasn't clear.

You can include such a declaration in the job application form or the employment agreement.

EMPLOYMENT

Case study
Dismissing someone for misrepresentation

An organisation dismissed its recently appointed chief executive after finding that he'd omitted negative events in his employment history from his CV. These events included involvement in a company failure. When the matter went to the Employment Tribunal (the predecessor to the Employment Relations Authority), the Tribunal agreed with the employer. It held that the former chief executive was justifiably dismissed. He had falsely represented himself by not mentioning the company failure, even though he knew such an experience was contrary to the 'proven track record' the organisation had sought. He had also signed a declaration that he had omitted nothing of relevance about his work record.

A quick guide to the Employment Relations Act 2000

The Employment Relations Act gives employees and employers a number of rights and obligations and regulates a number of different aspects of the employment relationship. These include:

- a definition of who is an employee and who the Act applies to
- a duty for employees, employers, and unions to treat each other in good faith
- freedom to join or refrain from joining a union
- provision for the registration and operation of unions and their right to represent members
- rules setting out the purposes for which unions may access the workplace and the procedure they need to follow in doing so

Types of employment

It is important to be clear about whether someone working for you is employed on a permanent or non-permanent basis and whether they are an employee or an independent contractor. This will have an impact on the employee's rights and your obligations under the Employment Relations Act and other employment legislation. It will also have implications with regard to income tax, goods and services tax, wages protection law, leave, and vicarious liability (your legal responsibility for damage done by people working for you).

Classifying employees as permanent, part-time, casual, or contractors is not as simple as you might think. In deciding what type of relationship exists, the Employment Relations Authority and Employment Court will look at the real nature of the relationship between the parties.

COMPLIANCE AND YOUR BUSINESS

- rules relating to the role of good faith in collective bargaining and how the collective bargaining process should be conducted
- a requirement to have a written employment agreement for all employees and the terms that must be included in collective agreements and individual employment agreements
- rules relating to bargaining for an individual employment agreement
- the rules governing employment relations education leave and how and when this can be taken
- obligations on both employers and employees in respect of strikes and lockouts, including defining what types of strike or lockout are legal and special provision for essential services
- the right for employees to take a personal grievance claim for unjustified dismissal, unjustified disadvantage, discrimination, duress relating to union membership or sexual or racial harassment and the time limit (90 days) for raising a grievance
- the remedies which are available for a successful grievance
- the right for both employees and employers to have disputes decided under the Act

That means even if you employ someone as a casual employee and have a signed agreement calling them a casual, the Courts can still decide the employment is permanent if the person has been working regularly, even with varied days and hours, for some time.

Casual employees

Casual employees are those who are employed on an irregular basis with no expectation of ongoing work by either party. An example could be a person who comes in to relieve when the receptionist is sick. However, if a person is being given regular shifts, has an expectation of ongoing work, or if you have an expectation of ongoing availability, then they are not normally truly casual.

If an employee's work is to be casual, make sure you explain that to him or her to avoid misunderstandings. It should be written clearly in the employment agreement. Don't promise, verbally or in writing, ongoing work. Of course, if you cannot offer as much work as the employee needs then they might find something more regular. If you have regular ongoing needs, you might be better to employ a permanent part-timer.

Remember, like all other employees, casual employees have a right to be treated fairly.

Casual employees have entitlements to holiday pay. See *Leave* page 31. For your obligations to deduct tax see the *Tax* chapter, page 141.

- the right for employees to take arrears of wage claims if they have believe they have not received their contractual entitlements
- provision for penalties to be given for breaches of the Act
- the way in which the employment institutions (Department of Labour provided mediation services, Employment Relations Authority and Employment Court) are made up and operate and the provisions which govern appeals to the Court of Appeal
- the powers and functions of Labour Inspectors under the Act.

Fixed-term employees

You can hire employees on fixed-term agreements. This allows you to end their employment either on a specific date or when a particular event occurs (eg when a project finishes). To do this you must have genuine reasons based on reasonable grounds for specifying a fixed term. These may be replacing another employee who is on extended leave, tiding the business through a short-term busy time, or completing a specific project. Both you and the employee must agree, preferably in writing, on how, why, and when the employment will end and you must inform the employee of the reasons for the fixed term (this is often done in the employment agreement).

Be aware that if your reasons for fixing the term of employment aren't valid, the employee might be able to bring a case for unjustified dismissal. Two reasons the Employment Relations Authority and Employment Court won't consider valid grounds for a fixed term agreement are:

- to limit the employee's legal rights
- to test the suitability of an employee for permanent work

COMPLIANCE AND YOUR BUSINESS

Seasonal employees

If you employ seasonal employees it can be useful to class them as 'fixed-term employees'. This is because:

- Seasons can vary in duration depending on the climate and other factors. It may be better to employ fruit pickers as fixed-term employees, who you employ as and when picking conditions dictate.
- Seasons recur, so the term 'seasonal employment' might raise expectations of recurring employment. Again, 'fixed-term employment' may be a better term. Ensure that there are no express or implied guarantees of further work given.

Remember: you don't have a free hand to sack an unsatisfactory employee at the end of a probationary period.

Probationary periods

If you want an employee to begin work on a probationary period you must specify this in writing at the time they are hired. But be aware that inserting a probationary period doesn't give you a free hand to dismiss an unsatisfactory employee during or at the end the probationary period. Employees on probationary periods still have the right to be treated fairly. This means that if you want to dismiss them because they are not performing, you need to follow a similar process as you would for a permanent employee. This includes informing the employee of the standards required and where their performance is lacking, providing extra training or support, and allowing the employee a reasonable time to improve.

Apprentice employees

The Modern Apprenticeship Training Act 2000 specifies that apprentices' training agreements are to be treated as part of the employment agreement. Before you take on an apprentice you should:

Once signed, an Apprenticeship Training Agreement is enforceable under the Employment Relations Act. By signing it you commit yourself to providing training.

- Contact the Education and Training Support Agency and Industry Training Organisation that look after apprentices in your industry. These organisations need to be satisfied that you can train the apprentice to industry standards.
- Don't enter any arrangement with the apprentice until it has been cleared by the Education and Training Support Agency. Once cleared, you can negotiate an employment agreement. This can include conditions to reflect the apprentice's status.
- The employment agreement must have an Apprenticeship Training Agreement attached (contact your industry's Education and Training Support Agency or Industry Training Organisation to find out how to get these agreements). The apprenticeship agreement must be signed by the employer and apprentice, and a copy must be sent to the Agency.

EMPLOYMENT

> **Case study**
>
> **Casual and permanent staff**
>
> Barnes signed an employment contact explicitly stating she was a casual employee. Initially she worked 'as and when' needed. But after 6 months she was rostered on regular days and hours, and had to let the boss know if she couldn't work.
>
> Seven months after starting work she was told a restructuring meant her services were no longer required. However, a few weeks later she discovered someone else had been hired and was working the hours she used to work.
>
> The Employment Court ruled that Barnes' 'casual' employment ended when the roster was introduced and she was required to get leave approved when unable to work. The Court said she had become a permanent part-time employee and her dismissal was unjustified.

Contractors

Independent contractors are not employees and therefore the Employment Relations Act, including personal grievance rights, does not apply to them. However, a person's status as a contractor must be backed up by the facts. If there is a dispute over whether someone is an independent contractor or an employee, the Employment Court or Employment Relations Authority will look at the real nature of your relationship with the person to determine the matter. If this relationship looks like employment, the Court or Authority might decide the person is actually an employee. This can happen even if you have a written agreement stating that the person is a contractor. If the person is an employee, you could be liable for PAYE, leave entitlements etc, as well as an action for unjustified dismissal if you have dismissed the person.

To minimise the risk that someone you consider to be a contractor is later found to be an employee:

- Look at how much control you have over the person. To what extent can they decide the number of hours they work or how the work is done? The less control you have, the more likely they are to be properly classified as a contractor.
- Look at whether the person runs their own business. Do they use their own equipment or hire their own helpers? Do they bear some financial risk for the work or stand to make a profit if it is done well? If a person runs their own business and provides services to you as part of this, they are more likely to be a contractor.

COMPLIANCE AND YOUR BUSINESS

- Look at whether the employee is their own person. Do they bear costs incurred in the job or carry the risk if the customer doesn't pay? Do they send invoices, pay GST and take full responsibility for ACC levies? If they do these things it is more likely that they are a contractor.

Other things the Court or Authority will look at is whether the person takes care of their own tax obligations and how they are paid – for example whether they submit an invoice or just get paid like all the other employees.

Part-time work

Make sure the employment agreement recognises that the employment is part-time. The document could be headed up 'Part-time individual employment agreement'. When providing for holidays, salary etc, you should ensure that the part-time nature of the work is taken into account.

Even more care must be taken with collective agreements. Unless these specifically allow for part-time work you can end up having to pay a part-time employee a full-time wage. To protect against this:

- Make sure the collective agreement includes a specific provision that allows weekly payment (including wages and allowances) to be paid on a proportional or hourly basis for part-timers.
- If your collective agreement doesn't include this provision, you need to get the employee's written agreement to make a deduction from their weekly wage/allowances. This deduction would reduce their payments to take account of the fact they are working part-time.
- Make sure that all leave entitlements, compensation for redundancy, bonus payments etc, can be pro-rated for part-time employees.

Employment agreements

Employment agreements set out the terms and conditions that govern the employment relationship between the employer and employee. The Employment Relations Act prescribes key information that must be included in all employment agreements. It also sets out rules for negotiating these agreements.

There are two types of agreements – individual employment agreements and collective agreements.

Individual employment agreements

An individual employment agreement is between one employer and one employee. To comply with the Act, an individual employment agreement must:

- be in writing
- include the names of the employee and employer
- include a description of the work to be done by the employee

- give an indication of the location where the work will be performed
- give an indication of the employee's hours of work
- specify the wage or salary
- contain a plain language explanation of how employment disputes will be resolved, including a reference to the 90-day time limit for raising personal grievance claims.

The agreement can include any other terms and conditions negotiated by the employee and employer. But it can't contain anything contrary to the law (eg, holidays and leave provisions must comply with legislative minimums).

Before entering into an individual employment agreement, you must provide a copy of the intended agreement to the employee. You must also advise them that they are entitled to seek independent advice on the terms of the agreement, and give them reasonable opportunity to seek that advice. Sometimes, the easiest way to do this is by including a note in the cover letter or a declaration at the end of the agreement that the employee can sign. If you don't follow these requirements, you can be ordered to pay a penalty by the Employment Relations Authority.

Collective agreements

A collective agreement is one that binds:

- one or more unions
- one or more employers
- two or more employees.

Collective agreements can only be negotiated between a union (or unions) and an employer or group of employers; not groups of employees on their own.

Collective agreements must contain a coverage clause that specifies what classes of employees the agreement covers. If there is a collective agreement in place, any employee who is a member of that union and whose work is covered by the coverage clause is automatically bound by the collective agreement.

As well as a coverage clause, a collective agreement must:

- be in writing and be signed by each union and employer who is a party to the agreement
- include a clause dealing with the rights and obligations of the employees and employer should any of their work be contracted out or the business (or part of it) sold.
- contain a plain language explanation of how employment disputes will be resolved, including a reference to the 90-day time limit for raising a personal grievance claim.
- outline a process for varying the agreement
- state the date the agreement expires or what events will cause it to expire.

After 1 April 2004, all employment agreements, including existing employment agreements, will also have to include a clause stating the employee's right to be paid at one and a half times their normal rate if they work on a public holiday. This is required by the Holidays Act 2003.

A copy of the collective agreement must be delivered to the Department of Labour as soon as practicable after it has been ratified by the employees (when an agreement has been reached between the union and the employer, a certain percentage of employees must vote in favour of the agreement before it will bind all of the employees covered). An employee covered by a collective agreement can negotiate other terms and conditions to apply to them individually, so long as those terms and conditions are not inconsistent with the collective agreement.

Collective agreements and new employees

If the work a new employee is to do is covered by a collective agreement, you must tell the employee that:

- a collective agreement exists and covers the work they will do
- they can join the union, and how to contact the union
- if they join the union they will be bound by the collective agreement
- during the first 30 days of their employment the collective agreement's terms and conditions will apply along with any other terms and conditions the employee agrees with the employer on an individual basis (as long as they aren't inconsistent with the collective agreement).

You must also give the employee a copy of the collective agreement, and if the employee agrees, tell the union that he or she has been employed.

Don't try to unduly influence the employee about whether to join the union, or put any form of pressure on them. However, you should ask the employee to inform you if they decide to join the union. If the employee does join they will be bound by the collective agreement from that date.

After the 30-day period has passed, if the employee has not joined the union then the employer and the employee can agree to vary the terms of the individual employment agreement.

Fair bargaining and individual employment agreements

Both collective agreements and individual employment agreements need to be bargained for in good faith. Employees can challenge an individual employment agreement and seek compensation (or a variation to or cancellation of the agreement) on the grounds it was bargained for unfairly. Under the Employment Relations Act the grounds for claiming unfair bargaining cover a range of circumstances, including:

- one party wasn't able to understand the agreement properly because of 'diminished capacity', eg their age, sickness, disability, or emotional distress
- one party relied on what the other party told them when they signed the agreement
- one party was forced to sign the agreement because they were oppressed, unduly influenced, or under duress

- the employee wasn't given the opportunity to get independent advice.

However, these only apply if the other party was aware of, or ought to have been aware of, the circumstances.

Fair bargaining and collective agreements

Usually, bargaining for collective agreements will be initiated by the union, although it can be initiated by the employer. There are certain restrictions on when bargaining can be initiated. Once a union approaches you to start bargaining, you are obliged to:

- try as soon as possible to set up a process for the bargaining
- meet with the union from time to time for the purposes of bargaining
- consider and respond to proposals from the union
- recognise the authority of any person appointed to represent the employees
- refrain from doing anything likely to undermine the bargaining
- provide information that is reasonably necessary for bargaining, when requested
- refrain from bargaining, directly or indirectly, with the union's members.

This last obligation limits the communication you can have with your staff about the bargaining process. Several companies have got into difficulty by trying to put their own interpretation on the union's approach to the bargaining talks. If you must communicate with your staff about the collective agreement bargaining process, stick to an update on the process, and don't discuss terms at all. One option is to put out an agreed statement with the union. The union is likely to want to communicate with its own members separately. That is the union's role, and the employer has no authority to vet what the union might say, unless it breaches the law. A recent attempt by an insurance company to take a union to court about its communications to members was substantially unsuccessful.

The Act also contains provisions on how the parties should go about requesting information from the other party during bargaining, and what process should be followed if the information is confidential or commercially sensitive.

The duty of good faith does not necessarily require you to reach agreement with the union. The Act recognises that even where good faith is present, negotiations may reach a stalemate. However, you must comply with the provisions of the Act, consider the claims made by the union and follow the processes in the Code of Good Faith. This Code may be downloaded from the Employment Relations Service website at *www.ers.dol.govt.nz/act/code.html*.

Both parties involved in collective bargaining must act in good faith.

If bargaining reaches an impasse – strikes or lockouts

The Employment Relations Act provides that strikes and lockouts are lawful in certain circumstances. Strikes and lockouts are sometimes used to place pressure on the other side if negotiations break down.

COMPLIANCE AND YOUR BUSINESS

It's a good idea to seek professional advice before suspending any staff because you may potentially be liable for unpaid wages.

In most cases, a strike or lockout must relate to collective bargaining and can only occur at least 40 days after bargaining has commenced. (Strikes and lockouts are also allowed on health and safety grounds and there are some limited exceptions to the 40-day rule.) In certain industries classified as 'essential', there must be 14 days' notice of a strike, but in most cases notice of strike action is not necessary.

Strikes or lockouts which take place while a collective agreement is in force, which relate to a dispute or personal grievance or which are about how employment agreements are interpreted, are illegal.

If your employees strike, you can suspend them until the strike has ended. Striking employees are not entitled to be paid for the period of suspension. You are also allowed to suspend non-striking employees if, as a result of the strike, you cannot provide them with work. When suspending any employees during a strike, you must tell them what provision of the Employment Relations Act you are relying on.

Some tips for preparing employment agreements

- When filling in the employer's name, be sure to use your company's full legal name, not your name or the trading name.
- One simple way to describe the employee's work is to attach a job description to the agreement. But as job descriptions can be incomplete and tend to date, it is prudent to add a sentence to the job description stating that the employee will carry out any other tasks the employer reasonably instructs him or her to perform, eg: 'Your primary duties are set out in the attached job description, but you may also be required to perform other functions from time to time.'
- For examples on how to describe the way employment relationship problems will be resolved see the Employment Relations Service website at *www.ers.dol.govt.nz.*
- You are not required by law to pay compensation for redundancy or even to mention it in individual employment agreements. However, it is prudent to set out whether or not there is any provision for redundancy compensation and, if so, what this is.
- If allowances are paid, spell out whether the value of these allowances changes if the employee does overtime. Ensure that all figures (eg salary and allowances) state whether they are gross or net.
- You may wish to incorporate your company policies and procedures (as amended by you from time to time) into your employment agreement.
- It is prudent to include a provision which allows the employer to terminate the agreement without notice in cases of serious misconduct and which allows the employer to suspend the employee in certain circumstances.

EMPLOYMENT

Check list for employment agreements

By law, individual employment agreements must:
- be in writing
- name the employer and employee
- describe the work to be done
- give an indication of the location where the employee will do the work
- state the wage or salary
- give an indication of the hours of work, or describe shift-work arrangements
- include a plain language description of how employment relationship problems will be resolved, including reference to the 90-day time limit for raising a personal grievance.

By law, collective agreements must:
- say what classes of employee are covered by the agreement
- outline employees' and employers' rights and obligations if the work is contracted out or the business sold
- include a plain language description of services to resolve employment relationship problems and refer to the 90-day time limit for raising a personal grievance
- include a clause outlining how the agreement can be varied
- say when the agreement expires (this can be a date or event).

Key points to cover in an employment agreement

The checklist above covers many of the key issues that you may want to include in an employment agreement. By law, you must include certain matters. However, you can add in other clauses as a way of clarifying the standards of behaviour you expect from an employee. The existence of these optional clauses, and their wording, can become important should you have to defend a personal grievance claim. However, remember that once something is in an employment agreement it can only be changed with the agreement of both parties. You may want to have company policy in a separate document that you can change as you wish and ensure that the employee agrees to comply with all company policies (as amended at your discretion from time to time).

COMPLIANCE AND YOUR BUSINESS

After 1 April 2004, all employment agreements, including existing employment agreements, will also have to include a clause stating the employee's right to be paid at one and a half times their normal rate if they work on a public holiday. This is required by the Holidays Act 2003.

> **Minimum clauses for individual employment agreements**
>
> **Employee:** *(insert name)*
>
> **Employer:** *(insert full company name, not your name or your company's trading name)*
>
> **Location:** The employee shall work at *(state location)* ie, employer's premises in Wellington.
>
> **Description of work:** This clause might state that the duties to be carried out by the employee are as set out in a position description attached to the agreement. The clause might also state that the duties, reporting relationships, or other matters covered in the position description may, from time to time, be altered by the employer following consultation with the employee.
>
> **Hours of work:** This clause should state the employee's normal hours of work – for eg: 'The normal hours of work are 40 hours per week, from 8:30am to 5pm, Monday to Friday.' It can be useful to include a description of break times – for eg: 'The employee is entitled to a half hour unpaid break for lunch and two paid breaks of 15 minutes each for morning and afternoon tea each day.' It may also be useful to spell out any overtime requirements. For eg, if overtime isn't paid the agreement might say: 'From time to time the employee may be required to work additional hours. The employee's salary shall be deemed to include compensation for all hours worked in excess of these hours.' Alternatively, the clause might spell out when overtime will be paid, at what rate and whether paid overtime must be pre-approved.
>
> **Salary:** This clause should state the salary or wage as a gross amount paid each week/fortnight/month/year, for eg 'the employee's salary is $20,000 gross per annum'. It should say when and how the money will be paid – for eg paid in arrears into the employee's bank account by direct credit each fortnight.
>
> **Fixed-term arrangements (if applicable):** If the employment is for a fixed term the agreement should state the start and expiry dates. It should also state the reason for the employment being on a fixed-term basis. This must be a genuine reason based on reasonable grounds, eg to replace an employee on parental leave or to perform a specific project.
>
> It can be useful to emphasise the temporary nature of the employment by including a statement along the lines of: 'Nothing in this Agreement shall be interpreted or understood to give to the employee any expectation that this agreement will be renewed, or that any subsequent agreement will be entered into. No assurance or arrangement for any renewal or subsequent agreement shall bind either party unless such assurance or arrangement is in writing and signed by both parties.'

Below is an explanation of dispute resolution procedures

Explanation of dispute resolution procedures

Here is a suggested clause you can use to explain the disputes process: 'We can save time and help preserve our working relationship by solving our own problems as far as possible. The following are suggestions for what you might do if you think there is a problem, and what help is available:

1. Clarify what the problem is from your point of view. Make sure there really is a problem. Check your facts and make sure you have not assumed or misunderstood something.

   You might discuss the apparent problem with family, friends, or advisers, and find out what the law is and/or what our employment agreement says. You can:
   - contact the Employment Relations Infoline by calling toll-free on 0800 800 863; or visiting the website at *www.ers.dol.govt.nz*.
   - get pamphlets or fact sheets from offices of the Employment Relations Service.
   - talk to your union, a lawyer, a community law office, or an industrial relations consultant.

2. Talk to us. We should discuss the problem, either directly or through our representatives. You may bring an advisor, a friend, relative, colleague, lawyer, or other representative to support you at the discussion. We should make sure that we discuss the facts so that we can clear up any assumptions or misunderstandings.

3. If we have not resolved the problem by talking to each other, one or both of us can do some or all of the following:
   - contact the Employment Relations Infoline, which may provide information and/or refer us to mediation
   - participate in mediation provided by the Employment Relations Service (or we can agree to get our own mediator)
   - if we reach agreement, a mediator provided by the Employment Relations Service can sign the agreed settlement, and that will bind us
   - if mediation does not resolve the problem, either or both of us can take the problem to the Employment Relations Authority for investigation
   - the Employment Relations Authority may direct us to mediation if it thinks that will still be useful
   - the Employment Relations Authority can investigate our employment relationship problem and make a determination
   - if one or both of us is/are dissatisfied with the determination of the Employment Relations Authority, we can take the problem to the Employment Court for a judicial hearing (the Court may also tell us to go back and have more mediation).

COMPLIANCE AND YOUR BUSINESS

4 If the problem is a personal grievance, you must raise it with us within 90 days after the action complained of, or the date on which you became aware of it (unless there are exceptional circumstances). A personal grievance is where you consider that you have been unjustifiably dismissed, unjustifiably disadvantaged in your employment, unlawfully discriminated against, sexually or racially harassed, or subjected to duress regarding union membership or non-membership. If the problem is about minimum entitlements under the law, you may ask a Labour Inspector to enforce your rights under minimum rights legislation, such as the Minimum Wage Act 1983 or the Holidays Act 2003. (NB: Prior to 1 April 2004, the Holidays Act 1981 will still be relevant.)

Below is a checklist for optional (but recommended) clauses for individual employment agreements

Deductions from salary: You may want to insert a clause that gives you the right to make deductions from wages. This clause would enable deductions to be made for unauthorised absence from work, absence due to sickness or injury when the employee is not entitled to any payment, or for authorised unpaid leave of absence. The clause should state that the deduction will be made in the relevant or subsequent pay period.

Company policies: It can be useful to insert a clause on compliance with company policies and procedures. The clause should state that policies and procedures, which can be amended at the company's discretion, form part of the terms and conditions of employment, and that the employee agrees to abide by them. Inserting this clause gives you flexibility to change the policies and procedures in a way that you cannot change your employment agreement. It also means your employee, or his or her union representative, has signed to say that they are aware of the policies and procedures, and will comply with them.

Annual leave: This clause should state the number of weeks' annual holiday allowed on completion of each 12-month period of continuous employment. It should say that these holidays will be allowed and paid in accordance with the Holidays Act, and are to be taken within 12 months of falling due, at a time to be agreed upon.

Closedown: If relevant, a clause can be inserted to say that the company observes a customary closedown of a certain number of days or weeks over a period like Christmas. It should say that the balance of an employee's annual leave entitlement may be taken at a time to be agreed upon. Closedowns are allowed under the Holidays Act.

Statutory holidays: This clause should state that statutory holidays will be allowed and paid in accordance with the Holidays Act. It should say that the following days are treated as statutory holidays on pay, where they fall on days that would otherwise be working days: New Year's Day, the day after New Years Day, Anniversary Day, Waitangi Day, Good Friday, Easter Monday, ANZAC Day, Queen's Birthday, Labour Day, Christmas Day, and Boxing Day.

If you run a seven-day operation the clause should state that the following days are treated as statutory holidays on pay, where they fall on days that would otherwise be working days: New Year's Day, the Day After New Years Day, Anniversary Day, Waitangi Day, Good Friday, Easter Monday, ANZAC Day, Queen's Birthday, Labour Day, Christmas Day, and Boxing Day.

The clause might go on to say that if an employee is rostered to work on a statutory holiday, they agree to attend work. If they work on a statutory holiday, an alternative paid holiday will be given on a date agreed by the employee and employer. If the employer and employee can't agree on an alternative day, it is the employee's choice (with certain conditions). From 1 April 2004, employers must pay employees at least time-and-a-half rate if they work on a statutory holiday. The Holidays Act 2003 requires employment agreements to state this right.

Sick and bereavement leave: This clause might state any provisions for sick and bereavement leave. For example, that on completion of 6 months' continuous service the employee is entitled to a certain amount of leave for sickness, bereavement, or to look after a sick relative. Any leave offered under this clause must be in accordance with the Holidays Act.

Parental leave: This clause should state that parental leave shall be allowed in accordance with the Parental Leave and Employment Protection Act 1987.

Jury service: This clause should state what happens when an employee is obliged to undertake jury service. For eg it might clarify that the difference between any fees (excluding reimbursements) paid by the court and the employee's ordinary rate of pay will be made up by the employer, for up to a maximum (say, 5 days) for any period of jury service. The clause might also include conditions before this top-up applies, such as requiring the employee to provide not less than 2 weeks' notice that they are required for jury selection. Employees might also be required to produce a court expenses voucher and to return to work immediately any day or part day that they are not required to serve on a jury.

Termination: This clause might state that the agreement may be terminated by either party giving a set period of notice (usually in writing). It may also spell out that wages can be paid out in lieu of notice, or that wages can be deducted if an employee does not give the required notice. Employers might also want to state that they can terminate the agreement without notice, for serious misconduct.

COMPLIANCE AND YOUR BUSINESS

> **Redundancy:** This clause might state that the employee's employment can be terminated if the position becomes superfluous to the needs of organisation. It should state the notice period required for redundancy, and if there is any entitlement to a redundancy payment. If there is no redundancy payment, this should be spelt out.
>
> **Technical redundancy:** This clause should state that where an employee ceases to work for the employer because all or part of the business has been sold, merged, or transferred, and the employee has been offered similar work and conditions by the new owner, they will not be entitled to any redundancy payment.
>
> **Confidentiality:** This clause should say that as part of normal duties the employee may have access to confidential information about the organisation, but that under no circumstances may the employee use this information, except for purposes directly related to the objectives of the organisation. The clause should state that the employee cannot, either during or after their employment, use or disclose any confidential information about the business or its clients, except where required to by law or where they have the company's written agreement. The clause can state that a breach of confidentiality while they are employed will be deemed serious misconduct, which may result in summary dismissal.

Restraint of trade

Restraint of trade clauses are sometimes included in individual employment agreements to protect company interests following the departure of a key employee. The courts will only enforce these clauses to the extent that they are reasonable. Restraint clauses are likely to be more robust if they:

- Say the former employee can't use your trade secrets, rather than saying they can't use the skills developed while working for you.
- Give you adequate, but no more than adequate protection. If the clause harms the employee more than you, it isn't likely to survive a legal challenge.
- Last only a reasonable time. What's reasonable will depend on the circumstances. But restraints of one year are viewed as being at the upper end of what's acceptable.
- Make a payment to the employee in consideration of the restraint or place the employee on 'garden leave'.
- Cover a reasonable geographical area. Preventing the employee from working in their trade in a large city (or throughout the country) might be viewed as too restrictive.

EMPLOYMENT

Internet and email

If your employees are being provided with internet and email access it is prudent to have a policy in place governing how these tools should be used. This can be spelt out in the employment agreement, or you can use a separate internet/email policy that the employee should agree to abide by.

Email/internet policies should specify:

- that email is the employer's property
- that email and internet are business tools, and there are limits on private use
- that the employer can, and might, access employees' emails, even deleted messages, at any time and for any reason
- the consequences of breaching the policy, including serious consequences like dismissal without notice
- rules for downloading material that could compromise the computer system – including software and attachments that might contain viruses
- rules for downloading other material – including a prohibition on pornography
- guidelines for sending emails, including avoiding inappropriate language
- guidelines for employee conduct including rules relating to email harassment and bullying.

Having a policy can strengthen your case should you decide to discipline or dismiss an employee who abuses the internet or email. It allows you to monitor employees' emails without running into problems with the Privacy Act.

Make sure you have a system for educating new employees about internet and email use.

Conflict of interest

You may want to include a clause in your employment agreements, or have a policy, about work done for other employers or organisations. This could state that employees are not permitted to work for any direct competitors or in any situation where a conflict of interest is likely to arise. Any employee wanting to carry out work where a potential conflict of interest may arise should seek written permission from the employer. You may also wish to ask employees to declare any other work they perform or business interests they have.

Alcohol and drug testing

New Zealand does not yet have a clear legal position on workplace drug testing. The courts have not yet issued rulings that clearly define the limits of any right to test, though in late 2003 the Employment Court was hearing a case involving a move by Air New Zealand to randomly test employees. In Canada, the Human Rights Commission has drafted a policy which requires that the testing be relevant to the job, and be conducted in good faith.

In essence, the Canadian policy allows:

- random alcohol testing where safety is an issue

25

- drug or alcohol testing where the employer can show they have reasonable cause to assume an employee has consumed drugs or alcohol
- drug or alcohol testing after an accident
- disclosure of present or past drug use in safety-sensitive positions
- random testing of an individual as part of a programme after an individual has disclosed a problem.

Union rights

The Employment Relations Act upholds the right to freedom of association, which includes the right of employees to form themselves into unions. It recognises that there is an inherent inequality in the relationship between employers and employees. It also encourages collective bargaining, which can only be carried out by unions.

For this reason, the Act sets out some union rights. There are also obligations on unions, which, among other things, need to be registered. Unions must operate democratically, and must also operate at arm's length from, and independently from, employers.

While unions are normally involved in collective bargaining and in personal grievance cases, they are entitled to represent their members on anything which relates to their members' employment interests.

Right of access

Representatives of unions are entitled to enter your workplace for purposes related to the employment of their members, including:

- to conduct union business
- to seek to recruit employees
- to explain about the union to members or potential members
- to deal with matters relating to individual employment agreements
- to bargain for collective agreements
- to monitor and seek compliance with employment agreements and other requirements
- on issues of health and safety
- on issues of statutory union rights such as employment-related education leave (see *Leave* section of this chapter at page 40)
- to advocate for or support an individual with a problem or grievance.

Union representatives must behave in a reasonable way when visiting your workplace. They must:

- introduce themselves and explain the purpose of their visit
- produce identification, and verify that they represent the union
- enter the workplace at a reasonable time during any period when any employee is employed to work

EMPLOYMENT

- not unduly disrupt business operations
- comply with legitimate health, safety or security requirements
- either have union members on site, or be from a union whose membership rule covers the employees on the site.

An employer is liable for a penalty of up to $5,000 for an individual or $10,000 for a company if he or she either refuses access or obstructs union access to the workplace.

Union meetings

Union members are entitled to attend two two-hour paid union meetings per year.

The union is required to give 14 days' notice of a meeting. After the meeting the union must supply you with a list of those who attended, so that they can be paid. The union must also tell you how long the meeting lasted.

The union is obliged to make arrangements with you to make sure normal business is maintained as far as possible during the meeting, and to ensure normal work resumes as soon as possible after the meeting. If the meeting lasts longer than 2 hours, this time need not be paid.

Union education

Unions have the right to allocate paid leave for union members, based on a formula relating to the size of your workforce. For more details on this, see the *Leave* section of this chapter at page 40.

Wages

The Wages Protection Act 1983 applies to all employees. Essentially, it states that the entire wage must be paid in cash (unless otherwise agreed), and spells out the circumstances under which deductions can be made. The definition of 'wages' includes holiday pay, allowances, lump sum bonuses, and redundancy compensation payments.

How to pay

Under the Wages Protection Act, you must pay wages in cash unless you have the employee's written consent to pay by some other means, for eg by:

- direct credit
- cheque
- money order.

Who to pay

You need an employee's written authority to pay their wages to someone else. If a employee dies, their wages are paid to the estate. However, you shouldn't release the final pay, until you have authorisation from the person legally responsible for the estate, such as a lawyer or the executor of the will.

Remember: the law imposes a duty of good faith, and includes an onus on employers, employees, and unions not to do anything likely to deceive or mislead.

Include the method and frequency of paying wages in the employment agreement.

When to pay

The employment agreement should specify whether payment is weekly, fortnightly, monthly, or some other period. If the payment date falls on a statutory holiday, it must be advanced, generally on the last working day before the holiday. Unless a striking employee has been suspended, the fact an employee is on strike doesn't negate an employer's obligation to pay any wages owing on the due date unless the employee is suspended.

Deductions from wages

Under the Wages Protection Act the only deductions you can make from wages are:

- deductions the employee has agreed to in the employment agreement
- deductions the employee has agreed to in writing, for eg social club fees or union fees
- deductions allowed by law, such as income tax, child support, ACC levies
- deductions authorised by the courts, for eg unpaid fines.

Recovery of overpaid wages

The Wages Protection Act allows you to recover wages that have been overpaid due to absences, strikes, lockouts, or suspensions. To be entitled to clawback wages, the payment method you use (for eg direct credit payments) must have made it impractical to avoid the overpayment.

You must tell the employee you plan to recover the money. This must be done on the first day the employee attends at the workplace, of if the employee has not returned to the workplace, within 10 days of the payday following the overpayment. The money must be recovered within 2 months of you notifying them. You have two options for recovering the money:

- using one or several deductions from the employee's future wages
- using the method spelt out in the employee's employment agreement.

If an employee is absent for a period where wages have been paid in advance, you are only entitled to deduct money from subsequent pays to cover the absence:

- with the employee's written permission; or
- if this is allowed under the employment agreement.

Sometimes employers want to deduct money from an employee's final pay to cover things like goods purchased through the company or tools that haven't been returned. To do this you must have the employee's consent.

Pay slips and unclaimed wages

There is no legal requirement to issue pay slips. However, you are required to keep records that show the method of calculating wages. Employees or their representatives must be allowed to see a copy of these records. Employees are legally entitled to claim wages at any time in the 6 years following the due date for payment.

Wage and time records

The Employment Relations Act requires you to keep the following information, which can be kept as one or more source documents:

- employee's name, postal address, and age if under 20
- the kind of work done and whether they are on an individual or collective agreement
- the actual hours between which the employee is employed each day, if needed to calculate wages
- wages paid and calculation method for each pay period
- details of any employment relations education leave.

If the employee is on a collective agreement you must have the title of the agreement, its expiry date, and the employee's classification.

The record must be kept for 6 years, for the purpose of claiming wage arrears, and for 7 years for tax purposes.

Individuals can be ordered to pay a penalty of up to $5,000 for failing to keep these records, and companies up to $10,000. Also, if you don't have these records and an employee takes a claim for unpaid wages to the Authority, it can choose to accept the employee's claim unless you have evidence to defend the claim. You can also be compelled to recreate missing records. If you don't produce them within a set time period, you can be ordered to pay a penalty.

Wage and time records can be inspected by:

- Labour Department inspectors
- Income tax inspectors
- the employee, or the employee's representative.

Recovery of wages

Claims for unpaid wages and unauthorised deductions can be made up to 6 years after the date the wages were due or the deduction was made. Unpaid wages can include things like allowances, bonuses, or leave payments. The Employment Relations Authority or Employment Court can order you to repay money owed due to an underpayment of wages or unauthorised deductions. Interest can be added to the money owed. However, action for the recovery of a penalty can only be taken against you within a year of the underpayment.

The arrears will be calculated either by comparing what was paid with:

- entitlements spelt out in the employment agreement
- entitlements contained in the Minimum Wage Act.

You can't protect yourself from a claim for unpaid wages by getting an employee to sign something saying they accept the underpayment.

COMPLIANCE AND YOUR BUSINESS

Minimum wages

The Minimum Wage Act 1983 sets minimum wage rates for adults and young adults.

The current rates as at January 2004 are:

Age	Per hour gross	Per day gross	Per 40-hour week gross
16 to 17 years	$6.80	$54.40	$272.00
18 and older	$8.50	$68.00	$340.00

Under the Minimum Wage Act every employment agreement must set the maximum number of hours worked each week at 40, preferably spread over not more than 5 days, unless the parties agree otherwise. There is no statutory obligation to pay overtime to someone who has worked more than 40 hours in one week, unless this is a condition of their employment agreement (ie, if they are being paid hourly or if the agreement provides for overtime payments).

The Minimum Wage Act allows for permits to be issued to some employees allowing them to be paid less than the minimum wage. These permits are issued if a employee is incapable of earning the minimum wage because, for eg they are disabled. The permits must be issued by a Labour Inspector and are granted for a set time.

Be aware that if payment is based on a system of piecework, the earnings may not be less than would equate with the minimum wage under the Minimum Wage Act 1983.

Penalties for breaching the Minimum Wage Act are imposed by the Employment Relations Authority or Employment Court and depend on the circumstances. At the higher end one employer said to be running a 'sweatshop' was ordered to pay $49,500 for various breaches to several employment laws, including the Minimum Wages Act. Another employer was ordered to pay $100 for underpaying an employee by $14.

Holidays and other leave

As an employer you have to obey laws in relation to minimum leave entitlements, and you cannot reach an agreement with your employees to contract out of this. The statutory requirements are a minimum, and employment agreements will sometimes provide for more leave. For example, an extra week's leave after a certain length of service is common. More generous sick leave provisions are also usual.

The laws relating to leave have recently changed and the Holidays Act 1981, which is quite complicated, is being replaced with the Holidays Act 2003 from 1 April 2004. The following pages take the changes into account.

There are nine different types of statutory leave. These are:
- annual holidays
- public holidays (often called statutory holidays)
- sick leave
- bereavement leave
- parental leave
- leave for health and safety representatives training
- employment relations education leave
- leave for defence force volunteers
- voting leave.

Annual leave

Annual leave is covered by the Holidays Act 2003, which replaces the Holidays Act 1981 from 1 April 2004. The core entitlement for employees is currently 3 weeks' annual leave on pay after each year's continuous service. However, this will be increased to 4 weeks from 1 April 2007 by the Holidays Act 2003. Employees will become entitled to the 4 weeks leave 12 months after 1 April 2007 (ie the leave accrues after a further 12 months of continuous service).

An employee must be allowed to take at least 2 uninterrupted weeks' leave if the employee wishes to do so. You must also allow an employee to take the remaining leave within 12 months after the date on which the employee becomes entitled to the leave.

The Holidays Act 2003 states that the decision as to when the employee takes annual leave is to be agreed between the employer and employee. If an employee requests the employer's consent to take annual leave, it must not be unreasonably withheld. If you and the employee are unable to agree on a time for leave to be taken, you may determine this. You must give the employee at least 14 days' notice of the date on which the leave is to commence (prior to 1 April 2004, the requirement was for 7 days' notice).

In most cases, the law requires that annual leave actually be taken as paid time off work. You cannot pay the money out instead, except in limited circumstances or for leave owing on termination of employment. It is also important from a health and safety perspective that you ensure that your employees take the leave that they are entitled to. In most cases, holiday pay must be paid at the time that annual leave is taken, rather than as a loading on to salary or on a 'pay as you go' basis.

Casual employees, or employees on a fixed-term agreement for less than a year, may agree that their holiday pay due on termination can be paid in advance as part of their wages. Any agreement with such employees should be very clear. It should state that holiday pay is being paid in addition to the payment for work, and should also state that the employee will have no further entitlement to holiday pay on termination or upon taking leave. Under the Holidays Act 2003, 'pay as you go' holiday pay must be paid as an identifiable component of the employee's pay.

COMPLIANCE AND YOUR BUSINESS

You should always seek some advice about 'pay as you go' arrangements before implementing them. Such arrangements have proven to be difficult and can lead to you having to pay twice unless the arrangement complies with the law.

Your obligation to allow annual leave to be taken continues until it is actually taken. In practice, that means that leave can accrue from year to year. For that reason, you need to keep a close eye on your leave obligations to ensure that leave balances do not build up. You should write to each employee to remind him or her that the leave is required to be taken by the appropriate date. If there is no step by the employee to take the leave, you should require that it be taken, after consulting about the dates.

Sickness or bereavement during annual leave

Until 1 April 2004, the Holidays Act 1981 (currently in force) technically prevents employees taking annual leave when they are sick, even if they have run out of sick leave. However, in practice, employers often allow this to happen.

From 1 April 2004, the Holidays Act 2003 allows annual leave to be taken when an employee is sick, or suffering a bereavement so long as the employer agrees to the annual leave being used in this way. It also allows employers to agree to allow employees to take sick leave if they get ill or are injured while they're on annual leave.

From 1 April 2004 an employer must allow an employee to take bereavement leave if they are on leave at the time of the bereavement.

Calculating what is due – employees who have worked more than a year

During annual leave the employee is entitled to be paid the greater of his/her ordinary weekly pay as at the beginning of the annual leave and average weekly earnings that were earned during the 12 months immediately before the end of the last pay period before the employee takes his/her annual leave. The term 'average weekly earnings' means 1/52 of the employee's gross earnings for the previous 12 months. The gross earnings figure must include any payments that you're required to make under the employment agreement, including salary or wages, allowances, payment for leave taken (annual, sick and bereavement leave and public holidays), productivity or incentive-based payments, overtime, the value of non-cash earnings, and first week compensation paid if the employee was off work with a work-related injury. It excludes payments not covered by the employment agreement, such as reimbursement for employment-related expenses, discretionary payments, weekly compensation under ACC.

Where you've agreed that unpaid leave counts towards the employee's 12 months of continuous employment, any whole weeks (or part weeks that add up to more than 1 week) of unpaid leave taken must be subtracted from the divisor of 52 used to calculate 'average weekly earnings'. For example, if the employee was on unpaid sick leave for three weeks, the divisor is 49.

After calculating the 'average weekly earnings' figure you then need to work out the employee's current 'ordinary weekly pay', that is, the amount of pay that the employee receives under his/her employment agreement for an ordinary working week.

You must then pay the higher of the 'average weekly earnings' and 'ordinary weekly pay' figures as the weekly payment for the annual leave.

If an employee leaves after a year and a bit and has not yet taken any annual leave, you must pay the employee the amount due as annual leave for the completed year and 6% of gross earnings earned in respect of the part of the second year. From 1 April 2007, this will increase to 8%.

Employees employed for less than a year

If there is a customary closedown for your business, any employee who you have employed for less than a year is entitled to 6% of the total gross earnings up to that date (this will increase to 8% from 1 April 2007), less any amount paid in advance for annual leave or any amount paid on a 'pay as you go' basis. The employee's 12 months of continuous employment (required to qualify for annual leave) then starts from the day closedown began. If you agree however, your employee may 'anticipate' leave on the expectation that they will accrue it soon after the closedown.

The Holidays Act 2003 got rid of the previous differences in holiday pay for employees whose period of employment was for less than 3 weeks. Anyone who leaves your employment before they qualify for annual leave must be given 6% of their gross earnings since they began working for you, minus any amount you've paid them for annual leave taken in advance or on a 'pay as you go' basis. This will increase to 8% from 1 April 2007.

'Gross earnings' includes any payments that you're required to make under the employment agreement, including salary or wages, allowances, productivity or incentive-based payments, overtime, the value of non-cash earnings, and first week compensation paid if the employee was off work with a work-related injury. It excludes payments not covered by the employment agreement, such as reimbursement for employment-related expenses and discretionary payments.

Public holidays

In New Zealand, the public or statutory holidays are set out in the Holidays Act and are taken in addition to annual leave. They are:

- Christmas Day
- Boxing Day
- New Years Day
- 2 January
- Waitangi Day
- Good Friday
- Easter Monday
- Anzac Day
- Queen's Birthday
- Labour Day
- Anniversary Day for the relevant province

COMPLIANCE AND YOUR BUSINESS

Your employees are entitled to a holiday on at least their relevant daily pay on each of these days, if they fall on a day which would normally be a working day for the employee (although special rules apply to four of those days, namely Christmas Day, Boxing Day, and the New Years holidays – those holiday days are transferred to the following Monday if they fall on a weekend, or if both fall on a weekend, Monday and Tuesday). However, this does not entitle an employee to take more than 4 days holiday.

If the holiday does not fall on a day that would otherwise be a working day for the employee, you do not need to pay the employee for it. For example, an employee who works Wednesday to Friday need not be paid for a statutory holiday that falls on a Monday.

If an employee works on a statutory holiday then they are entitled to take another full day off on pay in lieu of the holiday, as well as being paid for the time worked. The payment for the time worked is currently whatever is provided for in the employment agreement. From 1 April 2004, you must pay employees who work on a statutory holiday at lest one and a half times their relevant rate. Their employment agreement must state their right to this.

If an employee is on call on a public holiday, and that day would otherwise have been a working day for the employee, he or she will be entitled to a day in lieu if he or she is called by the employer or their representative to work that day or, is not called in to work but the nature of the restriction imposed by being on call is such that his or her freedom of action meant the employee didn't have a whole day holiday.

Under the Holidays Act 2003, the rules for Waitangi Day and Anzac Day have been made the same as for the other statutory holidays.

Other important matters you need to remember about the law relating to public holidays are:

- Unless the employment agreement specifies otherwise, you cannot require an employee to work on a public holiday.
- Even if an employee volunteers to work on a public holiday, the day in lieu obligation remains. Remember, however, that the day in lieu obligation only arises if the employee works on a day that would otherwise be a working day.
- Days in lieu accumulate until taken. However, an employer may require an employee to take an alternative holiday on a date determined by the employer if 12 months have past, the employee and employer can't agree and the employer gives 14 days' notice.
- Even if only an hour or two are worked, a full day in lieu must still be allowed.
- If one or more public holidays fall within a period of annual leave, that day is taken as a public holiday rather than a day of annual leave. This will also include days paid out as annual leave at the end of the employee's employment. For example, if an employee ends their employment on 22 December, and has 10 days annual leave owing, you will need to pay the employee for 14 days (10 days annual leave and 4 public holidays).

Sick and bereavement leave

When an employee has completed 6 months' continuous service with the employer, he or she is entitled to 5 days of paid sick leave per year from then on. Sick leave can be taken:

- if the employee is sick or injured
- if the employee's spouse is sick or injured
- if a dependent of the employee is sick.

As from 1 April 2004, sick leave can be accumlated if it it not used. The Holidays Act 2003 allows employees to carry over up to 15 days of unused sick leave to a maximum of 20 days' current entitlement in any year.

After 6 months' continuous service, employees also qualify for bereavement leave. Under the Holidays Act 2003 (which applies from 1 April 2004), employees are allowed up to 3 days of bereavement leave on the death of their spouse, parent, child, sibling, grandparent, grandchild, or their spouse's parent. They are also allowed 1 day of bereavement leave where you accept, in good faith, that they've suffered a bereavement. Relevant factors for determining if a bereavement has been suffered include the closeness of association between the employee and deceased person, whether the employee has helped arrange the ceremony or any cultural responsibilities.

Other important points about sick or bereavement leave are:

- Wherever practicable, the employee must notify you of their wish to take sick or bereavement leave before they were due to start work, and in any case as early as possible.
- Sick or bereavement leave is paid at the relevant daily pay, ie what they would have been paid if they had worked on that day.
- No sick or bereavement leave is payable if the employee is being paid by ACC, but an employee absent because of injury who is not receiving ACC can claim sick leave. In the first week after an accident, when ACC compensation or other compensation for wages is not usually payable, an employee will often claim sick leave.
- An employee who has run out of sick or bereavement leave may ask if they can use annual leave.
- You are entitled to ask an employee to provide proof of sickness or injury, eg a medical certificate, if the sickness or injury lasts for 3 or more consecutive days (whether or not those days would normally be working days for the employee).

Recent changes to holiday legislation

The Holidays Act 2003 replaces the Holidays Act 1981 on 1 April 2004, introducing major changes to holidays legislation.

The main changes include:

- Separate day in lieu arrangements for Waitangi Day and Anzac Day have gone, meaning those holidays are treated in the same way as other public holidays.

- Employees have separate sick leave and bereavement leave entitlements. Sick leave remains at 5 days a year, but unused sick leave can accumulate to a maximum of 20 days. Employers can require proof of sickness (such as a medical certificate) if an employee is sick or injured for 3 or more days in a row.
- Employees are entitled to bereavement leave of 3 days for a close relative, and one day for other bereavements.
- Those employees who have used up their sick or bereavement entitlements are able to use annual leave.

Another major change is that employees will be entitled to 4 weeks annual leave after a year's service, instead of 3 weeks. In order to give employers time to plan for this change, it does not become law until 1 April 2007.

The Department of Labour will publish a leaflet about leave changes, and will post any changes on its website, *www.dol.govt.nz*.

Parental leave

The Parental Leave and Employment Protection Act 1987 deals mainly with your employees' right to take unpaid leave from their jobs when they are having a baby or adopting a baby under 5 years old.

The Act also contains the various rules that protect the rights of employees during pregnancy and after parental leave is completed.

Employees whose employment agreement provisions compare favourably overall with the Act can choose to be covered by their agreement or the Act. That choice is only lawful if the employment agreement has effective arrangements dealing with:

- who can take parental leave
- how long the various types of leave last
- how well the employee's job is protected during and after parental leave
- whether or not the leave is paid
- what procedures employees must follow.

For more information see the brochure 'Parental Leave', published by the Employment Relations Service. This is available on the internet at *www.ers.dol.govt.nz*.

There are some parts of the Act which apply regardless of what is in the employment agreement (such as the protection against dismissal because of pregnancy or because an employee is taking parental leave, and access to complaints procedures).

In practice, most New Zealand employment agreements simply refer to the Act, and the Act forms the basis of the employees' rights and your obligations.

Employers do not have to pay for parental leave. The Act was amended in 2002 to allow the Government to pay for up to 12 weeks of parental leave, at a maximum rate of $334.75 before tax (this rate changes annually depending on the Consumer Price Index). Some employers include paid parental leave provisions in their employment agreements.

To be eligible for statutory parental leave (paid or unpaid), an employee must have worked for you for an average of 10 hours per week for 12 months before the expected date of birth or date of adoption. The 12-month period applies again after returning to work from parental leave – that is, no further parental leave may be taken until another 12 months has elapsed.

There are four types of parental leave (the paid portion of parental leave is usually taken as maternity and/or extended leave):

- **Special leave** – a pregnant employee can have up to 10 days' unpaid leave before maternity leave begins, for reasons connected with pregnancy.
- **Maternity leave** – female employees may have up to 14 continuous weeks of unpaid maternity leave. This can commence up to 6 weeks before the expected date of birth or adoption. Leave may begin sooner on medical advice. In addition, if by reason of the pregnancy, your employee is (a) unable to continue to work without endangering herself and others or (b) is incapable of performing her work adequately and there is no other work available, you can require that the employee commence maternity leave early.
- **Paternity leave** – a male partner can have up to 2 continuous weeks' unpaid leave around the time of the birth or adoption. The leave may be taken within the period 3 weeks before and 3 weeks after the expected date of confinement or adoption.
- **Extended leave** – a total period of unpaid leave of 52 weeks (less any maternity leave, but not paternity leave, taken) is available to the parents after the birth or adoption. That leave may be shared by the parents, but the total taken by both parents may not be more than 52 weeks.

The following example is given in the Employment Relations Service publication, 'Parental Leave', of how parental leave may be shared between partners:

Julie may take 14 weeks' maternity leave and then 26 weeks extended leave. Her partner Jason could have 2 weeks' paternity leave when the baby is born. Jason could then take the remaining 12 weeks' extended leave while Julie returns to work.

Some other options for a woman and her spouse/partner sharing leave are:

- the mother takes 14 weeks' maternity leave and 38 weeks' extended leave (totalling 52 weeks)
- both parents take 26 weeks leave together (totalling 52 weeks)
- both parents take a total of 52 weeks between them, either separately or partly separately and partly together.

As an employer you are obliged to allow employees to take the parental leave (provided they are eligible, ie have worked an average of 10 hours per week for the past 12 months).

An employee is not eligible for parental leave unless they apply for it under the terms of the legislation. However, if you have a pregnant employee, an employee whose spouse/partner is pregnant, or an employee intending to adopt a child, you

COMPLIANCE AND YOUR BUSINESS

may want to be proactive about discussing their leave intentions, as many employees are not aware of what they need to do under the Act. You may receive a letter like this one from your employee, which comes from the Parental Leave brochure:

> Dear Employer
>
> I wish to inform you that I want to take parental leave.
>
> I attach a medical certificate saying when my baby is due.
>
> I wish to take leave between [date] and [date] as extended leave.
>
> My partner [name] is also seeking leave from his job at [   ]. He will take 2 weeks' paternity leave when the baby is born and extended leave between [date] and [date].
>
> The total leave we are applying for is no more than 52 weeks, including paternity leave.
>
> Yours faithfully
>
> Employee

You then have 7 days to respond to ask for any required information that the employee has not given. Any such extra information must be provided by the employee within 14 days.

You must reply to the substantive application within 21 days of receiving it. Your response must be in the form required by the Act. You will find the appropriate form in the Parental Leave brochure which may be obtained online at www.ers.dol.govt.nz.

Reasons for refusing parental leave include: the employee's service is less than the required 12 months, the employee has returned to work for less than 12 months after a previous period of parental leave, or the employee has a position that is classified as a 'key position' and a temporary replacement is not suitable. This last circumstance does not mean the employee is not entitled to leave, rather, that their job cannot be held open. The onus is on the employer to prove that a position is a 'key' position and that a temporary replacement is not practicable. In practice, very few jobs are considered key positions under the Act. If the position cannot be kept open (eg if the employee is a key employee and a temporary replacement is not suitable) you must inform the employee of this, and tell them that your decision may be disputed and that, for a period of 26 weeks after their leave ends, they will have preference for any substantially similar vacancy.

Your reply must also state what the employee's rights are in relation to parental leave, including the right to end it early or extend it in some circumstances.

There is a presumption that if the parental leave is less than 4 weeks, the employee's position can be kept open. That is, you must re-employ the employee unless there is a genuine redundancy in the meantime.

For periods of leave greater than 4 weeks, there is also a presumption that the position can be kept open unless you can show that a temporary replacement is not reasonably practicable because the position is a key position (or there is a genuine redundancy in the meantime).

If the position is to be kept open you must give notice in the prescribed form within 21 days of the leave commencing, including what date the leave will end and at what date the employee will be obliged to give 21 days' notice of their return.

If the position is not to be kept open, you must give notice in the prescribed form, including the date on which the leave will end and the dates for the preferential rehiring.

Generally speaking it is not easy for an employer to escape the obligation to re-employ by asserting that the employee filled a key position. The courts tend to lean in favour of employees.

Case study

Who is a key employee?

Ms Topia, an office assistant for Unitech, applied for 6 months' parental leave. Her employer advised her that her position could not be held open. The company told the Employment Relations Authority that it had a small clerical staff carrying out a wide range of duties and her absence would place a burden on the remaining staff. Replacing her for 6 months would not be justified because of the training needed. The Authority found however that it was not a key position, and training a replacement would be necessary whether or not Ms Topia returned to her employment. It also stated that a person could perform the duties adequately while under training and found that sufficient efforts were not made to ascertain whether the position could be filled by a temporary employee (especially as the employer was based in Auckland, a city with a large population base). The Authority commented that the company has lost sight of the fact that parental leave was a right rather than a privilege.

Unitech was ordered to keep the position open.

Other important points to remember about parental leave are:
- You should not pay out holiday pay to employees when they go on parental leave, as you would when an employee is leaving. However, employees may elect to use up any remaining annual leave before going on parental leave – so their first few weeks off are annual leave on full pay. If the employee has superannuation obligations they may be required to continue paying those while on leave, depending on the scheme.

- Any parental leave does not break continuity of service, but is treated as continuous service upon resumption of employment.
- There is no entitlement to payment for public holidays during parental leave except during the first fortnight.
- You may, but are not obliged to, agree to convert a full-time employee to a part-time or temporary part-time employee upon their return from parental leave (although you are likely to be required to agree to any small variation in duties eg leaving 15 minutes early and taking a short lunch break to pick up a child).
- If an employee fails, without good cause, to return to work at the conclusion of the parental leave period, their employment terminates. Similarly, an employee who fails to take up a 'preference' position is deemed to have had their employment terminated.

Remember that an employee may make a complaint if you breach your obligations under the Parental Leave and Employment Protection Act. Generally speaking, the complaint will go to mediation and then, if not settled, to the Employment Relations Authority.

Employment relations education leave

Union members have the right to take employment relations education leave under the Employment Relations Act 2000. The union has the right to allocate this leave to 'eligible employees' (ie union members bound by or bargaining for a collective agreement in your workplace).

The number of days that a union is entitled to allocate depends on the number of full-time equivalent eligible employees you employ. If you employ between one and five eligible employees, 3 days a year are available to be allocated by the union. If you employ between six and 50 eligible employees, 5 days are available for the union to allocate to employees. Larger enterprises will be liable to provide a greater number of days.

You are obliged to pay employees who take this leave. Payment is calculated in the same way as 'relevant daily' pay in the Holidays Act 2003.

Leave for Defence Force volunteers

An employee who undertakes:
- full time voluntary training in the armed forces for periods of up to 3 months
- part time voluntary training in the armed forced for periods of up to 3 weeks in any training year (ie 1 April to 31 March each year)

is entitled to have their job protected.

Under the Volunteers Employment Protection Act 1973 there is no obligation to pay wages for this type of leave, but service-related benefits are not affected by the leave. Service is deemed to be continuous when an employee takes this type of leave.

Voting leave

You must allow an employee to take time off work on pay to cast their vote in a General Election if they have not had a reasonable opportunity to vote before commencing work. The employee can leave work no later than 3pm and is not required to return to work for the rest of the day. You must pay the employee for the period that they are absent, up to 2 hours.

Jury leave

Jury service is compulsory, and in most cases you will be required to grant unpaid leave if an employee is called up for jury service. There are exemptions. Most of these relate to the personal circumstances of employee – family commitments, health concerns, recent or onerous previous jury service. However, your employee can be exempted for work reasons if the nature of their occupation, or pressing commitments related to their occupation, may cause undue hardship or serious inconvenience.

There is no legal obligation to pay for jury service. However, the fee paid by the court to jurors is minimal and many employment agreements include a commitment to pay the difference between ordinary wages and the jury service fee (to a maximum number of days).

Discipline and dismissal

Although discipline and dismissal are dealt with under the same section in this chapter, remember that disciplining an employee is not necessarily a step on the way to dismissal. Dismissal is a relatively rare event, and it has serious consequences for the employee. Because of this, the Employment Relations Authority and Employment Court closely scrutinise any cases about dismissal that come before them, to make sure that the employer has acted fairly and in good faith. This doesn't just mean following a process that looks 'fair', it means genuinely treating the employee fairly, so that he or she is given a reasonable opportunity to improve their performance, or explain an allegation of misconduct.

The Authority and Court will look at how you actually treated an employee when disciplining and dismissing them. An employer who follows a textbook process, but who intends to dismiss an employee from the start is likely to have predetermined the matter and therefore acted unfairly. Adopting a fair mindset can be difficult, but it is your legal obligation as an employer.

If you act unfairly, you risk a successful personal grievance claim being taken against you. You could be ordered to reinstate the employee, or to pay them lost wages and/or compensation. You could also be liable for a portion of their legal costs in bringing the claim. In addition, the case can give you bad publicity, will be expensive to defend, will take time, and may negatively influence your reputation with other staff or in the market.

It is important to remember that the Employment Relations Authority and the Employment Court will look, not just at whether you had a good reason to sack an employee, but at the way you did it. This process is where many employers are held to have acted unlawfully – they follow a process that is later held to be unfair to the employee.

Getting the process right can be time consuming and even costly. But it is unlikely to be as expensive as having to defend a personal grievance case and having an award made against you (or the employee reinstated!).

It must be fair

In judging whether a dismissal is justified, the Court and Authority considers a number of matters including:

- did you have a good reason to dismiss or discipline the employee?
- was the decision to dismiss or discipline made in a fair manner?
- did you comply with your obligations under the employment agreement?
- was the act of dismissal or providing a warning or caution carried out in a fair way?

Personal grievances

Employees can raise personal grievance claims for the following reasons:
- unjustified dismissal
- unjustified action of the employer which affects the employee's employment to their disadvantage
- discrimination on the grounds set out in the Human Rights Act or because of involvement in a union
- duress – related to involvement or non-involvement in a union
- sexual or racial harassment.

The claims are investigated by the Employment Relations Authority, whose determination can be challenged in the Employment Court and, in some cases, appealed to the Court of Appeal.

Getting the process right

No legislation spells out the process you should use to dismiss or discipline a staff member. However, the Employment Relations Authority and Employment Court have said a lot about what they consider to be fair process in their decisions on dismissal and warning cases. What is a fair process will depend on the individual circumstances of each case. In most cases, the Authority or Court will be deciding whether your actions would have been open to a reasonable employer in those circumstances.

The most common problems that may lead to dismissal are:

- failure to perform
- misconduct
- serious misconduct
- unauthorised absence.

Remedies for personal grievance claims

The Employment Relations Act sets out a range of remedies for successful personal grievance claims. These are:

- reinstatement – this is the primary remedy the Authority or Court will consider
- reimbursement of all or some of the wages or other money lost
- compensation for loss of a benefit (monetary or non-monetary)
- compensation for humiliation, loss of dignity, and injury to feelings – awards of $5,000 are common, though they can run as high as $35,000.
- awards often include an amount to cover a contribution towards the employee's legal costs
- in cases of sexual or racial harassment, the Authority or Court can make recommendations to the employer to prevent similar incidents in future.

Failure to perform

If one of your staff is not performing, you cannot just sack them. You have an obligation to manage their performance. First, you must tell the employee they aren't performing to the expected standards and give them an opportunity to improve. In doing this, you must be very clear as to what the expected standards are, how they are not being currently reached, and what needs to be done to reach them. You should try to set measurable targets. In many cases, employees do improve.

But, if the employee fails to improve within a reasonable time despite getting additional training and guidance, you can take further action.

COMPLIANCE AND YOUR BUSINESS

It is important that you do not begin performance management with dismissal as the inevitable endpoint. You must approach each step in this process fairly and with an open mind.

A performance management process can take several months, but, depending on the employee's position and the effect of their performance on the viability of your business, it can be truncated – for eg if an accounts person keeps making mistakes like double-paying your suppliers.

Performance management – how to meet the legal requirement to be fair

Here are some guidelines to help you develop a fair procedure for managing an employee whose performance is not meeting your expectations. However, it is important to note that these guidelines are general in nature and may not apply to your specific situation.

If you are unsure about how to manage an employee's performance, get professional advice on the process to follow.

1. Before you do anything else, double check that the employee really understands what is required of them in the job, and that they've had all the necessary training. Check the employment agreement. Did it include a full job description or performance agreement? Many employment problems result from a communication breakdown, and can be overcome with goodwill. Make sure you have some written record that all of the necessary training was done. The Authority and Court are likely to take a dim view of any employer who sacks someone for poor performance without first checking that the employee was adequately trained for the job.

2. Set up a performance review meeting with the employee. Give the employee advance warning of this meeting – at least a day's notice - and briefly outline what it is about. Say something like: 'I've got concerns about how you are performing in the job and I want to talk them through with you.' Let them know that they are entitled to bring a support person or representative with them.

    At the meeting tell the employee that their performance is not meeting the expected standards and that improvement is required. The employee must be given specific details of how and why they are not meeting the required standards. Don't make vague statements like 'you've got a bad attitude'. Instead talk about how this attitude is manifesting itself – for example say: 'You are not courteous to customers' or 'you don't communicate well with other staff'.

    Give the employee an opportunity to explain why they haven't been able to meet your expectations. Listen to what they say and discuss ways of solving the problems. It might be necessary to go away and investigate the issues they've raised. Try to reach agreement with the employee on a plan to help them improve, (eg by giving more training or mentoring), and get the employee to sign it. This training doesn't have to be expensive. It can be as simple as sitting with the receptionist showing them how to answer the phone in a pleasant and polite manner.

Take notes about what's been discussed during the meeting and get the employee to sign these too. At the end of the meeting, summarise your expectations, the timeframe for improvement, and the consequences if the employee doesn't improve – which might include some disciplinary action such as issuing a written warning.

Give the employee their own copy of the improvement plan within 2 days of the meeting. Put the plan into action and hold regular, say weekly, meetings with the employee to review progress. At these meetings you must clearly tell the employee if they are still falling below standard and why. You must listen to their explanations, and if possible act on them. Take notes and get the employee to sign them.

Options for disciplining employees

These include:
- placing a note on their employment file – the comments contained in this note might be taken into account when deciding bonuses or pay rises
- demotion
- verbal or written warnings
- dismissal.

3. If an employee fails to improve after a reasonable period of time, you can consider a more formal performance management process. Again, you will need to commence this process by meeting with the employee (and their support person or representative). Briefly tell them the meeting is about their performance. But don't tell them they are going to get a warning or write a warning letter beforehand. You are required to go into the meeting with an open mind and to consider what the employee says. Stating the outcome before the meeting even starts is a clear sign you don't have an open mind and this could be used against you during a personal grievance claim.

When the meeting begins, outline the steps that have been taken to date to improve the employee's performance and specify how they are still falling short of expectations. Explain that you are considering more formal disciplinary action in respect of their performance, but would like to hear their comments before you make a decision. Listen to the employee's explanation. However, if you don't think the explanation is genuine, say so. Take time to consider what the employee has said. This may involve adjourning the meeting until later that day or the next day. If you consider that the circumstances warrant it, you may wish to issue a warning, preferably in writing.

When you write the letter make sure it actually contains a warning. This warning would be that unless the employee's performance improves to an expected level within a specified timeframe you will take further action (for example further warnings or dismissal). Give the warning letter to the employee. The warning needs to be explicit. It should describe how an employee has failed to meet the required standard, what has been done to date to help them, that improvements are required, what these improvements are, how those improvements will be measured, and the consequences or possible consequences of not improving.

Case study

The importance of giving employees a fair hearing

Trotter, a senior manager for Telecom, was demoted by a new supervisor and given 2 months to improve his performance. At the time the supervisor said she didn't think Trotter could do his job adequately. Two months later he was sacked. Trotter gave his supervisor a report about his situation a day before he was dismissed. But the decision to dismiss wasn't revisited in light of his report. The Employment Court said Telecom had never fairly tested Trotter's abilities, so had no reasonable basis for concluding that he should be dismissed for poor performance. Among other things, the Court said Trotter was not given specific reasons for Telecom's dissatisfaction with his performance. The company did not specify reasonably specific and measurable improvements required of Trotter. He was not given a reasonable time to establish whether he was able to improve and his previous good record was not taken into account. His dismissal was considered to be unjustified, and he was awarded $200,000 in lost wages, $40,000 for humiliation, and about $120,000 to cover other lost benefits.

EMPLOYMENT

> ### Warnings
>
> Warnings are a way to tell an employee that they are under-performing or are behaving in a way that is considered inappropriate. They tell employees that further instances of this behaviour will not be tolerated, or that performance will need to improve, and if there is no change, the employee could be given a further warning or dismissed. Employment legislation doesn't say how many times you must warn an employee before dismissing them. What is fair will largely depend on the circumstances and what the employee did. However, the process used by many employers is to issue:
>
> - a preliminary verbal warning
> - a formal written warning
> - then a final written warning.
>
> Whatever process you use, the warning must be explicit. You can't just say: 'I'm warning you' or write 'warning' at the top of a letter. You must state what you are warning them about. This is that the consequences of future under-performance or misconduct might include a more serious warning or dismissal.

4. If the employee's performance doesn't improve during the warning process you can issue a final warning. The employee must get advance warning of the meeting – at least a day's notice – and be invited to bring a support person or representative. They must be told the meeting is about their performance and the outcome could be serious. Again, you must tell the employee how their work is falling below standard and that efforts to help them have failed. You must give the employee the right to explain and allow them to make suggestions as to what else could be done. Listen to what they say. Take time – which may even be overnight or over a weekend – to consider what the employee has said and come back to them with your decision. If the circumstances warrant it, you can issue a final warning. In the warning you will need to state that if the employee's performance does not improve within a specific reasonable timeframe, you will need to consider dismissal.

5. If there is still no improvement you can prepare for the possibility of dismissal. Many employees will have resigned before the process gets to this stage. Again, the employee must get advance warning, be invited to bring a support person or representative, and be told the meeting is about their performance and that the consequences could be serious. Note that the employee already has a final warning, so the consequences could include dismissal. At the meeting, you must once again outline how their work is falling below standard, and that efforts

COMPLIANCE AND YOUR BUSINESS

Remember: If an employee thinks you have been unfair in warning or disciplining them they can raise a personal grievance claim. They don't have to wait to be sacked to take these claims. You must be able to justify your decision to take disciplinary action or issue a warning. If you can't, you risk a successful grievance claim against you.

to help them have failed. Tell them that the circumstances might warrant dismissal and on what grounds. Give them a chance to respond and take time to consider this response. If circumstances warrant, you can come back and inform the employee of your decision. If this decision is to dismiss them you should put it in writing.

It is important that during this process you don't get angry or become too embarrassed to be frank with the employee. If you shout down their explanations or mislead them about how seriously you take the problem, this could work against you in future. And remember you need to keep an open mind. Placing a job advertisement or talking to anyone about filling the role is a clear sign you've already made up your mind to dismiss an employee. This could be used against you during any personal grievance claim.

Misconduct

You are entitled to discipline an employee whose behaviour amounts to 'misconduct'. Misconduct isn't defined in employment legislation, but it can be described as when an employee does something that harms or potentially harms your business, themselves, or another person. It can range from swearing at a customer, to taking home company property, to breaches of safety rules.

If an employee continues to behave in a way that amounts to misconduct you might eventually have the right to sack them. However, you must have a justifiable reason and you must treat the employee fairly during the discipline and dismissal process.

Remember that many instances of misconduct may be isolated and, after taking disciplinary action, there may be no further problem.

The process

To reduce the risk of a successful personal grievance claim there are certain steps you must take when disciplining or dismissing an employee for misconduct. Here are some guidelines to help you set up that process:

1. **Conduct an investigation.** You must do this whether you are making the allegation of misconduct yourself, or if it comes from a third person. The investigation aims to establish the facts of what happened. However, if you are closely involved in the incident giving rise to the allegation against the employee (eg he/she has sworn at you), you are essentially the victim and will not be objective enough to fairly conduct the investigation. To help make sure your investigation is fair you should:
   – Check the employment agreement. It might include information on how investigations are to be conducted.

EMPLOYMENT

- Check whether your company has guidelines or manuals for conducting investigations and if so, follow them. Look at what has been done during past investigations. You could risk a successful personal grievance claim against you if you don't follow your own procedures or if you treat employees differently in similar circumstances.
- Check the facts. Relying on information from other people, including the police, without verifying it and making your own decision can lead to a finding of unjustified dismissal. If the allegation comes from someone else, get a signed, written statement from them. Also get signed, written statements from any witnesses.
- If your inquiries suggest there's an alternative explanation for the alleged misconduct – for example, someone else had a key to the empty petty cash box – you must investigate it.
- The next step is to put the allegations to the employee to give them an opportunity to explain. You must show them the evidence against them. An employee has a right to be told of all information you are going to take into account when making a decision. In most cases, you must say who has made the allegation and name the witness.
- The employee should be given the right to have a support person or representative with them during any interviews.
- As the overall requirement is to be fair, the employee will need to have the opportunity to respond to the allegation in a meeting with the person who makes the ultimate decision. It would be unfair for a person to be sacked for misconduct if the person who makes the decision has not heard the employee's explanation themselves.

Document what you do during an enquiry. You may need to show you had an open mind and that the investigation wasn't a sham.

COMPLIANCE AND YOUR BUSINESS

> ### Case study
>
> #### Allegations of dishonesty
>
> Porter was a cleaning supervisor at a school. She was called into see the Principal and told she was being suspended while the school investigated allegations of dishonesty. She was told a meeting would take place the next day and she could bring a representative. The only detail of the dishonesty Porter was given was that she had taken bus tickets.
>
> At the meeting the next day, Porter was told unnamed students had alleged she had stolen bus tickets. The school declined to name the students. Further allegations were made at the meeting that she had breached school security rules by allowing her stepson to lock up the school and that she had stolen alcohol from the staff room and consumed it with student cleaners. Porter was also asked about an item of lost property she had allegedly given to a student. Porter denied some of the allegations but was unable to respond to others as she was not provided with enough detail.
>
> She was dismissed the next day due to the school's 'loss of trust' in her.
>
> The Employment Tribunal held that Porter's dismissal was justified and the case was then appealed to the Employment Court. The Court held that using 'loss of trust' as a reason for dismissing an employee cannot be used as a short-cut method of depriving an employee of a full and fair investigation.
>
> The Court held that although the school's decision not to name the students was fair in the circumstances, it was still incumbent on the school to ensure that the investigation was conducted fairly in other respects. The school failed to do this because it did not adequately inform Porter of the allegations made against her, she was not given adequate opportunity to respond to the allegations, evidence was collected by the school in the course of the investigation which was not put to Porter for her response, and she was only told of 3 out of 11 complaints made against her.
>
> However, the Court also held that the evidence presented in respect of Porter's dishonesty was such that no remedies should be payable to her, even though the dismissal was unjustified.

2 **Inform the employee of the allegations**. You can do this either by a letter to the employee, setting out all of the information you have to date and asking the employee (and their support person or representative) to a meeting to provide a response to the allegations. Alternatively, you can meet with the employee to inform them of the allegations and then ask the employee to attend a second

meeting to provide a response. In any case, you should give the employee time to consider their response. You should not put an employee under pressure to respond immediately, especially if they do not have a support person or representative present.

3. **Meeting with the employee.** Ask the employee to attend a meeting to discuss the allegations and the explanation they've offered. Give them at least a day's notice and tell them they can bring a support person. Be quite sure the employee understands the purpose of the meeting. Briefly outline the nature of the allegation that has been made against them, that this has been investigated, and that the allegation and results of the investigation will be discussed at the meeting. You are expected to enter this meeting with an open mind and to give the employee a fair hearing. Telling the employee you plan disciplinary action or writing a warning letter before the meeting could be used as evidence that you'd already made up your mind on the employee's guilt.

At the meeting you should:

- Reiterate the main issues relating to the allegation. The employee should already be aware of these. Listen to the employee's explanation and, if necessary, go away and investigate the facts further. If you don't believe the employee's explanation, tell them why. For example, 'John I don't believe your suggestion that someone else took the money from the petty cash because no one else has a key and the lock wasn't forced.'
- If you decide that you need to conduct further investigation into some of the matters raised and you obtain further information as a result, you will also need to get the employee's response to this additional information. This may necessitate holding another meeting.
- At the end of the meeting you should take time to consider the facts and their explanation. Tell them when you will make a decision on the matter.
- End the meeting and consider the matter carefully with an open mind before making your decision. Fully consider the employee's explanation, taking the time you need to do so.
- If you believe, given the facts and taking into account any explanation, that the employee is guilty of misconduct you will need to consider what penalty is appropriate, given the circumstances. You might decide to take some disciplinary action, including issuing a warning. If you do decide to issue a warning, it is important to ensure that the process you have used is valid. If you want to rely on the warning later (ie, for a further warning or to dismiss) any mistakes you have made here can make the first warning (and potentially the whole process) unjustified.

COMPLIANCE AND YOUR BUSINESS

4. If a warning is issued and there is a subsequent similar allegation of misconduct against the employee, you must conduct another investigation and meeting, using a similar process to the one outlined above. Don't make the mistake of assuming that the allegation will be true just because the employee has been warned in the past. You must again give the employee a chance to explain. Listen to their explanation and make enquiries to see if it is plausible.

Once you have followed the process, if the circumstances warrant it, you can issue another warning. Depending on the circumstances and the severity of the conduct, a final warning or even dismissal may be an option here. However, you will need to have spelt this out to the employee as a possible outcome of your investigation.

Dismissal

If another allegation of misconduct is made you must investigate, as outlined above. Depending on the conduct, if this is the third time that similar misconduct has occurred, you may be considering dismissal.

Your behaviour during this meeting is important. You must treat the employee fairly and be able to show this.

Prior to making a decision, you will of course need to conduct a full investigation and meet with the employee. You should refer to the previous warnings/final warning and make sure that you tell them the outcome of the investigation could be serious and, if the misconduct is established, may result in their dismissal. Although you have flagged dismissal as an option, you are still expected to enter this meeting with an open mind and to listen to any explanation the employee might offer. Writing a dismissal letter or placing a job advertisement beforehand is a clear sign you don't have an open mind. This would be used against you in any personal grievance claim.

After the meeting you should once again consider the facts and their explanation, taking the time you need to do so (when you are considering dismissal, this may often be overnight or over a weekend). Tell them when you will make a decision on the matter.

After considering all the relevant comments and facts, if you believe, given the facts, that the employee is again guilty of misconduct, dismissal may be an appropriate penalty in the circumstances.

If so, you should advise of your decision at a face-to-face meeting – this will give the employee the opportunity to make any final comment before you actually dismiss them, and will also allow you to discuss final issues such as pay and return of property. You should then confirm all of this in a letter to the employee.

> ### Case study
> #### The dangers of firing staff 'on the spot'
> Barker was a bar employee for Stonewin until she was dismissed for theft after giving a fellow employee a drink that was rejected by a customer. The director of the group that owned Stonewin saw Barker giving away the drink and took her into his office. There he dismissed her for theft on the spot. The director and Barker then returned to the bar so she could get her things and the director told the bar manager to make Barker leave through the back door.
>
> Barker claimed she gave her fellow employee the drink instead of disposing of it. She said she was too busy to fill out Stonewin's wastage record, as this was usually done at the end of her shift.
>
> The Employment Relations Authority upheld Barker's personal grievance claim for unjustified dismissal. It said she wasn't given any notice of the allegation prior to her meeting with the director. There was no suggestion she could have a representative present and she wasn't given any chance to refute the allegation. The whole meeting took place in less than a minute, suggesting the director had decided to sack her before the meeting began.
>
> However, it said Barker had contributed to her dismissal by giving away the drink, and her compensation – $9,000 for lost wages – was reduced by a quarter to reflect her contributing conduct.

Dismissing an employee without warning: serious misconduct

In some cases, employers have the right to dismiss employees without going through a warning process if the employee has done something that amounts to 'serious misconduct'. You are still obliged to investigate and treat the employee fairly during the dismissal process and give them a chance to explain.

Serious misconduct is not defined by legislation. But it can be described as 'behaviour that badly damages or destroys your trust and confidence in the employee'. Examples of how an employee can destroy this trust and confidence are:

- If the employee steals or commits some other act of dishonesty. You don't have to prove beyond doubt that an employee was dishonest but you must have reasonable grounds to suspect them. Be aware that dishonesty outside of work, for eg shoplifting, doesn't necessarily amount to serious misconduct. It depends on the type of work the employee does and how much trust you place in them.
- Physical violence towards customers or other employees.

- drinking or possessing drugs while working or being under the influence while working,
- bringing the company into disrepute (eg acting in a disorderly manner while in company uniform or badmouthing the company to clients),
- when an employee does something that creates a conflict of interest – such as doing work for a competitor while still employed by you. Many employment agreements specifically state that leaking documents or confidential information will be regarded as serious misconduct.

The position an employee holds within the company is relevant to a decision about whether an action is serious misconduct. For example, you are likely to place more trust and confidence in a manager than an apprentice.

If an allegation of serious misconduct is made against an employee you should:

- conduct an investigation using the guidelines for misconduct in step one above.
- when the investigation is completed, inform the employee of the allegations and hold a formal meeting with the employee.

You must give the employee notice of the meeting, ensuring adequate time to prepare. Tell them they can bring a support person or representative and inform them that if the allegations are established, they could be dismissed. It is important to tell an employee that dismissal is a possible outcome to give them fair warning of the potential consequence but you must still have an open mind about any explanation the employee might offer.

The meeting

You are expected to enter this meeting with an open mind and to listen to any explanation the employee might offer. Writing a dismissal letter beforehand is a clear sign you'd already made up your mind and this would be used against you in a personal grievance claim.

Your behaviour during this meeting is extremely important. You must be able to show you treated the employee fairly.

At the meeting you should:

- Go over the facts gathered during your investigation (the employee should already have been provided adequate information to enable them to respond to the allegations). Give the employee a reasonable time to explain their conduct.
- Listen to the employee's explanation and if necessary go away and investigate the facts further. If further information is uncovered as a result of this, you will need to meet with the employee again.
- At the end of the meeting consider the facts and their explanation. Tell the employee when you will make a decision on any disciplinary action, and what this action might be.
- After the meeting, consider carefully any points the employee has made.

- If you consider that the employee has committed serious misconduct, you will need to consider what the appropriate penalty is given the circumstances (and taking into account how you have acted in any previous similar situations). Alternatives to dismissal may be a final written warning, demotion, or transfer to another part of the business (either temporarily or permanently) or reduction of benefits (eg taking away a company credit card or car).
- If you decide that dismissal is justified in the circumstances, you will need to meet with the employee to inform him or her of your decision and the reasons for dismissal. You should also put your decision in writing.

Was it misconduct or serious misconduct?

Many employers have learned the difference between these terms the hard way – when the Employment Court ruled that an employee they sacked without warning for serious misconduct was only guilty of misconduct, so was unfairly dismissed. The difference isn't spelt out in any legislation. To decide if an action is misconduct or serious misconduct you should:

- Look at the wording of the staff member's employment agreement. Some agreements spell out whether some activities are considered to be misconduct or serious misconduct. For example, one agreement might describe breaching client confidentiality as serious misconduct, while another classes it as misconduct. You will be on shaky ground if you dismiss someone for serious misconduct when the activity they've been involved in is described in their employment agreement as misconduct.
- Look at any HR manuals, or employee 'code of conduct' your company might have. These might say what behaviour/activities are considered to be misconduct and what is serious misconduct. They might also spell out what disciplinary action you would expect to take.
- Look at what the company has done in the past. The last time an employee punched the foreman at a work social was it treated as misconduct or serious misconduct?
- Talk to a HR professional or lawyer. Yes, this will cost you money. But not as much as defending and then paying damages for a successful personal grievance claim.
- Look at the circumstances and what harm was done. An electrician who flouts safety rules on storing equipment might be guilty of misconduct. However, flouting safety rules when wiring a primary school sprinkler system might be serious misconduct.

> ### Case study
> #### Was it misconduct or serious misconduct?
> Taranaki Sawmills sacked an employee, Maxwell, after he stole five biscuits belonging to another employee and ate them. Theft of personal property was listed in the company's rules as serious misconduct. The employee had seen the open packet of biscuits in the staff cafeteria and had helped himself to them. When the owner of the biscuits found out he complained to the employer. An investigation took place and Mr Maxwell admitted taking the biscuits, saying he was sorry. He was sacked and claimed unjustified dismissal.
>
> The Employment Tribunal (the predecessor to the Employment Relations Authority) ruled that the decision to dismiss was an extravagant overreaction given that the theft involved only five biscuits. It awarded reimbursement of 6 months' wages.

Suspension

You must have a good reason to suspend an employee. Generally, the courts don't accept misconduct or poor performance as reasons to suspend. In addition, the courts are less likely to consider that a suspension is justified if the power for the employer to suspend is not specifically provided for in the employment agreement.

The most common situation where suspension is used is when having the employee at work might hinder an investigation into serious misconduct, where the employee may hurt themselves or others or where serious financial misappropriation is suspected. In the vast majority of cases, suspension will be on full pay.

Before you suspend an employee you must tell them that suspension is being considered and why. They should be given reasonable time to provide their comments and state why suspension is not appropriate in the circumstances. You need to do this even if the employment agreement specifically states that an employee may be suspended during any investigation into misconduct.

> ### Case study
>
> #### Suspending employees
>
> A women's refugee centre in Marlborough suspended an employee without pay while it looked into an allegation of misconduct. The employment agreement stated that employees would be 'stood down' during investigations, and the employee was told about the suspension in a letter that was left on her desk.
>
> The Employment Court said that the employee should have been given an opportunity to prevent the suspension or to argue that it should be on pay. The Court of Appeal upheld this decision. The Employment Court said even though the agreement allowed employees to be stood down during investigations, the employer had some discretion over whether it actually did this. The Court also said the suspension shouldn't have started until the employee was told of the alleged misconduct and given the right to argue against the suspension.

When an employee quits while being investigated

Be aware that you don't have to actually dismiss an employee for them to claim unfair dismissal. If an employee resigns because:

- you have given them a choice between resigning or being dismissed
- the employee believes you have purposely acted in a way designed to force them to resign
- the employee believes you have breached your duties to such an extent that he or she has no choice but to resign

the employee may be able to claim constructive dismissal.

To help avoid a successful claim for 'constructive dismissal' you must not:

- make life unpleasant for an employee in the hope they'll resign
- lumber them with unpleasant tasks or take away perks
- reduce their wages and conditions
- do anything to suggest you've made up your mind to sack them and are just going through the motions of the warning process.

COMPLIANCE AND YOUR BUSINESS

> ### Case study
> #### The dangers of 'encouraging' an employee to resign
> Baldwin was a branch manager for RMS Shopfitters, where she managed several sales and factory staff. She was also responsible for a sales manager, who was later promoted to North Island operations manager, meaning Baldwin began reporting to him.
>
> Following his promotion, the operations manager changed Baldwin's job description so she spent more time in sales-related work, including cold-calling customers. Baldwin, who wasn't consulted on the change, objected but complied. After this the working relationship between the two began to deteriorate.
>
> The operations manager only communicated with Baldwin using memos, and in one of these memos he said if her sales efforts didn't improve her job was in jeopardy. RMS then required that Baldwin accept changes being made to her job or resign. She was required to respond within a few days.
>
> On the day the ultimatum expired Baldwin was told her company car was being taken away. Baldwin then wrote to RMS saying that in her view she was being constructively dismissed. She said the company hadn't treated her in 'good faith' and was trying to force her to do work outside the scope of her employment.
>
> The Employment Court agreed, saying the company, through its operations manager, had deliberately tried to coerce Baldwin into resigning. The changes to her duties went against what was in her employment agreement, meaning she had been constructively dismissed. She was awarded $7,000 in compensation and $2,000 towards legal costs.

Remember: you don't have to actually sack an employee for them to bring a personal grievance claim involving hurt and humiliation.

Why it pays to keep your temper

There is a strong financial reason why you should make sure that you act fairly and reasonably when disciplining or dismissing an employee. Under the Employment Relations Act employees can claim compensation for the hurt, loss of dignity, and injury to feelings you've caused them. The Act doesn't spell out what behaviour can amount to hurt or humiliation. Shouting or swearing at an employee, or 'tearing strips' off them in public can all lead to claims for hurt and humiliation. In addition, if your process is unjustified in any way, you will usually be found to have caused the employee hurt or injury to feelings and an award of compensation under this head will be made. If an employee has a successful personal grievance claim against you, there will almost always be an aspect of this claim that relates to hurt and humiliation, unless the employee significantly contributed to the action you took.

Calling the police

Be aware that if an allegation of misconduct or serious misconduct involves a crime and the police are called, the employee may exercise their right to silence. That means they don't necessarily have to answer questions during your investigation or give their own explanation of what happened if that may incriminate them in terms of the police investigation. Because a full employment investigation hasn't been possible, and the employee hasn't been able to explain, any dismissal would be unjustified. Anyone caught in a situation like this should seek advice from a human resources professional or lawyer.

Abandonment of employment

If an employee fails to show up for work for a period of time without any explanation, he or she can be dismissed. There are no rules on how long the absence must be to amount to abandonment, but many employment agreements will specify this. But in the past, the courts have accepted that an unexplained absence of 3-5 consecutive days can be considered abandonment. Before you terminate someone for abandonment you must take reasonable steps to contact them and find out why they are away. You must be able to show you made reasonable efforts to contact the employee. If you don't do this, the courts might override your right to terminate their employment for abandonment.

Terminating an employee because of illness

In some circumstances, long-term or ongoing absences from work due to illness justifies dismissing an employee. Where an employee has been absent from work for some time or is consistently absent for short periods of time, an employer will not be expected to hold their job open forever. However, you are required to treat sick employees fairly. To prove to the Authority or Court that you have been fair when terminating employment due to ill health you must:

- Wait a reasonable time for the employee to recover.
- Provide the employee with reasonable assistance to aid their return to work (this may involve being flexible with their duties or hours for a period).
- If the employee has not been able to work for some time, enquire in an open-minded way as to whether the employee has any realistic prospect of returning to work within a reasonable time.
- Get all the relevant information from the employee, making it known that the information might be used to help decide whether or not to discontinue their employment.
- Make your decision using all possible information, checking that the information is up to date when you use it. You may need to seek information from the employee's doctor (you will need the employee's consent to do this) or send the employee to a doctor nominated by the company for an examination (unless the

employee consents, you can only do this if it is provided for in the employment agreement).
- Consider alternatives, like alternative duties, a graduated return to work, or the use of temporary employees.

Taking into account all the relevant information, and balancing fairness to the employee with practical business requirements, decide if you can keep the position open until the time the employee is likely to be well enough to return to work.

There is no legal definition of how long you should wait for an employee to get well. It just has to be a 'reasonable time'. However, indications in case law are that a 3-4 month absence would justify termination. Things you need to consider in deciding what's reasonable include:

- conditions contained in the employment agreement, such as sick leave available to the employee
- how long the employee has been with the company, and whether they were likely to be employed long term if they hadn't got sick
- the employee's role within the company, for example, whether they do a key job that can't be left vacant for long
- the nature of the illness and the prospects of recovery.

It is important to be upfront and discuss the situation with the employee. Long-term illness is often very difficult to manage because the employee does not want to lose their job and is likely to have other pressures connected with the illness (eg family, financial). In most cases, if you are considering terminating an employee's employment due to ill health, you should consult a human resources professional or lawyer. This is especially the case if the employee is suffering from a work-related illness (eg workplace stress resulting in illness), as you may later be held liable for their ongoing lost wages.

> **Case study**
>
> **Dismissing a sick employee**
>
> When Wilson Parking dismissed an employee with a serious injury the court decided in favour of the company. Wilson Parking waited 6 weeks before raising the issue of the employee's future. It deferred any decision until it received a specialist report, then it held the job open for another 6 weeks. The company then sought positive reassurance, unsuccessfully, about the employee's future health before terminating the employment.

Notice periods and final pay

When an employee is dismissed, whether you must give notice will depend on what is in the employment agreement. If notice is provided for, you will need to give the employee the specified notice. If the agreement allows, you may pay the employee instead of requiring them to work out the notice period.

Many agreements will explicitly state that notice is not necessary if an employee is dismissed for serious misconduct. If your agreement does not say this, remember that even in cases of serious misconduct, you will need to pay for the appropriate notice period. There is no legal right to waive notice unless it is an express term of the agreement.

If the employment agreement is silent on the amount of notice required (which would be unusual) the courts will require you to give 'reasonable' notice. 'Reasonable' is not defined and will depend on the nature of the position, length of service, and other factors.

When making up final pay, you are also liable for holiday pay and any public holidays which fall in the period for which you are paying holiday pay. You must also pay out for any days in lieu owing in respect of work done on a statutory holiday. You should also consider whether any other payments are owing, such as bonuses or superannuation payments.

In addition, when any employment relationship is terminated, unless you have made other arrangements, it is important to ensure that the employee returns all of your property, including uniforms, access cards, cars, computers, cellphones, confidential information, intellectual property etc.

Redundancy

Redundancy occurs when the employer terminates an employee's employment because their position is superfluous to the operation's needs.

A redundancy is a dismissal and like any other dismissal, an employee who is made redundant can raise a personal grievance if they think that the dismissal was unjustified.

Fairness in redundancy situations as required by the courts includes the following:

- You should consult with employees as soon as possible about any proposed changes you plan to make to the workplace which may affect the employees. Consultation does not require that you reach agreement with employees about how to handle the situation, but it normally requires that you present your proposed action to the employees before you have made any final decision, listen to what the employees have to say, and take their comments into account when deciding what you will do.

- Fair treatment will often require that you investigate and consider alternatives to redundancy such as an alternative position for the surplus employee, transfer to another site, retraining, etc.
- You will always be required to follow the terms of the employment agreement, regardless of how inconvenient that may seem to you. You should carefully check your obligations relating to notice of termination, redundancy compensation, notification to unions, etc.
- Remember that the overriding principle is fair and reasonable treatment. You have a right to manage your business in the way that will be the most efficient for you, but the courts will normally require that you have some regard for the serious consequences that redundancy dismissals have for employees.

Currently, you are not required to pay redundancy compensation unless that obligation is contained in the employment agreement. You may of course make such payments if you wish.

There are no specific rules as to who to select when making employees redundant. Some employers adopt a last-on, first-off principle, and others select on the basis of skills and experience. Others do not lay anyone off until they have asked for volunteers. In some circumstances, calling for volunteers may be a requirement of fairness. You need to be careful when offering voluntary redundancy that you do not commit yourself to accepting any particular volunteer as a candidate (eg if that person is a key staff member and necessary for your business).

Although the courts do not impose any specific selection rules, they require that any selection criteria be fair and transparent, and be applied fairly and even-handedly.

Case study

A non-genuine redundancy

Mrs Palmer worked for the Nelson Aero Club as club secretary. The club reduced her hours of work from 40 to 30 per week without proper negotiations and she lodged a personal grievance. She was then made redundant. The Employment Authority found that the redundancy was not genuine as the evidence established that the employer wanted 'to get rid' of Mrs Palmer. The redundancy was found to be substantially unjustified and procedurally unfair. The case was appealed to the Employment Court, which upheld the Tribunal's decision and awarded $5,000 in compensation for lost wages, $8,000 as compensation for humiliation, and costs of $1,500.

Sale of a business

If a business is sold what happens to employees depends on the nature of the sale. If the shares in your company are sold the employment relationships are not usually affected as the employees remain employed by the same company on the same conditions. However, if you sell your business by selling the assets you will in effect be terminating the employment agreements with your staff, and the ordinary rules as to dismissals apply.

As with any other redundancy situation, if you are selling or intending to sell your business you are obliged to treat your employees fairly, and this includes giving them notice of your intentions, and consulting them about the likely impact on their employment. If your staff are employed under a collective agreement, you are also likely to be required to consult with the union or unions who are party to the agreement.

A problem can arise with what's called 'technical redundancy' where employees are offered re-employment under the same terms with the new employer. In this situation, in spite of the fact that they have been offered new jobs, you have still made the employees redundant and they can claim notice of redundancy and redundancy compensation under their employment agreements with you. To prevent this, it is a good idea to include a technical redundancy clause in your employment agreements that stipulates that in such a redundancy situation, you are not required to give notice of redundancy or pay redundancy compensation.

Retirement

Remember that there is no statutory age for retirement in New Zealand. Under the Human Rights Act you cannot discriminate on the grounds of age. This means that you cannot force an employee to retire when they reach a certain age. Generally speaking, an employee can choose to retire at whatever age they wish.

The employment institutions

The Employment Relations Service

The Employment Relations Service (part of the Department of Labour) offers a free confidential mediation service to help resolve employment relationship problems. If you have a problem you can ring the Employment Relations Service on **0800 800 863**. The staff of the Employment Relations Service can give advice over the phone, or, if the problem warrants it, set up a formal meeting for both parties. A mediator will attempt to help the parties reach their own solution at mediation, which will then be put in writing and signed by both sides. The idea of the Employment Relations Service is to help you reach your own agreement, rather than having one imposed. It is also a cheap, quick way of resolving problems.

Mediators can help because they can clarify what the real issues are for the parties, they can help each side communicate their issues clearly, they can help each side see the other's point of view, and, because of their experience in the workplace, they can often identify solutions that are not readily apparent.

Although Employment Relations Authority hearings are relatively informal, mediation meetings are even more so. You do not need a lawyer, advocate, or advisor to accompany you to mediation, even though your employee may have a union representative. The mediator makes sure neither side is disadvantaged by not having an outside representative. However, it is still common for employers to take a lawyer or adviser to mediation.

Obviously, it pays to prepare for the meeting, as much to save time as anything else. You need to work out: What the problem is, what underlying factors contribute to the problem, what evidence you have for your position, and what resolution would satisfy you.

The advantages for you reaching agreement at mediation level are costs, that you have some control over the process and the outcome, and you can explore 'non-legal' options. It is also less time-consuming than going to the Employment Relations Authority.

The disadvantage, of course, is that any solution is likely to involve some compromise, and agreement is dependent on whether you and your employee can both be flexible.

If you reach agreement at mediation, it is a full and final settlement under the Employment Relations Act. You cannot change your mind. It is up to you and your employee to put the decision into practice, although you can of course contact the mediator or the Employment Relations Authority if you think the employee has breached the agreement.

If you cannot reach agreement, you can ask the mediator to make a decision. This too is a cheaper and quicker option than the Employment Relations Authority. If you do this, the mediator's decision is binding and cannot be appealed.

Mediators can also be involved in collective bargaining. This is a useful free service for employers who are not used to dealing with unions and with collective bargaining. The Employment Relations Service suggests it is best to get a mediator involved early on. Later in the bargaining process positions may have become entrenched.

The mediator may be needed just to help set up the process, or to help sort out how any agreement may be ratified, or just when negotiations reach a particularly contentious matter. The mediator can attend bargaining sessions or be available informally as an advisor.

Unlike anything you say at mediation meeting about an employment problem, what you say during collective bargaining using a mediator is not confidential.

Mediators can also get involved in disputes in essential industries where a strike or lockout has been notified.

If an employee issues proceedings against you in the Employment Relations Authority and you have not already attended mediation, the matter will almost always be referred to mediation first.

The Employment Relations Authority

The Employment Relations Authority is an investigative body that resolves employment relationship problems by establishing the facts and making a determination one way or the other. It is not like a court, in that it is required to observe natural justice rather than legal technicalities, and is expected to be practical and act swiftly according to the merits of the case.

If an employee issues proceedings against you in the Authority you will receive a Statement of Problem setting out the facts relied upon and the remedies sought.

You will be obliged to file a Statement in Reply setting out your view of the facts and attaching any documents within 14 days of receiving the Statement of Problem. It is important to be quite detailed with your statement, so that the Authority member investigating the case has a good understanding of the facts. You should provide a chronology of the events leading up to the problem. Your statement can include material that would be considered evidence before a court. As a general rule you will be obliged to attend an investigation meeting. The Authority may arrange a conference call, to deal with any other documents or material needed, and to arrange for witness statements to be made, and for a date for the investigation meeting. Generally, witness statements need to be filed a week before the meeting, so that each side has a chance to read them in advance.

The Authority has wide powers to act flexibly to carry out its investigation. It may require the parties to narrow down their issues, and may exclude witnesses if it considers they are not relevant to the key issues. The Authority may decide for itself what the key issues are, which may be different than those outlined in the Statement of Problem. Usually, cross examination of witnesses is not allowed at investigation meetings, although the Authority has discretion in this area.

The Authority can also order people to appear before it, and can call its own witnesses and experts to help with the investigation.

The investigation meeting is quite informal, and occurs around a table, but it is open to the public, including the media.

It is important that you take legal or professional advice about an Authority matter. In any Authority proceedings you are at risk financially and could be ordered to pay compensation and costs to the employee who is suing you.

The Employment Court

The Employment Court considers challenges to determinations made by the Authority. The challenges can be a rehearing of the entire matter (a de novo challenge), or can concern an appeal relating to part of the matter only.

The Employment Court also has exclusive jurisdiction to deal with a number of matters directly. These include certain matters relating to strike or lockouts and matters transferred to the Court by the Authority.

The process in the Employment Court is a full hearing before a judge (or sometimes a 'full bench' of judges). Most employers have a lawyer or advocate to represent them in the Employment Court. It is like a High Court hearing in that lawyers' gowns are worn.

On certain limited grounds, Employment Court matters can be appealed to the Court of Appeal.

HEALTH AND SAFETY

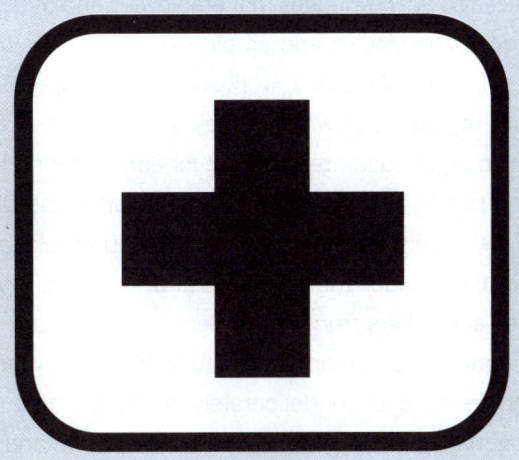

As a business owner or manager you have a legal obligation to provide a safe and healthy workplace. You must protect your employees, and others who come into contact with your workplace, from harm.

The main piece of legislation setting out your obligations is the Health and Safety in Employment Act 1992. Important amendments to this Act came into force in 2003. Other duties relating to the workplace are included in the Health and Safety in Employment Regulations, other Government regulations, and guidelines published by the Department of Labour.

Every employer, big or small, must comply with health and safety legislation

The Health and Safety in Employment Act clearly states that the responsibility for making a workplace safe lies primarily with the employer.

But the Act also acknowledges that employees and other parties have a role to play, and it requires employers and employees to work together to tackle safety issues. It applies to virtually every workplace, and imposes strict obligations on all businesses regardless of whether they are big or small.

The main organisation responsible for administering the Act is the Occupational Safety and Health Service (OSH), which is part of the Department of Labour.

There are three compelling reasons why you should take the time to comply with your obligations under the Act. First and foremost, it will help protect you, your employees and others from harm. Secondly, there are stiff penalties for failing to comply – employers face fines of up to $500,000, 2 years in prison, or both, if they are found to have been deliberately reckless about workplace safety. Thirdly, complying may help bring down your accident rate and ACC levies.

Who the Act applies to

The Act applies to:

- employers
- employees
- principals
- contractors and sub-contractors
- self-employed people
- people who control a place of work
- volunteers doing work activity
- people on work experience or getting on the job training
- people who design or make machinery and plant.

Managers, team leaders, supervisors and forepersons all have duties under the Act. It also applies to company directors and office holders within organisations such as schools, cooperatives, trusts and clubs.

Where the Act applies

The Act applies to any 'place of work'. The definition of 'place of work' is broad and includes physical premises and outside worksites. Vehicles and commercial vessels are defined as places of work while they are being used for business purposes. Areas of a home used for business are also counted as places of work.

That means the Act applies even if your employees are not working at your business premises, eg if they are working at another business, at home or in a public place. And it covers mobile employees, such as truck drivers or sales reps who work mainly from their vehicles. Their vehicles must be safe, the staff driving them must be properly trained, and they must understand the vehicle's limitations. Employers aren't responsible for normal traffic hazards. But they are obliged to warn employees about known hazards, like dangerous dogs on a motorbike postal round.

Employers' responsibilities

The Act imposes more than 30 duties on employers. But the over-riding duty is to take 'all practicable steps' (see key terms p70) to make the workplace safe, and to protect employees and others who come into contact with the workplace from harm. Employers must also provide appropriate health and safety equipment, and make sure any plant and equipment is arranged, used, and maintained in a safe way.

The Act uses a broad definition of employee. It includes permanent and casual staff, people working for you from their own home, unpaid 'on the job' trainees, and people on work experience. The Act also covers employees on secondment, and in some cases, volunteers. Independent contractors are not treated as employees under the Act, though they still have rights to protection from harm, along with several obligations.

To help achieve the goal of keeping the workplace and employees safe, the Act spells out particular things employers must do in four main areas:

Managing hazards

Employers must:

- set up and use a system for identifying hazards and assessing whether any hazards are 'significant hazards'
- set up and use a system for managing any hazards that are identified
- when managing significant hazards – take all practicable steps to eliminate them, isolate them, or minimise them (in order of preference).

Where a significant hazard can't be eliminated or isolated, employers must provide suitable protective clothing and equipment to staff and, with their consent, monitor their health in respect of exposure to the hazard.

Informing and training employees

Employers must:

- take all practicable steps to provide staff training and supervision so work can be done safely

COMPLIANCE AND YOUR BUSINESS

- provide employees with information regarding the hazards they will be exposed to while at work, the steps put in place to protect them from those hazards, and the location of safety clothing or equipment
- put in place systems for dealing with emergencies at work.

Recording accidents and notifying OSH
Employers must:
- maintain a register of accidents and 'near misses' at work
- report accidents and incidents involving serious harm to OSH.

Involving staff in workplace safety
Employers must:
- provide staff with reasonable opportunities to be involved in ongoing process for improving workplace safety
- have a formal system enabling employees to participate in health and safety issues (this does not apply to all employers – see *Involving staff in workplace safety* on page 91).

Key terms

Three key expressions are used repeatedly in the Act. It's important to understand what they mean because they define legal obligations for employers, employees, and others covered by the Act.

All practicable steps

The meaning of this term is important because it defines the lengths employers and others covered by the Act must go to in order to comply with the Act. Under the Act, employers are required to take 'all practicable steps' to protect themselves and others from workplace harm. The same duty applies to employees, contractors, principals, the self employed, and people in charge of a workplace.

The Act doesn't impose an absolute obligation on employers to maintain a safe workplace or give an exhaustive list of what practicable steps should be taken. Instead it says 'all practical steps' means what is reasonable and practical given the circumstances. Whether a safety measure is reasonable will largely depend on things like how much harm could be done, how much is known about the hazard, and how difficult or expensive it is to put protections in place.

You aren't expected to do everything humanly possible to protect people. And you are only required to deal with problems that you knew, or ought to have known, about. But that doesn't mean you can turn a blind eye to danger. You are expected to put in place systems to identify and manage hazards.

One approach that you may take to decide what is 'practicable' is to list every safety measure that could possibly be taken, then list the reasons why it hasn't

HEALTH AND SAFETY

been taken. If you can't come up with good reasons why the safety measure hasn't been put in place, then it probably should be. Although the Act imposes safety duties on every workplace, a business' size and financial resources may be a consideration in deciding what is reasonable. Cost alone, however, isn't an excuse for failing to take action.

Taking all practicable steps also means you must comply with the mandatory steps set out in the Act (see *Dealing with hazards* on page 75). Employers and others covered by the Act must also comply with:

- Government regulations that cover particular industries and work situations
- guidelines prepared by OSH
- manufacturers' guidelines for using equipment safely
- codes of practice prepared by relevant industry associations.

Taking all practicable steps means actively seeking out potential hazards, rather than fixing problems after an accident. That means it's advisable for workplaces to have a formal, preferably written, plan for dealing with health and safety at work. They should keep a written record of safety activities undertaken as part of this plan. This record may be an important defence if safety issues in the workplace are ever investigated by OSH.

Hazard

'Hazard' has a broad definition under the Act. It means much more than obvious things like loose floorboards or faulty wiring. Hazards include activities, processes, substances, and circumstances (even people) that have the potential to cause harm. This harm can be physical or mental – so it can include things like exhaustion, shock, or stress.

The Act's main focus is on dealing with 'significant hazards'. These are hazards that can cause:

- serious harm such as death, injury, or sickness
- harm that occurs because of repeat or extended exposure, eg hearing damage caused by very noisy workplaces
- harm that might not be detected until some time after exposure to the hazard, eg illnesses caused by handling chemicals.

If an employer comes across a significant hazard in the workplace they have a legal obligation to (in order of preference) eliminate or isolate it, or to minimise its impact on employees (see *Dealing with hazards* on page 75). There are penalties for failing to deal with a significant hazard.

Information about regulations, guidelines, and codes of practice is available from the OSH website at *www.osh.dol.govt.nz* and the ACC website at *www.acc.co.nz*.

Serious harm

Under the Act, serious harm means death, or harm that results in:

- permanent loss of bodily function or temporary, severe loss of bodily function, respiratory disease, noise-induced hearing loss, neurological disease, cancer, dermatological disease, communicable disease, musculoskeletal disease, illness caused by exposure to infected material, decompression sickness, poisoning, vision impairment, chemical or hot-metal burns to the eye, penetrating wounds to the eye, bone fracture, laceration, or crushing
- amputation of a body part
- burns requiring referral to a specialist registered medical practitioner or specialist outpatient clinic
- loss of consciousness from lack of oxygen
- loss of consciousness, or acute illness requiring treatment by a registered medical practitioner, from absorption, inhalation, or ingestion of any substance
- a person being hospitalised for a period of 48 hours or more, starting within 7 days of the harm occurring.

Whether something can cause serious harm is important in determining an employer's duties to manage a hazard, the filing of official reports on accidents, employees' rights to refuse to do dangerous work, and inspectors' powers to shut down a workplace.

> **Case study**
>
> **People can be hazards**
>
> Several hospital employees went on strike, claiming that one of their patients posed an unacceptable health and safety risk. The patient had a history of mental illness, drug dependency, and was violent (having seriously assaulted two staff members in an unprovoked attack). The Employment Court ruled that a person might be a hazard, and a significant hazard, under the Health and Safety in Employment Act.

HEALTH AND SAFETY

> ### Case study
> #### Stress can be a hazard
> A probation officer claimed that stress was a big factor in him developing heart disease, which eventually forced him to retire for medical reasons. The court ruled that his employer hadn't taken all practicable steps to ensure a safe working environment. Its health and safety policies didn't identify stress as a hazard, or a significant hazard, and no steps were taken to eliminate or monitor it. Damages were initially set at $189,000, though the final amount could be higher as there is a lost wages component yet to be determined by the Employment Court. Since this case began, the Act has been amended to make it even clearer to employers that stress is considered to be a workplace hazard.

Managing hazards

Identifying hazards

The Act requires all employers – big and small – to be proactive about identifying hazards. You must have systems in place to identify existing hazards and any new hazards that may be created, eg when a new piece of machinery comes on site. To make sure these systems work and to prove you have them, you should formalise them – preferably by writing them down. Draw up a form that states what the hazard identification system is, who is responsible for what, the dates that checks are made, and who does them.

Ways to identify hazards include:

- physically inspecting the workplace and equipment
- listing the tasks that are regularly done in your workplace and watching to see how they are carried out by employees
- analysing the processes carried out in your workplace, eg do things get so busy at the end of the month that employees risk suffering from stress or occupational overuse syndrome?

Remember, under the Act it isn't enough to check that all your equipment is in working order and has the appropriate safety guards. You are also obliged to make sure that hazards aren't created by the way equipment, and other things in your workplace, are moved around, stored, maintained, or disposed of. It may be useful to include a checklist in your hazard identification system. The one below will give you an idea of the sorts of things to watch out for. However, it is only an example and there may be other hazards or potential hazards in your workplace which you may need to check for.

COMPLIANCE AND YOUR BUSINESS

Hazard checklist

- are work areas kept clean and tidy?
- are floors kept clean and free of things that could trip people up?
- do stairs and high platforms have railings?
- do you have clearly marked safe walkways through areas where forklifts or other machinery operate?
- do you have enough storage room so boxes and other waste don't encroach into work areas or walkways?
- are items that are stored up high secured in place?
- do you have systems for disposing of hazardous substances?
- do you have systems for tracking the use of hazardous substances?
- are incompatible chemicals stored apart?
- are hazardous substances labelled and stored safely?
- does your machinery have appropriate safety guards?
- are all electrical leads and switches maintained to safe standards?
- are transformers or earthing devices used where there is a danger of electrocution?
- do you have clear rules for dealing with dangerous equipment or situations, and do you check that staff follow these rules?
- is appropriate safety equipment available and is it being used correctly?
- is protective clothing available and is it being used correctly?
- is the workplace adequately ventilated?
- do you have a system for extracting dust and fumes?
- is the workplace big enough? (as a general rule each person requires 12 cubic metres of space)
- is the workplace at a comfortable temperature? (the usual comfortable range is 18-22ºC in winter and 19-24ºC in summer)
- is there enough light?
- could glare or reflections cause a problem?
- are you protecting employees from noise or providing them with adequate hearing protection? (normal office noise is about 65dB(A), while a jet taking off is about 135dB(A), and the maximum exposure at 85 dB(A) is 8 hours)
- are workstations set up to suit individual users?
- do employees know how to adjust their workstations for comfort?
- are employees warned of the dangers of occupational overuse syndrome?
- are they taught how to minimise this danger using good posture, exercises, and taking regular breaks?

HEALTH AND SAFETY

Hazard checklist (continued)

- ❑ do you have a system for training new and existing staff on how to do their jobs safely?
- ❑ are employees trained in the safe use of all plant, equipment and clothing they may use or handle?
- ❑ are employees who don't have the knowledge to perform a task alone properly supervised?
- ❑ are employees provided with information about all hazards to which they are exposed?
- ❑ do you have procedures for dealing with an emergency, and is everyone familiar with the procedures?
- ❑ do you have enough fire extinguishers, and are they properly serviced?
- ❑ are emergency exits clearly marked and clear of obstructions?
- ❑ do you have a clearly identified first aid cabinet?
- ❑ are accidents investigated to identify what caused them?

Dealing with hazards

When you've identified the hazards in your workplace you need to rank them. If any are considered significant hazards (ie ones that could cause serious harm) the Act sets out the steps you should take. You are obliged to take all practicable steps to:

- **eliminate** the hazard. This may involve replacing an unsafe machine, putting lights in a badly lit area or clearing boxes away from a fire exit. If this can't reasonably be done the next option is to:
- **isolate** the hazard by putting in place processes or mechanisms that isolate people from the hazard. This may mean building an enclosure around a noisy machine or permanently fixing a guard-rail that can't be removed by staff. If this can't be done your next option is to:
- **minimise and monitor** the risk of harm being done by the hazard. This could involve providing employees with suitable instructions, giving people breaks to limit their exposure to a hazard, providing protective clothing and equipment, and monitoring their exposure to the hazard.

Once you've dealt with significant hazards you must turn your attention to other, less serious, hazards.

75

COMPLIANCE AND YOUR BUSINESS

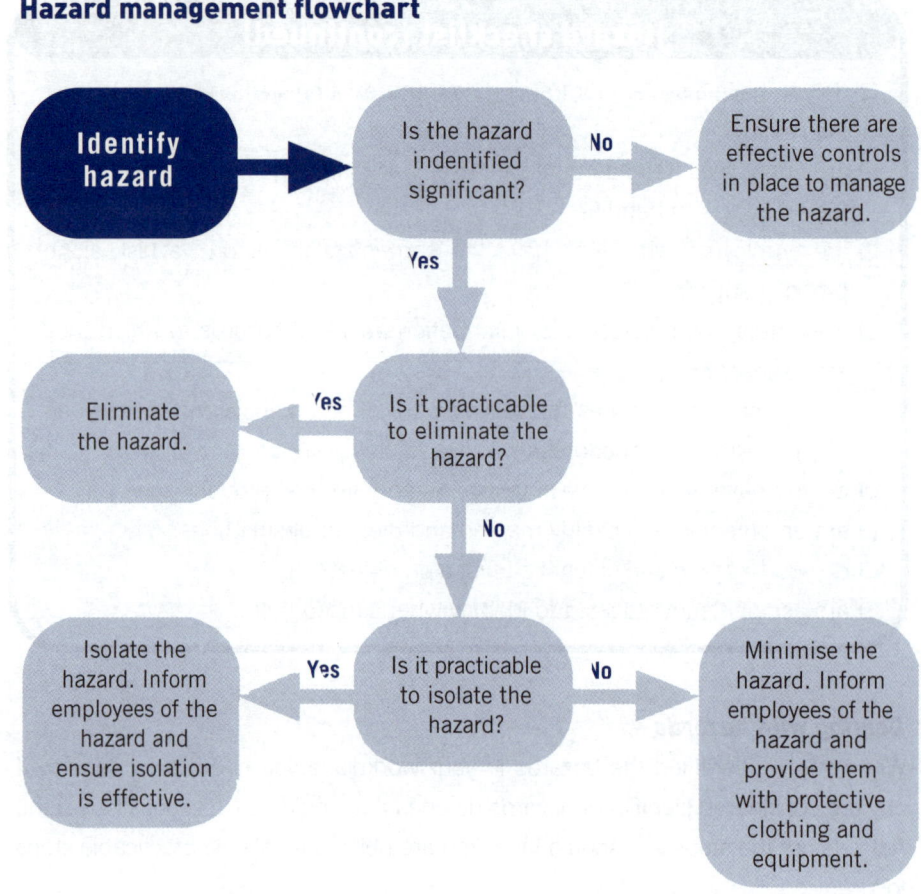

Case study

Failure to properly guard machinery

Carter Holt Harvey pleaded guilty to a charge of breaching the Act after an employee's hand was crushed in a machine's rollers during a rethreading procedure. The machine couldn't be operated while the service door was open. Contrary to the stipulated operating procedure, Carter Holt's procedure was for another employee to close the service door and to keep using the machine.

The court said Carter Holt had failed to identify the hazard associated with its non-standard operating procedure. It said the company was 'highly culpable' because its practice was contrary to the required procedure. Carter Holt was fined $12,000, with the amount having been reduced to take account of its early admission of guilt and the immediate steps it had taken to prevent a recurrence. The victim received $2,000 of the fine.

HEALTH AND SAFETY

Protective equipment and monitoring

Where a hazard can't be eliminated or isolated, employers must provide suitable protective clothing and equipment to staff to minimise the risk the hazard poses, and must monitor their exposure to the hazard and the effect it is having on their health. Employers are obliged to take all practical steps to get the employees' consent to this monitoring. However, they are still obliged to do it, even if employees don't consent.

Under the Act it is the employers' duty to provide, pay for, and ensure that employees use protective clothing and equipment. You cannot satisfy this duty by paying a clothing allowance or giving the employee money to buy the equipment. And you cannot satisfy it by requiring the employee to provide protective clothing and equipment as a condition of employing them.

The only exception is if the employee voluntarily chooses to supply their own protective clothing because they find it more comfortable and convenient. This exemption only applies to clothes, not safety equipment, and the employer is still obliged to check that the clothing is suitable. In addition, at any time, an employee providing their own clothing can give the employer notice that they wish the employer to provide the clothing.

Employers also have a duty to ensure that protective clothing and equipment is worn or used. If an employee refuses to use necessary protective equipment or clothing you should not let them work. Employers are entitled to take disciplinary action against employees who unreasonably fail or refuse to use protective gear after being instructed to do so. This might include verbal or written warnings. See chapter 1, *Employment* for more information.

Hazard identification form

It is important to keep a written record of whether you find any hazards and the steps taken to deal with them. If you are ever investigated following an accident, these records will show the efforts you made to protect people in your workplace. You may want to use the hazard identification form below, which comes from the Department of Labour.

Hazard	Significant	Practical to eliminate	Practical to isolate	All practicable steps to minimise	Controls requiring (Incl. existing)	Person responsible	Date to be completed by	Completed (initials/date)
	Yes No	Yes No	Yes No	Yes No				

COMPLIANCE AND YOUR BUSINESS

A single person can supervise a group of untrained employees, depending on the complexity of the work and the nature of the hazards.

Informing and training employees

Employers have a duty to take all practicable steps to provide employees with training and supervision so their work can be done safely.

They must take all reasonable steps to make sure employees:

- have the knowledge and experience to do their job safely, or are supervised by someone with sufficient knowledge and experience
- are adequately trained in how to safely use all plant, machinery, and substances
- are adequately trained in the use of all protective clothing and equipment.

All training must be in an understandable form. In some situations this may mean you have to run through information verbally or have material translated into another language. This may apply, for eg if most of your employees are poor readers or speak English as a second language.

If employees don't have the skills or experience to do a job safely they must be supervised by someone who does. The supervisor should make sure that employees doing the work are not likely to cause harm to themselves, another employee, or anyone else.

The supervisor must be adequately trained in the safe use of all materials, machines, tools, and equipment that the employee may need to use. They must also be trained in safety and emergency procedures.

You are obliged to inform employees about:

- what hazards they might be exposed to at work, including tangible hazards like potentially dangerous machines and long-term hazards like exposure to noise and chemicals
- what hazards they might create at work
- how they can minimise the risk of harm done to themselves and others from those hazards
- the results of any monitoring done in relation to exposure to a hazard.

Individual results from monitoring should be made available to the individual involved. You must also make available generalised results from monitoring to any employee involved in the monitoring. This information should be presented in a way that protects the privacy of individuals. You must also supply these generalised results to other employees who aren't involved in the monitoring but who request this information.

Employees must be told what to do if an emergency or accident happens. They must be told where emergency equipment, including the first aid kit, is located. There should be staff trained to deal with emergencies, and other employees must know who they are.

You should also inform employees about the legal requirement to report accidents or near misses to you so these can be recorded in a formal register. They must know that if the accident or near miss involved serious harm that the event must be reported to OSH (see *Recording and reporting accidents* on page 83). Employees should also be told that they have a legal requirement to cooperate with OSH inspectors.

Keeping track of the training and information given

It is important to keep a record of the training you are planning to do in your workplace, the training that has been done, who participated, and the information supplied to staff. This will support your claim that you have complied with your obligations should OSH ever investigate your workplace. You can draw up your own form, or use the one suggested by ACC below.

Training plan – example

XYZ company		For the year: *April 2004–March 2005*
Training topic or course	Names of staff to attend to attend	Date (due and completed)
First aid refresher course	Linda Richardson	Due June 2004
		Completed 6/6/04
Safe computer use	Andrea Olsen, Ben Warden	Due September 2004

Some employers get new staff to read through, and sign, a safety checklist when they first start work. This checklist covers things like emergency procedures and accident reporting requirements. The employee ticks each box to show they have read and understood the checklist.

Written statements can also be used to confirm that a qualified person has demonstrated to an employee the safe way to use a piece of equipment, including its safety features, and that the employee understood this instruction. This process can be repeated with existing employees as an update process, when new machinery or procedures are introduced, or when an employee changes jobs.

Employers should keep a record of these checklists and declarations. They should also record demonstrations given to employees, including the date and who gave the demonstration.

Safety information can also be posted around the workplace, in lunchrooms and – where appropriate – beside machinery.

Case study

Failure to ensure employee has sufficient experience

Three divers drowned and three were seriously injured while on a diving course in the Marlborough Sounds. Six charges were filed against Nelson Dive Centre (one for each student killed or injured) for failing to take all reasonable steps to ensure employee action did not harm any person. Stuart, the dive instructor was also charged. He pleaded guilty and was fined $15,000. Nelson Dive Centre didn't plead guilty, alleging that Stuart was an independent contractor so the company wasn't liable for his actions.

The District Court ruled that Stuart was an employee, and that Nelson Dive Centre had breached the Act. The company knew the French Pass area should not have been used for training and that Stuart didn't have enough experience to teach 'drift' diving. The company was $75,000 out of a possible $300,000 maximum ($50,000 per student involved).

Nelson Dive Centre appealed to the High Court, among other things claiming the penalty should have been $50,000 as there was only one charge rather than six. The High Court allowed this part of the appeal and returned the matter back to the District Court who awarded a $50,000 penalty.

Case studies

Failure to train

- Kiwi Packaging was convicted of breaching the Act after an employee lost four fingers in a rotary die cutter machine. The employee had been shown a method of operating the machine that was dangerous and contrary to good practice. The court said the staff performing safety checks on the machine didn't know how to operate it properly. Kiwi was fined $10,000, of which $6,000 went to the injured employee. Costs of $285 were also ordered.
- Tranz Rail admitted breaching the Act after an employee suffered a serious hand injury because the company hadn't told the employee not to lift rail wheels off the track until the correct pressure had been reached. Tranz Rail was fined $15,000. The court said Tranz Rail's culpability was in the 'medium range'.

HEALTH AND SAFETY

Dealing with emergencies at work

You should have a system in place for dealing with accidents or emergencies at work. These emergency plans or procedures may include:

- identifying types of emergencies that could arise in your business, such as fires, chemical spills, or civil defence emergencies
- developing procedures for protecting people in the workplace during these emergencies, such as making individual staff members responsible for shutting off gas or electricity
- establishing the need for emergency equipment such as fire extinguishers
- making sure employees know about the emergency procedures
- developing a warning system
- making sure employees knows where emergency equipment is stored
- making someone responsible for keeping emergency equipment well maintained, and checking that they do this job
- clearly displaying evacuation plans and emergency phone numbers
- having clearly marked assembly points and a system for accounting for all persons on site, including visitors
- developing an all clear system for returning to work
- marking emergency exits and keeping them clear at all times
- appointing wardens to take charge in an emergency and making sure everyone knows who they are
- keeping a fully-stocked first aid kit
- advising employees to keep emergencies supplies (eg food, clothing, water)
- holding a regular emergency drill or fire drill (depending on your particular circumstances).

Regularly review your emergency plans and procedures and tell employees about them.

First aid

Employers are obliged to provide first aid equipment that is suitable for their workplace, kept in good condition and easily accessed by staff. The Act doesn't spell out what must go into a first aid kit but OSH has provided guidelines that can be found on their website. However, you are expected to tailor the kit to your individual circumstances. You are also expected to check the kit regularly, replenish stock, and remove out of date items.

The guidelines refer to the need to have first aid personnel. This can be you or an employee who holds a valid first aid certificate awarded by a trainer operating under an organisation accredited by the NZQA. The OSH website (*www.osh.dol.govt.nz*) contains information about the training requirements.

OSH's guidelines suggest:

- All employers should provide first aid equipment and (where appropriate) trained first aid personnel, that is available during all hours of operation.

COMPLIANCE AND YOUR BUSINESS

- In offices and shops with up to 50 employees, there should be at least two first aid personnel. There should be an additional first aid person for each additional 50 staff.
- In all other workplaces with up to 25 employees, there should be two first aid personnel. There should be an additional first aid person for each additional 25 employees.
- Where employees of more than one employer are working together, eg on a building site, employers can arrange to share first aid provisions (this arrangement should be made in writing).
- Employers should provide adequate first aid provisions for employees working away from their usual workplace. What is adequate will depend on the work they do. If employees are in remote locations far from medical care, at least two first aid personnel should be provided for every 10 employees.
- Employers should take into account their duty to protect other people, including the public. Depending on the risks to the public, this might mean they need additional first aid provisions.
- Employers must review their first aid needs on a regular basis, particularly after operational changes, such as introducing new equipment.
- Employees should be given information about first aid facilities and the location of first aid personnel. This information should be given when they are first employed, when there is a change in the nature of their duties, and at regular intervals after that.

Every employer should have at least one first aid kit in each workplace. The kits should be visible and easily accessible to all employers, and unlocked where possible. First aid kits should be located close to a wash basin with hot and cold water, soap, and a clean towel. If there is no running water a saline solution should be provided.

Kits should be immediately accessible in areas that are particularly hazardous and there should be at least one kit on each floor. There should be at least one kit for every 50 employees. Work vehicles should also contain basic kits.

There is no mandatory list of items that should be in a first aid kit. The requirement is to have a kit that includes suitable and sufficient items for your workplace. If your workplace has no specific hazards OSH suggest the kit contain as a minimum:

- a first aid manual (available from the Department of Labour, Department of Health, or St Johns)
- 20 individually-wrapped sterile adhesive dressings (assorted sizes)
- 2 sterile eye pads
- 2 individually-wrapped triangular bandages (preferably sterile)
- 6 safety pins

- 6 medium-sized, individually-wrapped sterile unmedicated wound dressings (approximately 12cm x 12cm)
- 2 large sterile individually-wrapped unmedicated wound dressings (approximately 18cm x 18cm)
- 1 pair of disposable gloves
- 1 resuscitation mask.

For company vehicles or employees working on their own, OSH suggests:

- a first aid leaflet
- individually-wrapped sterile adhesive dressings (assorted sizes)
- individually-wrapped triangular bandages (preferably sterile)
- 2 safety pins
- 1 large, sterile, individually-wrapped, unmedicated wound dressing (approximately 18cm x 18cm)
- individually-wrapped moist cleansing wipes (not alcohol-based)
- 1 pair of disposable gloves
- 1 resuscitation mask.

Workplaces with more than 100 employees are expected to provide a first aid room. First aid rooms may also be required by those with less than 100 employees if the location of the work makes access to medical facilities difficult, or if there is a high risk of harm to employees or the public. If you think you might fall into this category contact OSH to clarify your obligations.

Recording and reporting accidents

Under the Act you are obliged to maintain a register of all work-related injuries, illnesses, or near misses. In particular, the register should include any incidents that have caused, or might have caused, serious harm, ie serious injury or illness.

You can create your own register using a book or folder. The details you need to record are set out in Government regulations and are listed below. Alternatively, you can buy a pre-printed register from OSH or an office stationery shop.

You should tell all employees how to report accidents. You may also wish to tell them what accidents have happened in a workplace, so they can contribute to improving workplace safety.

Prescribed form for recording accidents in the register

The register must record every accident, incident, or illness that harmed or might have caused harm to someone in a workplace. The information to include is:

- the place of work involved, including a reference to the shed, floor, building, street number, street, locality, suburb, and postal address or, where applicable, a reference to the identification of a vehicle, ship, or aircraft
- the time and day of the incident, and if it was during a shift, the shift

- the nature and cause of the incident
- any investigation carried out
- any significant hazard involved
- if someone was injured, the person's name, residential address, date of birth, sex, and employment or other status (eg visitor or contractor)
- if the person was:
  - an employee, the person's occupation or job title, and length of employment by the employer, and the time between the person's arrival at work and the occurrence of the harm
  - self-employed, the person's occupation or job title, and the time between the person's arrival at the place of work concerned and the occurrence of the harm
- the treatment the person was given, at work or elsewhere
- the part or parts of the person's body that were harmed and the nature of that harm
- the name and position of the person recording the details.

What to do if someone is seriously harmed at work

If an accident, incident, or illness involves serious harm you must:

- Make sure anyone injured or suspected of being injured gets medical attention.
- Notify OSH by phone or fax (not mail) as soon as possible, telling them what happened and to whom, and where the incident occurred.
- Refrain from interfering with the accident scene unless:
  - it is to save someone's life, prevent injury, or relieve suffering
  - you need to maintain public access to an essential service
  - it is to prevent serious damage to property
  - you have been given permission by OSH.
- Notify the nearest OSH branch of the event in writing within 7 days, using the prescribed form. A copy of this form is included below. Alternatively you can get one from the OSH website (*www.osh.dol.govt.nz*). If you are involved in the maritime or aviation industries you may have to report the event to the Maritime Safety Authority or the Civil Aviation Authority. This may occur if the event involved a plane or boat – call these organisations to clarify.
- Deal with any hazard that contributed to the event (once OSH gives permission). You must investigate all accidents, incidents, illnesses, or near misses to see if they were caused by a 'significant hazard'. If a significant hazard was involved, then the statutory requirements to manage hazards kicks in. This means you are obliged to, in order of preference, eliminate the hazard, isolate it, or minimise its impact.

HEALTH AND SAFETY

Below is a copy of the official OSH form you should use to report accidents or incidents involving serious harm. The form should also be used to report near misses that may have caused serious harm, in which case you only fill in the relevant questions. You can photocopy the form, or download an online version from the OSH website (*www.osh.dol.govt.nz*).

Form of register of notification of circumstances of accident or serious harm

Required for section 25(1), (1A), (1B), and 3(b) of the Health and Safety in Employment Act 1992.

For non-injury accident, complete questions 1, 2, 3, 9, 10, 11, 14 and 15 as applicable.

1 Particulars of employer, self-employed person or principal *(business name, postal address and telephone number)*:
   _____
   _____

2 The person reporting is:
   ❏ an employer
   ❏ a principal
   ❏ a self-employed person

3 Location of place of work *(shop, shed, unit nos., floor, building, street nos. and names, locality/suburb, or details of vehicle, ship or aircraft)*:
   _____
   _____

4 Personal data of injured person:
   Name _____
   Residential address _____
   _____
   Date of birth _____ Sex (M/F) _____

5 Occupation or job title of injured person *(employees and self-employed persons only)*:
   _____

6 The injured person is:
   ❏ an employee
   ❏ a contractor (self-employed person)
   ❏ self
   ❏ other

COMPLIANCE AND YOUR BUSINESS

7   Period of employment of injured person (employees only):
    ❏ 1st week   ❏ 1–5 years
    ❏ 1st month   ❏ over 5 years
    ❏ 1–6 months   ❏ non-employee
    ❏ 6 months–1 year

8   Treatment of injury:
    ❏ none
    ❏ first aid only
    ❏ doctor but no hospitalisation
    ❏ hospitalisation

9   Time and date of accident/serious harm:
    Time _____ am/pm
    Date _____ Shift: ❏ Day   ❏ Afternoon   ❏ Night
    Hours worked since arrival at work *(employees and self-employed persons only)*
    _____

10 Mechanism of accident/serious harm:
    ❏ fall, trip or slip   ❏ hitting objects with part of the body
    ❏ sound or pressure   ❏ being hit by moving objects
    ❏ body stressing   ❏ heat, radiation or energy
    ❏ biological factors   ❏ chemicals or other substances
    ❏ mental stress

11 Agency of accident/ serious harm:
    ❏ machinery or (mainly)   ❏ environmental exposure
      fixed plant   (eg dust, gas)
    ❏ mobile plant or transport   ❏ animal, human or biological agency
    ❏ powered equipment, tool,   (other than bacteria or virus)
      or appliance   ❏ bacteria or virus
    ❏ non-powered handtool,   ❏ material or substance
      appliance, or equipment   ❏ chemical or chemical product

12 Body part:
    ❏ head   ❏ lower limb
    ❏ neck   ❏ multiple locations
    ❏ trunk   ❏ systemic internal organs
    ❏ upper limb

HEALTH AND SAFETY

13 Nature of injury or disease: ❏ fatal

(specify all)

❏ fracture of spine ❏ puncture wound
❏ other fracture ❏ poisoning or toxic effects
❏ dislocation ❏ multiple injuries
❏ sprain or strain ❏ damage to artificial aid
❏ head injury ❏ disease, nervous system
❏ internal injury of trunk ❏ disease, musculoskeletal system
❏ amputation, including eye ❏ disease, skin
❏ open wound ❏ disease, digestive system
❏ superficial injury ❏ disease, infectious or parasitic
❏ bruising or crushing ❏ disease, respiratory system
❏ foreign body ❏ disease, circulatory system
❏ burns ❏ tumour (malignant or benign)
❏ nerves or spinal chord ❏ mental disorder

14 Where and how did the accident/serious harm happen?

(If not enough room attach separate sheet or sheets)

_____

_____

15 If notification is from an employer:
    a Has an investigation been carried out? ❏ yes ❏ no
    b Was a significant hazard involved? ❏ yes ❏ no

Signature and date   / /

Name and position *(capitals)*

Accidents – who has a duty to record and report them

The following people must keep a register of accidents and serious harm arising from hazards at work:

- **Employers:** record in an accident register all events that harm, or might have harmed, employees and other people in the place of work.
- **Principals** (people who hire others on contract): record in an accident register all events that harm, or might have harmed, self-employed people at work and contracted to the principal and other people, as a result of the work of the self-employed person.
- **Self-employed people:** record in an accident register all events that harm, or might have harmed, themselves or any other person as a result of the work of the self-employed person.

The register can be your own forms or a photocopy of the Department of Labour's form.

Employers, principals, and the self-employed are required to:

- notify OSH as soon as possible (by phone or fax) of any of the above events that resulted in serious harm
- provide OSH written notice (using the prescribed form) of the circumstances within 7 days.

Recording accidents and incidents that don't result in serious harm

When events do not result in serious harm, complete your own accident investigation and take whatever steps are needed to eliminate, isolate, or minimise any identified significant hazard. Then record the details in your accident register.

Occupational overuse syndrome

Some hazards – like unguarded chainsaws – are easy to spot and eliminate. Others are less tangible – making them harder to recognise and protect against. One such hazard is occupational overuse syndrome (OOS).

OOS is an umbrella term covering a range of injuries that are characterised by pain and other sensations in muscles, tendons, nerves, soft tissue, and joints. Although OOS is generally associated with using computers, it can affect people operating any machinery or doing any task that involves prolonged muscle tension, repetitive actions, forceful movements, or an awkward posture.

Here are six things OSH suggests might help reduce the incidents of OOS in your workplace:

1. **Ergonomics:** employers should ensure equipment (particularly workstations) is designed and set up in a way that is ergonomically sound. The *Visual Display Unit (VDU) Code of Practice* (available on the OSH website at *www.osh.dol.govt.nz*) will assist with basic standards.

2. **Work organisation:** changing your processes can reduce the incidence of OOS. Examine job descriptions, workloads and workflow, deadlines, break times, incentive payments, and supervision practices. All can contribute to OOS.

3. **Monitoring:** if OOS is a potential hazard in your workplace you need to put in place effective measures to monitor employee exposure to this hazard. These measures might include providing a form so those using equipment, particularly computers, can report aches and pains. They might also involve periodically interviewing staff, or asking them to fill in questionnaires, to ensure you are aware of any problems.

4. **Information:** employers should provide information and training to employees to prevent OOS. This must include information about the risk of OOS and techniques for preventing it. The information should say what you've done to minimise the risk and tell employees what to do if they experience pain.

5. **Training:** this should cover:
    - the use, maintenance, and adjustment of the workstation
    - working techniques, including posture, relaxation exercises, breaks, and micropauses
    - work organisation – scheduling work to avoid peak pressures and repeated urgent deadlines
    - reporting systems for pain and discomfort.

    This training should be provided by a person with the necessary knowledge and experience. It should be ongoing.

6. **Rehabilitation:** Although this is not a specific requirement under the Act, rehabilitation is an essential element of OOS management, and will assist in the prevention of further harm. Rehabilitation is a planned process, to assist employees to return to their work as early as possible.

COMPLIANCE AND YOUR BUSINESS

> ### Case study
> #### OOS injury 'largely avoidable'
> Price Waterhouse's culpability was assessed as being high in relation to an OOS injury where the firm had failed to ensure that an employee's VDU was ergonomically set up. The firm also failed to adequately train the employee and structure her work so necessary breaks could be taken. It failed to manage her workload so as to comply with a doctor's certificate limiting the amount of typing she did each day and failed to have a system for monitoring employee's health.
>
> The court said the injury was largely avoidable if the firm had given the necessary thought and planning as to how the employee might fit into the organisation, instead of promoting her beyond her abilities, giving her inadequate training, and leaving her to adjust her workplace. They also had no structured approach to communicating with her, other than in a formal way. A fine of $15,000 was imposed.

Signs of workplace stress include higher rates of sickness, absenteeism, and turnover, or declining productivity and industrial relations problems.

Workplace stress

An amendment to the Act that came into force in May 2003 confirmed that stress is regarded as a workplace hazard. When the Act talks about stress it means stress which causes someone to become physically or mentally ill (eg with depression, heart problems etc). It doesn't mean the short-term stress that might come with deadlines and project work.

OSH have defined workplace stress as resulting from the interaction between a person and their environment. It involves an awareness of not being able to cope with the demands of their working environment and a negative response associated with that awareness.

Employers' obligations

Under the Act, stress is a hazard like any other. As a hazard which is capable of causing serious harm, depending on your workplace, you may need to:

- put systems in place to identify and monitor signs of workplace stress
- take employee's concerns seriously and try to address the issues they raise
- put mechanisms in place to deal with stress on a general level and in specific circumstances
- take action when it is clear that an employee is not coping or others have expressed concern about the employee.

Under the Act employees have a duty to minimise their own stress. However, they need to be told who they can talk to if they feel unable to cope, and that there are options that could make their situation easier. Employees should be reassured that they will not be punished for using these mechanisms.

Employers have an obligation to provide information and training to employees. This should include information about the types of things that may cause stress at work and how to minimise its impact. It should also include information about the consequences and external signs of stress. Employees should be encouraged to monitor the stress they are under and to notify the employer if they or a colleague are showing signs of stress.

If you wish to obtain further information on workplace stress, OSH have published a detailed guideline which is available from the Department of Labour or which may be downloaded from *www.osh.dol.govt.nz*.

Involving staff in workplace safety

Under the Act, employers must give employees reasonable opportunities to participate in developing and maintaining systems to improve health and safety in their workplace. There are three other good reasons why you should involve employees. First, the penalties imposed for any breach of the Act are likely to be higher if employees haven't been involved in safety issues. Secondly, employees are generally at the 'coal face' of a workplace, meaning they know what hazards can arise and have good ideas on how to avoid them. Harnessing this knowledge may save you from future prosecutions and fines. Thirdly, you have an obligation to do so under the Act and can be fined if you do not.

Following changes to the Act that came into force in May 2003, some workplaces are now required to set up what is known as an employee participation system. This is a formal system that spells out how the employer will provide opportunities for employees to participate in improving health and safety.

Employers required to have an employee participation system are those with:

- 30 or more employees, either at one site or in several places
- fewer than 30 employees, but where at least one employee, or a union representing them, makes a request for an employee participation system.

Employers obliged to have an employee participation scheme, or where a request is made, have two options. Employers, employees, and unions can work together to develop their own system before deadlines set out in the Act (if you had more than 30 employees in May 2003 the deadline was November 2003, or otherwise 6 months from when you first have 30 employees or from when the request was made). If the employer, employees, and any unions can't agree on a system, or don't want to develop their own, they will be obliged to adopt the system set out in the Act.

Even if a workplace isn't required to set up an employee participation system, employers are still required to provide reasonable opportunities for employees to participate in improving workplace health and safety.

COMPLIANCE AND YOUR BUSINESS

Employee participation systems

Workplaces that are obliged to have an employee participation system are probably better to develop their own, rather than rely on the one in the Act. Developing your own system enables you to tailor the system to your own needs, although you can use the statutory provisions as guidelines. Some requirements in the system that is set out in the Act, such as the need to hold elections for health and safety representatives, may also be time-consuming for small businesses with limited resources.

Developing your own system

Under the Act, an employee participation system must give employees reasonable opportunities to have input into health and safety, and must be negotiated in good faith between employees, employers, and any unions. There is only one mandatory clause – the employee participation system must spell out a review period.

Your employee participation systems should detail the process for ensuring regular contact between the employer and employees on health and safety matters. For small workplaces that aren't particularly hazardous, employers can probably fulfil this requirement by:

- having a committee involving management, staff, and any relevant unions which meets quarterly to discuss safety issues
- bringing up health and safety issues once a month or quarter at regular team meetings
- mentioning health and safety issues in regular emails or newsletters sent to all relevant staff.

The system should include a way of recording input, suggestions, and concerns voiced by employees, and checking that this input is acted on. Employers should document the efforts they take to involve staff by keeping copies of emails and taking notes at team meetings. They should also record their responses to issues and concerns raised by staff. This will support their claim to have complied with their duties under the Act, should the workplace ever be investigated by OSH.

The Act sets out provisions regarding the powers and duties of health and safety representatives. These will apply if you use the default system or if your agreed system contains provision for health and safety represenatives. However, the election of health and safety representatives is not mandatory. Under the default employee participation system the role of these representatives is to encourage safe practices, identify hazards, and bring them to the employer's attention, and to consult with OSH inspectors. If you choose to have health and safety representatives in your agreed system, they can have any functions which you agree to confer on them.

HEALTH AND SAFETY

Under the Act, if you have health and safety representatives, these representatives will also be entitled to a certain number of days of paid training leave (the exact number of days will depend on the number of employees in your workplace, but it is usually around 2 days per year).

Default employee participation system

Under the Act, employers with 30 or more employees were required to have an employee participation system in place by November 2003.

Employers, employees and/or unions also have to agree on a system within 6 months of:

- an employer first employing 30 employees
- an employee first requesting an employee participation system (where the workplace has less than 30 employees).

If employers, employees, and unions can't agree within this time the default system contained in the Act applies. This system differs depending on the size of the workplace.

For workplaces with fewer than 30 employees, the employees (and where relevant their union) must elect at least one health and safety representative. If there are more than 30 employees, employees must elect between one and five representatives.

Under the default system, health and safety representatives are entitled to paid training leave, with the number of days depending on the size of the workforce. (see *Calculating maximum leave for health and safety training* below). Paid leave can only be taken if the representative is attending a safety course approved by OSH. Employers are obliged to pay for these courses. Health and safety representatives must give at least 14 days' notice before going on paid training leave. If the potential disruption is unreasonable, the employer can refuse to give leave at a particular time.

Workplaces that had an employee participation system before November 2003

The requirements relating to employee participation changed in 2003, after the Act was amended. Before an employer relies on an old participation system to meet their obligations under the revised Act they should check that it:

- complies with general health and safety duties under the revised Act
- includes a process for reviewing the system
- is acceptable to the employees and any unions.

The easiest way to implement a system may be to email a document setting out the proposed system to employees (and unions) and seek their comments on it.

COMPLIANCE AND YOUR BUSINESS

What's a health and safety representative?

Under the default structure in the Act, the function of health and safety representatives is to:

- foster positive health and safety management practices
- identify hazards, tell the employer about them, and discuss with the employer ways to manage hazards
- consult with Department of Labour health and safety inspectors
- promote employees' interests with regard to health and safety, particularly the interests of employees who have been injured at work.
- carry out other functions conferred on them by the employee participation system.

Trained health and safety representatives have the power to issue 'hazard notices' (see *Hazard notices* on page 102) to the employer. A 'trained' representative is one who reaches a level of competency in health and safety practice by attending a training course approved by the Minister of Labour. Representatives can issue hazard notices if they have tried to talk about ways of dealing with a hazard with an employer and the:

- employer refuses to discuss or take steps to deal with the hazard
- steps cannot be agreed upon
- representative believes on reasonable grounds that the employer has failed to comply with its general duty to ensure the safety of its employees.

Calculating maximum leave for health and safety training

A health and safety representative's entitlement to paid training leave varies depending on the number of employees in their workforce. The requirement is:

Employees	Maximum number of paid leave days a year (calculated from 1 April to 31 March)
1–5	2
6–50	6
51–280	1 day for every 8 employees, or part thereof

Employee participation system checklist

Below is a list of issues you might want to think about when developing an employee participation system:

- do you want to develop your own system or use the default system in the Act?
- will you have health and safety representatives or does a committee or team meetings better suit your workplace?

HEALTH AND SAFETY

- who is eligible to be a health and safety representative?
- what's the process for selecting representatives? (eg an election, nominations, asking for volunteers)
- if you decide to set up a health and safety committee who else will be on it? (eg management, union reps)
- what will be the responsibilities and functions of your health and safety representatives and/or committee? Suggestions include:
  - fostering good health and safety practices
  - identifying hazards and employee concerns and communicating these to the employer
  - working with employees and the employer to manage identified hazards
  - consulting with inspectors on health and safety issues
  - promoting the health and safety interests of employees – particularly those who've been harmed at work
  - participating in health and safety committee meetings
  - assisting with employee induction programmes and/or training
  - helping with decisions about purchasing equipment
- how many paid training leave days will your health and safety representatives get? (see the minimum legal entitlements under the default system above)
- what notice must they give to take training days? (usually 14 days and by mutual agreement)
- how often will health and safety committee meetings be held?
- what notice must be given of these meetings and how will people be told about them?
- what will be discussed at meetings?
- how will decisions be made and implemented?
- what is the process for reviewing the employee participation system? (remember, it is mandatory to have a review process)
- how often will the system be reviewed? (under the Act employers must allow an employee-initiated review 12 months after the system was developed)
- how will the review be conducted?
- how will decisions be made during the review?

Volunteers

There are two categories of protection for volunteers under the Act. Volunteers who work on an ongoing and regular basis, in a role which is integral to the business of the 'employer' are treated similarly to employees under the Act, unless they fall into one of the exempted categories. Employers are required to take all practicable steps to protect volunteers health and safety. There are some exceptions, but usually it is prudent to treat volunteers as any other employee.

COMPLIANCE AND YOUR BUSINESS

Some volunteers, even though they may work on a regular basis in an integral role, are not covered in the same way as employees. The following are volunteers who are not treated as employees, but fall within the more general category of volunteer protection:

- participating in a fundraising activity (eg door to door collector or raffle seller)
- assisting with sports or recreation at a sports club, a recreation club, or educational institution (eg children's sports coach)
- assisting with activities for an educational institution outside the premises of the institution (eg camp Mum or Dad)
- providing care for another person in the volunteer's home.

The general category of volunteer protection applies to all other volunteers. If volunteers under this category work for you, you should take all practicable steps to ensure the health and safety of the volunteers and should take hazards into account when planning the activity. However, there is no penalty under the Act if you breach this duty. If an OSH inspector becomes aware of a significant hazard relating to your work with volunteers, the inspector will contact you to discuss ways of eliminating, isolating, or minimising it, but there is no legal enforcement mechanism.

People on work experience or getting on-the-job training

People on work experience or getting on-the-job training have most of the same rights as employees, regardless of whether they are paid or not. Employers are obliged to protect them from harm. However, this category of worker doesn't have the right to formally participate in the system to manage health and safety issues. However, there is nothing stopping an employer letting them join in.

Duties of employees

Under the Act, employees have obligations as well as rights. They have a duty to take all practicable steps to protect their own health and safety at work, and that of the people around them. The obligations imposed on employees particularly apply to managers, team leaders, supervisors, and forepersons.

To comply with their obligations, employees should:

- not do any work that is unsafe, and make sure their actions or inactions don't cause anyone harm
- learn and follow their workplace's health and safety rules, including the requirement to report accidents at work
- use the protective equipment and clothing provided or their own clothing that the employer has approved
- cooperate with the monitoring of workplace hazards and employees' health
- comply with any improvement and prohibition notices issued by OSH for their workplace.

Employees who fail to comply can face prosecution themselves. However, only a small percentage of prosecutions under the Act involve employees.

> ### Case study
> #### Employees responsibility to look after workmates
> Adams, a crane driver, caused another employee to be fatally electrocuted when a metal object his crane was lifting came into contact with power lines. Adams was charged with failing to take all practical steps to ensure no action at work would cause harm to another. In the decision, the District Court judge cited a code of practice and a safety manual for crane drivers that said operators had a high duty to watch out for hazards like overhead power lines. The Judge emphasised that the Act created positive duties to seek out hazards, and that this duty applied to employers and to employees. Adams was fined $5,000.

Right to refuse to do dangerous work

Employees have the right to refuse to carry out work that is likely to cause serious harm so long as they try to resolve the matter with their employer as soon as possible after stopping work. If the problem isn't resolved and the employee still has good reason to believe the work will cause harm, they can continue to refuse to do it.

If the work the employee does is inherently risky, they can only refuse to work if the danger has become greater than normal. Employees who refuse to do a task on the grounds it is dangerous must still do any other work that is part of their job.

Duties of principals

Principals are people who contract in services or labour. These contractors can be individuals or companies. There can be more than one principal in a workplace. Take the example of a building site, where a property developer has contracted in a builder, who in turn contracts in three labourers. Both the property developer and builder may be principals. Under the Act, principals must take all practicable steps to ensure that no contractor, or employee of a contractor, is harmed at work.

Principals are expected to include health and safety issues in all their planning processes and contracting arrangements. They must actively discuss health and safety issues with all their contractors. Principals cannot contract out of this obligation, eg by inserting a clause in a contract saying the contractor takes all responsibility for health and safety issues.

Principals must maintain a register of workplace accidents, incidents or near misses that harmed or potentially harmed a self-employed person working for them. They must also record accidents, incidents, and near misses involving any other person, where the situation resulted from the work of a self-employed person working for the principal.

When an incident involving serious harm occurs at work, principals must:

- advise the local OSH branch office as soon as possible by phone or fax.
- mail or fax a written notice to the nearest OSH office within 7 days using the prescribed form (see page 85).

Case study

Duties of principals and contractors

Central Cranes Ltd contracted Skytech to erect a tower crane on an Auckland construction site. Skytech employees were seen working 41 metres above the ground without fall prevention equipment or helmets. Skytech admitted breaching the Act and was fined.

Central Cranes was also charged with failing to take all practicable steps to ensure that employees of contractors aren't harmed. The charge related to the fact it had failed to ensure Skytech's employees followed appropriate safety guidelines. Central Cranes claimed it wasn't its duty to ensure Skytech's employees took appropriate precautions.

The High Court upheld the charge. Central Cranes appealed, and the Court of Appeal also upheld the charge.

The Court said that while an employer's duty under the Act was greater than a principal's, the Act imposed a straightforward duty for principals to take all reasonable steps to ensure no employee of a contractor was harmed. The Court rejected Central Cranes claim it had fulfilled its duty by engaging a 'competent' contractor. It said there were steps the company should have taken.

Duties of contractors

Under the Act, a contractor is someone engaged by another person to do work, other than as an employee. Contractors have the same duties as the self-employed. If they employ staff, they have the same duties as other employers. If they engage sub-contractors they have the same duties as other principals.

Contractors need to think about health and safety issues. They should inform the person who hires them of any hazards that arise from the work they are doing, and any safety measures or equipment needed to protect people from harm that may be caused by the work they are doing.

They should make sure they have received all relevant health and safety information from the person they are working for. This includes hazards existing in the place they are working, company rules on health and safety, emergency procedures and first aid facilities, and procedures for reporting new hazards.

Contractors who work in someone's home have the same responsibilities under the Act as any other contractor. They must ensure that their work practices are safe and do not harm any other person, such as the homeowner. The homeowner, on the other hand, does not have any responsibilities to ensure the safety of contractors doing residential work on or in their home.

A self-employed contractor must record in a register any accident, incident, or near miss that involves harm to themselves, or harm to another person where the situations resulted from the work being done by the contractor.

If serious harm was involved they must:

- advise the local OSH branch office as soon as possible by phone or fax
- mail or fax a written notice using the prescribed to the nearest OSH office within 7 days (see page 85).

Duties of self-employed people

Self-employed people must take all practicable steps to not harm themselves or others while at work. This includes co-workers, visitors, and passers-by. They cannot contract out of this obligation.

Self-employed people must maintain a register of workplace accidents, incidents or near misses that involved harm to themselves or another person, where the situation resulted from the work being done by the self-employed person.

If serious harm was involved they must:

- advise the local OSH branch office as soon as possible by phone or fax
- mail or fax a written notice using the prescribed form to the nearest OSH office within 7 days (see page 85).

Where a self-employed person hires another person as a contractor they have the same duties as other principals (see page 97).

Duties of people who control a work place

This is a broad category and can cover anyone from mall operators to factory supervisors. Under the Act a person who controls a place of work is defined as anyone who owns, leases, sub-leases, occupies, or possesses a place of work, or who owns, leases, sub-leases, or possesses any plant or equipment in a place of work.

More than one person can control a workplace. For example, on a building site the owner of the building, the construction company, and contractors involved in the work may all be people who control that place of work.

The Act places different duties on those in control of a workplace, depending on the sorts of people who are in and around the workplace. Below are a few examples provided by OSH:

- A person who controls a workplace must take all practicable steps to ensure no hazard harms anyone working at the workplace or any member of the public nearby, eg a lawnmowing contractor must ensure that stones flying out from under the lawnmower do not injure passers-by.
- A person who controls a workplace has obligations towards customers, eg a dairy owner must ensure that people who enter the dairy to buy goods are not harmed while they are inside the dairy.
- If people pay you to undertake an activity, whether on your premises or otherwise (eg camping or horse trekking) you must take practicable steps to keep these people safe. It is not necessary for the activity to take place on your premises for you to be found 'in control of a place of work'.
- A person who controls a workplace has duties towards authorised visitors. These duties include warning visitors about significant and unusual hazards in the workplace, eg if an employer invites an employees' friends to attend an office party, and construction work is being done in the office, then the employer must warn the visitors about any hazards.
- If you are authorising people to be in a place of work you control, you must provide hazard warning at the time you give the authorisation. If the warning needs to be given to a group of people (eg a tramping club), then it can be given to a representative of a group.
- If you are aware of any unexpected significant hazard likely arise from work being conducted you must take all steps to make this hazard known to people you've authorised to be in the workplace or people you know will be there under the authority of any law.

It is possible to be a person in control of a workplace and a principal, employer, or contractor. Anyone in this situation must comply with all their obligations under the Act.

Selling and supplying plant

Anyone who sells or supplies plant for use in a workplace must take all practicable steps to ensure the plant is arranged, designed, made, and maintained, so it is safe for its intended use.

If you hire, lease, or loan plant that can be used in a place of work, before handing it over, you must find out whether the plant is to be used in a workplace, and if so, what the plant will be used for. If the plant will be used in a workplace you must take all practicable steps to ensure it is designed, made, and maintained, so it is safe for the intended use.

If you sell or supply plant that can be used in a place of work, you must take all practicable steps to ensure the plant is designed, made, and maintained, so it is safe for any reasonably expected use or for anything which you know the plant will be used for.

If you agree to install or arrange the plant, you must take all practicable steps to install or arrange it so that it is safe for its intended use.

There are exceptions to these obligations for plant which is sold as second-hand or 'as is'.

Administration of the Health and Safety in Employment Act

The Act is primarily administered by OSH. However, in some circumstances, such as when a plane is flying or a ship is at sea, the relevant aviation or maritime agency oversees health and safety issues. The Civil Aviation Authority administers the Act for aircrew while in flight, while the Maritime Safety Authority administers it for most ships at sea. If you work in these industries you should contact these authorities to clarify your obligations.

OSH has a network of 14 regional offices. Its health and safety inspectors provide information and check the Act is being complied with. The agency develops and publishes codes of practice and other guidelines relating to specific industries and safety issues. This material can be found on the OSH website (*www.osh.dol.govt.nz*).

Health and safety inspectors

Inspectors provide information and education, and investigate accidents and complaints. During an investigation they have the right to enter a workplace, to ask questions, take statements and information, and take samples. They can conduct tests, take photographs, and require you to produce documents. They can require that a workplace is to be left undisturbed, particularly after an accident. It is an offence to obstruct or delay an inspector in the course of performing their duties.

If the workplace is in or through a home, inspectors can only enter if they get the homeowner's permission or a warrant issued by a judge.

After investigating an accident or near miss an inspector can decide to take no action, talk to you about your safety practices, or use a range of enforcement tools. Inspectors also have the right to commence prosecutions for breaches of the Act.

Enforcement tools

The Act includes a range of enforcement tools that can be used when someone has failed to comply with their obligations.

Hazard notices

These can be issued by 'trained' health and safety representatives. The Minister sets out the criteria for what is necessary to become 'trained'. Before a hazard notice can be issued, the representative must have tried to discuss the problem with the employer, but they have failed to agree on how to resolve the issue or on what timing is reasonable for resolving the issue. The Act obliges the employer and representative to try to resolve the problem in 'good faith'. This may mean that they have to seek expert advice, either from someone else at work or an outside expert.

A hazard notice doesn't have any penalty or fine attached. However, after issuing a hazard notice a representative may call OSH to inform them that a hazard notice has been issued and they should schedule an inspection. If an inspector comes to the workplace and notices the same hazard, the inspector may treat the hazard notice as prior warning and issue an infringement notice (which can include a 'spot fine').

Improvement notices

If an OSH inspector finds that a verbal or written discussion or a hazard notice hasn't been enough to persuade an employer to deal with a breach of the Act, they can issue an improvement notice requesting compliance.

The notice will specify what part of the Act is involved, the nature of the breach, and how long the employer has to rectify the problem. If an employer disagrees with the inspector's assessment they have 14 days to appeal to the District Court. The court will decide whether or not the improvement notice is unreasonable in the circumstances.

Prohibition notices

These oblige an employer to stop whatever activity is referred to in the notice. They are issued when an inspector believes that a workplace situation is so dangerous someone is likely to be seriously harmed.

The notice will specify what the hazard is and why the inspector thinks it will cause serious harm. The prohibition notice remains in force until the inspector considers that the problem has been rectified. Employers have 14 days to appeal to the District Court. But in the meantime they must comply with the notice.

HEALTH AND SAFETY

Compliance orders

A compliance order is when the Employment Relations Authority orders someone to comply with the requirements of the employee participation provisions contained in the Health and Safety in Employment Act. If the person ordered to comply still fails to do so, then they may become subject to certain penalties set out in the Employment Relations Act.

However, before the Authority will involve itself in considering an application for a compliance order, it will usually want to have the parties get together with a mediator to see if the issues can be resolved by agreement.

Infringement notices

OSH inspectors can issue an infringement notice to employers who fail to deal with a problem they've been previously warned about or prosecuted for. An infringement notice contains an instant fine as a penalty. A previous warning can consist of a written warning from an inspector, an improvement, prohibition or infringement notice, a prior conviction, a hazard notice (issued by a trained health and safety inspector), or a compliance order. Employers who disagree with the inspector's assessment or the amount of the fine can appeal to the District Court.

There are two categories of infringement fees:

- $800-$4,000 (in $100 increments) for breaches of the requirement to have a system for hazard identification
- $100-$3,000 (in $100 increments) for all other breaches of the Act.

The inspector who issues the infringement notice has to decide what fee the offending warrants. To do that the inspector will look at:

- what harm was done or might have been done
- how serious the harm or potential harm was
- the size of the business and the financial circumstances of the offender
- the workplace safety record of the offender.

An inspector can revoke an infringement fee before it is paid, for eg if the breach of the Act is minor and is promptly remedied by the employer.

Prosecutions by inspectors

If a breach of the Act is very serious, inspectors can decide it is in the public interest to prosecute the offender. The case will be heard in the District Court and the inspector has to prove beyond reasonable doubt that the person charged committed the offence.

The inspector has to start the proceedings within 6 months of when the Department of Labour found out about the offence, or should have known about the offence, eg because it was reported in a newspaper. The inspector can't prosecute if an infringement notice has already been given for the same incident.

Prosecution by others

In limited circumstances people other than inspectors can take a prosecution. This is only possible if an inspector (or any other appropriate authority such as the Maritime Safety Authority) has looked at the matter and decided not to take any action against any of those involved. Someone taking a private prosecution normally needs to do so within 6 months of OSH finding out about the offence. However, they can get an extension if OSH took several months to decide whether or not to prosecute.

Offences and penalties

There are two types of offence under the Act – ones committed under section 49 and ones committed under section 50.

Section 49 offences

This section deals with the most serious offences under the Act. It covers people who know that an action is a breach of the Act and is likely to cause serious harm and take that action anyway. Likewise, section 49 also provides that a person commits an offence if they know that failing to take an action breaches the Act and is likely to cause serious harm, but still fail to take that action.

The maximum penalties for this type of offence are severe – a fine of up to $500,000 and/or up to 2 years in prison. Prior to the changes to the Act in 2003, it was very rare for charges to be laid under this section of the Act. This is likely to continue to be the case. However, it is important to remember that there is no requirement that somebody be hurt for a charge to be laid under this section. You can be prosecuted for 'an accident waiting to happen' within your workplace. In addition, this section applies to managers, supervisors, employees, the self-employed, principals to a contract, company directors and office-holders within organisations like school boards, as well as employers.

Section 50 offences

The second type of offence occurs under section 50 of the Act and is when someone breaches their obligations under the Act, in a way that does not fall under section 49. This can include a breach of the obligation to:

- identify and manage significant hazards
- report incidents involving serious harm to OSH, to comply with notices issued by OSH, or to not interfere with OSH investigations
- comply with duties set out in the Government regulations.

The penalty for the above offences is a fine of up to $250,000.

Under the same section of the Act a fine of up to $10,000 can be imposed if the person in control of a workplace fails to comply with their duties under the Act.

HEALTH AND SAFETY

It's important to note that these are 'strict liability' offences. That means OSH doesn't have to prove the person knew what they were doing might contribute to an accident or was a breach of the Act. OSH simply has to show that the person failed to comply with their duties.

Again, employers aren't the only ones who can be charged. The Act, and the penalties, also apply to managers, supervisors, employees, the self-employed, principals to a contract, company directors, and office-holders within organisations like school boards.

When deciding on the size of the fine the court will look at things like:

- the offender's ability to pay the fine
- what (if any) harm was caused
- the offender's previous safety record
- whether the offender has cooperated with OSH to take corrective action.

With legislation changes in 2003, the court can no longer order that any of the fine be paid to a victim. The fine goes to the Government. But the court must look separately at whether any victim should receive reparation for emotional harm or consequential loss. Reparation cannot be paid for physical harm as this will be covered by ACC.

Case study

Size of fines imposed

Department of Labour v De Spa & Co Limited (1994) involved Labour Department appeals over the sentences imposed for three different offences committed by three different employers. Under the Act the offenders faced fines of up to $50,000. But each was fined considerably less, despite the events involving serious harm.

In one case, *De Spa*, an employee was killed when he was trapped in a wool bale elevator. The defendant was fined $6,500. In *Westland Funeral Services*, a fine of $2,000 was imposed after an employee suffered the amputation of part of a finger and lacerations when a circular saw was not properly guarded. A fatal accident to an employee caught under a pneumatic out feed gate in *Gordons Wool and Skins Limited* attracted a fine of $5,000.

The High Court ruled that the fine in *De Spa* should be increased from $6,500 to $15,500. The fines in the other two cases were described as being on the low side, but within the judge's discretion and not manifestly inadequate. It is expected that fines will increase following the five-fold increase in the maximum fine levels in May 2003. This is a clear statement by the Government that they considered the previous fine levels did not present an appropriate deterrent to those committing offences under the Act.

Insurance against fines not allowed

People are not able to insure against the fines that might be imposed for breaching the Act. Offering insurance against these fines or buying it is in itself a breach of the Act. However, you can take out insurance policies to cover the cost of defending a prosecution and the amount of any reparations you may be ordered to pay the victim.

> **Case study**
>
> **Accident waiting to happen**
>
> In *Department of Labour v De Spa* (a different case from the previous *De Spa* case mentioned above) make-shift arrangements by which employees climbed up a ladder to reach a conveyor led to the amputation of an employee's arm when his hand went into the unguarded opening of a machine after the ladder slipped. This was described by the court as 'an accident waiting to happen'. No assessment of the obvious and easily remedied hazard presented by the opener had been carried out and the company was aware of the common practice of climbing onto the machine to free blockages. The degree of culpability was said to be high. A total fine of $50,000 (for two charges under the Act) was imposed.

Smoking in the workplace

Smoking in the workplace is covered by the Smoke-free Environments Act. This Act restricts smoking at work.

Under the Smoke-free Environments Act:

- employers are obliged to have a smoking policy (containing certain minimum requirements) that must be reviewed each year
- employees are entitled to help develop this policy
- smoking is not allowed in shared office accommodation, unless all employees agree in writing to allow it
- if the workplace is not an office, employees can ask that there be no smoking within two metres of the employee's workstation
- schools and early childcare centres must be smoke-free, both indoors and outdoors, 24 hours a day and 7 days a week
- employees after consulting together, can insist on a completely smoke-free workplace.

Employees can complain to their employer or to the Director-General of Health if the terms of the Act are not complied with.

HEALTH AND SAFETY

The Smoke-free Environments Act was amended in December 2003. Most of the changes have a 'lead in' time. The main changes are:

- from December 2004, smoking is banned in all indoor workplaces (limited exceptions apply for some work vehicles and home-like environments such as individual prison cells, resthomes, hospitals, hotel rooms, and residential care facilities)
- from December 2004, smoking is banned in hospitality venues such as bars, clubs, cafes, and restaurants that are workplaces or serve alcohol.

Retailers are also affected. From December 2004, the display of tobacco products is restricted at each point of sale to 100 packages/40 cartons, unless the retailer is a specialist tobacconist. Tobacco products must be at least one metre away from products such as confectionery that are marketed for children. Prominent 'smoking kills' signs will be required at each point of sale.

Individuals who smoke in a workplace or other public place can be fined up to $400. Employers or company owners who allow smoking indoors can be fined up to $400 for individuals, and $4,000 for companies. They will not be liable for someone smoking if they have taken all reasonably practicable steps to prevent it.

Friday night drinks

An employer's duty to keep employees safe extends to socials events at the workplace, particularly those involving alcohol.

At work social functions where alcohol is served employers should:
- ensure food is available
- restrict the amount of alcohol available
- restrict the duration – don't let people drink for hours on end
- make sure a senior manager remains on the premises (and relatively sober) during the social occasion.

If employees are attending social events in a work capacity where they are likely to drink alcohol, you should consider providing taxi chits to ensure they get home safely.

If an incident occurs at a work social function, eg one employee assaults or sexually harasses another, you have a duty to do what you can to restrain the aggressor and protect the victim. You must also investigate the incident and consider whether you need to take disciplinary action or other action to prevent a recurrence of the incident.

Employers and employees are not allowed to sell liquor without a liquor licence.

107

Hazardous Substances and New Organisms Act

Employers and other involved in workplaces also have duties under the Hazardous Substances and New Organisms Act. Hazardous substances include things like poisons, pesticides, and other dangerous goods.

The Act contains rules on things like how these materials should be stored and handled, and who should have access to them. Penalties for breaching the rules include imprisonment for up to 3 months or a fine of up to $500,000.

See chapter 6, *Environment* for more information on the Hazardous Substances and New Organisms Act.

Asbestos

Along with the Hazardous Substances legislation there are regulations covering potentially dangerous substances, particularly asbestos. These regulations are particularly relevant to builders and renovators, who may encounter asbestos in ceiling, floor coverings, and other building products. The regulations cover your duties to find out whether asbestos might be present and how workers and other can be protected. Details of the regulations are available on the OSH website.

Health and Safety in Employment Regulations

Under the Health and Safety in Employment Regulations, employers are required to provide certain facilities in their workplace – like toilets, ventilation, and drinking water.

The regulations state that employees mustn't be exposed to noise above a certain level, overcrowding, or other specific hazards that are outlined below. They also impose specific duties in relation to particular workplace situations such as scaffolding, excavations, agricultural employees, manufacturers, and dangerous goods.

Duties imposed on employers under the regulations

Under the regulations employers must take all reasonable steps to provide the following facilities:

- toilets
- drinking water
- hand-washing facilities
- emergency exits from the workplace
- first aid equipment
- adequate lighting for safe work and movement
- ventilation to provide fresh or purified air
- a way to control steam and other atmospheric conditions, including air velocity and air temperature

HEALTH AND SAFETY

- a place where employees can eat meals in reasonable comfort (separate from any plant and materials, and protected from dirt, noise, and other hazards produced in the workplace)
- equipment to expel harmful air pollutants
- seating for employees who are required to stand so they can take rests
- somewhere for employees who are feeling unwell to rest.

If employees are working in wet or dirty conditions employers must also take reasonable steps to provide:

- showers or baths
- wet weather gear and facilities for changing clothes
- clean and dry storage for employee's non-work clothes
- a way of stopping employees becoming wet when working on a wet floor, for eg drainage.

Employers must take all reasonable steps to keep the workplace clean and hygienic.

Noise

Employers must take all practicable steps to make sure employees aren't exposed to noise above a certain level. OSH says normal office noise is about 65dB(A), while a jet taking off is about 135dB(A). The maximum exposure at 85 dB(A) is 8 hours. If you can't eliminate or isolate the noise, you must provide signs and labelling to warn employees and others about it. You must also tell them that hearing protection devices need to be worn and say where these devices are stored.

Overcrowding

You must make sure the workplace doesn't become so overcrowded that it creates a hazard, particularly when people are moving around. As a rule of thumb, each staff member needs about 12m^3 of space.

Other specific hazards

The Health and Safety in Employment Regulations contain specific regulations that cover common but potentially dangerous workplace situations, such as scaffolding on construction sites. There's a different regulation for each situation. Details of these individual regulations are available from OSH (*www.osh.dol.govt.nz*). The regulations and the workplace situations they apply to are:

- Regulation 14: containers of liquids – this covers things like sewage pits or any other pits containing a liquid that is sunk in the ground
- Regulation 15: loose but enclosed materials – this covers things like silos of grain and cheese vats

COMPLIANCE AND YOUR BUSINESS

- Regulation 16: raised objects – this applies, for example, if machinery has been raised to enable cleaning to take place underneath it
- Regulation 17: cleaning, maintenance, or repair of machinery
- Regulation 18: woodworking and abrasive grinding machinery
- Regulation 20: roll-over and seat belt protection for self-propelled mobile mechanical equipment – some forklifts and tractors must have seat belts and roll protection (eg a rollbar) fitted
- Regulation 21: working at heights of more than 3 metres
- Regulation 22: scaffolding in construction work
- Regulations 24 and 25: excavation in construction work
- Regulation 26: the notification of certain types of hazardous work, such as asbestos work, logging, some construction and excavation work, and explosives work (the definition of 'notifiable work' is included in regulation 2 of the regulations).

Young people

Employers must take all reasonable steps to make sure someone aged under 16 years doesn't:

- work in an area where goods are manufactured, construction work is done, logging or tree-felling is undertaken, or other potentially dangerous work is done
- lift weights or do any task likely to harm the employee's health
- work or assist with any machinery
- drive or ride on any vehicle
- work between the hours of 10pm and 6am the next day, unless an approved code of practice is in place.

Agricultural workers

If an employer provides accommodation to agricultural workers the accommodation must have the following facilities:

- toilets and a shower or bath
- furniture and somewhere to sleep
- lighting and ventilation in all rooms
- heating, a fridge, and laundry facilities
- rubbish disposal
- drinking water.

Employers must also provide meals or have cooking and eating facilities in the accommodation. The accommodation must be made of permanent materials, maintained in good order, and have facilities that are suitable to the number of people living there.

HEALTH AND SAFETY

Designers, manufacturers, and suppliers

The regulations impose special duties on designers, manufacturers, and suppliers of plant, protective clothing, and protective equipment. This is to ensure that the goods are safe to use and will not cause harm.

Designers of plant

Designers must ensure their plant is:

- designed ergonomically, including the positioning of any power control
- designed in such a way that if it is manufactured, installed, used, maintained, and repaired in line with the designer's instructions then it is unlikely to cause any harm.

Designers must ensure that manufacturers of the plant get complete and easy-to-understand information on:

- the use for which the plant has been designed
- how to install, adjust, use, clean, maintain, repair, and dismantle the plant safely
- and any other relevant information.

Manufacturers and suppliers of plant

Manufacturers and suppliers of plant must take all practicable steps to make sure that there is no likelihood that their goods will cause harm if they are:

- used for the purpose they were designed for
- installed, adjusted, used, cleaned, maintained, repaired, and dismantled in line with the designer's instructions.

Taking all practicable steps might mean preparing a manual that includes information on using and maintaining the equipment, using any safety equipment or guards, and spelling out the risks if these instructions aren't followed.

Designers of protective clothing and equipment

Designers of protective clothing and equipment must ensure the design of their goods incorporates all relevant ergonomic principals, eg chairs designed for a workplace must not cause harm to someone if they sit in them for 8 hours.

Goods must also be designed so that if they are made, installed, used, maintained, and repaired in line with the designer's instructions they will give adequate protection from the harm they are intended to protect against.

Designers must make sure comprehensive and easy-to-understand information is given to the manufacturers.

Penalties

Failing to comply with the regulations may result in a maximum fine of:

- $250,000 (a section 50 fine).

More information

For general questions about the Health and Safety in Employment Act and how it applies, or developing a health and safety plan:

- visit the OSH website on *www.osh.dol.govt.nz*
- call the Department of Labour's Workinfo service on 0800 209020 or visit their website at *www.workinfo.govt.nz*.

If the problem is a matter of appropriate health and safety practice, the following people and resources may be able to assist:

- your own employees or their union – you should talk to them first
- experts within the workplace
- a lawyer or HR consultant
- specialist workplace health and safety companies
- external experts in the field, such as scientists or engineers
- unions
- employer associations and sector organisations
- other publications, such as codes of practice, guidelines, and material safety data sheets
- manufacturers, suppliers, or designers
- health and safety inspectors.

You can also contact the Maritime Safety Authority on 0800 22 55 22 or visit their website at *www.msa.govt.nz*.

ACC can provide you with information on injury prevention and safety issues. Contact them on 0800 THINK SAFE (0800 844 657) or visit *www.acc.co.nz/injury-prevention*.

Health and safety checklist

At first glance the obligations imposed by the Act can seem overwhelming, especially for small businesses with limited resources. But when these obligations are broken down into bite-sized chunks and listed systematically they seem more manageable. The checklist below will help clarify what you must do to comply with the Act. You can use it to help draw up a health and safety plan for your workplace.

- ❑ who is going to have input into the health and safety plan?
- ❑ who is responsible for implementing the health and safety plan and distributing it among staff?
- ❑ what goals and deadlines will you set? (eg train all employees to use the fire equipment within 6 months)
- ❑ how are you going to check the workplace for hazards or potential hazards?
- ❑ do you have a system for employees to report real or potential hazards?
- ❑ do you have a system to make sure your employees' concerns are acted on?
- ❑ do you check for hazards when new equipment arrives or procedures change?

HEALTH AND SAFETY

- when you buy new machinery, do you check that you have all relevant safety information and equipment so the machinery can be used safely?
- what training and operational changes need to be done to prevent new equipment creating a hazard?
- do you tell contractors about hazards in your workplace and find out what hazards they bring into your workplace?
- are you managing hazards properly, ie identifying them, deciding if they are significant and taking the appropriate action?
- are you complying with your legal obligations regarding significant hazards?
- if significant hazards can't be removed or isolated, are you monitoring any impact they may be having on employee health?
- do you have a plan for dealing with non-significant hazards and is someone responsible for this?
- do you tell contractors and visitors about workplace hazards and how they can keep safe?
- do you make sure that contractors have the knowledge and skills to do the job safely?
- do you provide staff with health and safety information and training?
- do people at all levels understand their responsibilities?
- do employees know about their legal duty not to harm themselves or others at work?
- how are new employees told about health and safety issues?
- are health and safety responsibilities included in the job description?
- have particular health and safety duties been assigned to particular individuals?
- do you tell employees about real and potential hazards in your workplace and how to protect themselves?
- do you have a system for making sure all employees have the skills and experience to do their jobs safely and if not, do you have a system for making sure they are supervised until they have sufficient training and experience?
- do you have a legal requirement to have an employee participation system?
- if so, do you have one, or are you complying with the requirements of the default system?
- if not, how are you fulfilling your legal duty to give employees a chance to participate in improving workplace safety?
- do you have emergency procedures and equipment in place?
- do employees know about these procedures and how to use any emergency equipment?
- are staff reporting incidents and injuries?
- are you investigating incidents and injuries?
- do you maintain a register of accidents and serious harm?
- is your accident register in the required form?

COMPLIANCE AND YOUR BUSINESS

- are all incidents of serious harm reported to OSH?
- do you and your staff understand your legal duty not to interfere with an accident site that will be investigated by OSH, except in special circumstances?
- are you aware of the codes of practice, OSH guidelines, Government regulations, or industry standards that apply to your workplace and are you complying with them?

Accident compensation

All employers must belong to the Accident Compensation Corporation's (ACC) workplace insurance scheme. The scheme provides 24-hour, no-fault insurance for anyone injured in an accident in New Zealand. It covers medical care as well as reimbursing employees for some loss of earnings. ACC is the sole provider of this insurance.

Employers are obliged to pay levies to cover work-related injuries involving themselves and their staff. Their employees also pay levies to cover non-work injuries. These levies are deducted from salary at the same time as PAYE. The Government picks up the tab for non-income earners.

Employers can choose between two types of insurance:

- ACC WorkPlace Cover – under this option ACC automatically sends out information about the workplace insurance scheme, calculates the levy and sends an invoice. This is the cover taken by most small- and medium-sized businesses.
- ACC Partnership Programme – this option lets employers take on some or all the workplace insurance risk themselves. Generally, the amount of effort involved in being accredited to the programme means it is only worthwhile for big employers.

See chapter 4, *Tax* for more details on the amount of ACC levies and the way they are calculated.

Levies

ACC levies are set each year by Government regulations. Employers pay different levies depending on the activities they are involved in. Levies are payable in advance and are based on the previous year's payroll. They are re-calculated the following year based on the actual payroll. The employer is then sent a levy adjustment.

Discounts on the WorkPlace Cover levy

Levy discounts are available to employers who can demonstrate that they have a relatively safe workplace. Discounts of 10%, 15%, and 20% are available on the ACC WorkPlace Cover levy for employers who qualify under ACC's WorkPlace Safety Management Practices Programme.

Participation in a workplace safety programme is optional. It is also fairly time-consuming, meaning an employer may need a fairly large workforce to make going through the process worthwhile. However, the programme will also go a long way to taking the practical steps required by health and safety legislation – so it has a double benefit.

To qualify, employers must apply to ACC, go through a workplace self-assessment, then go through an independent workplace safety audit. ACC provides an audit tool that employers use for the self-assessment. The tool enables employers to assess safety standards in their workplace and helps them decide it they would pass an independent audit. If an employer passes the self-assessment, they send a completed application form to ACC. ACC then tells them if they've qualified for the next step – the independent audit.

ACC will pay for the independent audit. The auditor will assess whether the workplace meets the requirements for a levy discount, and the level of discount. The level of discount depends on the extent to which the employer's workplace meets the requirement of having a safer working environment. Workplaces are graded on three levels:

- **primary:** the workplace conforms to a basic level (10% discount)
- **secondary:** the workplace conforms above specified requirements (15% discount)
- **tertiary:** awarded to workplaces that conform to a high level of requirements and shows continuous improvement (20% discount).

As well as examining the workplaces, processes, and safety systems, they will conduct interviews with staff. If the workplace doesn't meet the required standards but the problems are minor, the employer has 30 days to come up to scratch and have this verified by the same auditor. After 30 days, the auditor completes the report and gives ACC their recommendation.

ACC makes the final decision on whether a discount is awarded based on the recommendation of an auditor's report. Discounts apply for 2 years. To keep the discount the employer must reapply every 2 years.

If the problems are extensive, or if the employer fails the audit, they aren't able to reapply for the discount for 12 months.

Self-employed

Self-employed people are also required to have workplace accident insurance through ACC. They pay a self-employed levy, with the amount depending on the activities they are involved in. The self-employed have two choices when it comes to protecting their earnings after an accident. They can pay:

- a higher premium and insure themselves so they will receive a guaranteed level of weekly compensation if injured in a workplace accident
- the standard premium and receive weekly compensation for loss of earnings based on their actual earnings before the accident.

See chapter 4, *Tax* for more details on cost of self-employed ACC levies.

The claims process

When an employee is injured at work you will receive a letter from ACC saying if the injury is covered by ACC.

ACC will assign a case manager to the claim, and contact you to discuss a rehabilitation plan for getting the employee back to work. ACC will continue to work with and monitor the employee's progress until a sustainable return to work or other outcome has been achieved.

Employers' obligations to pay weekly compensation

Under the Injury Prevention, Rehabilitation and Compensation Act (IPRC Act), employees are entitled to receive weekly compensation for loss of wages resulting from any injury that is covered by ACC. Most of this compensation is paid for by ACC. However, compensation for the first week of incapacity comes from the employer if the injury was:

- work related, or
- a work-related injury caused in a motor vehicle accident.

If a claimant has more than one job, and suffered a loss of earnings from all their jobs in the first week, the employer in whose employment they suffered the injury is responsible for all the first week of compensation.

The employer must pay the injured person 80% of the amount of the earnings lost by the employee during the first week of incapacity.

Before making the payment, an employer can ask the employee to produce a certificate from a registered health professional nominated and paid for by the employer.

Under the IPRC Act employees are entitled to use any special leave they are entitled to under the Holidays Act during the first week they are incapacitated due to a non-work injury. This is provided the injury is not work related, or due to a work-related motor vehicle accident.

Weekly compensation after the first week of incapacity

ACC's liability to pay weekly compensation commences only after the first week of incapacity. Generally, ACC is liable to pay weekly compensation to earners, and potential earners, for loss of earnings and loss of potential earnings capacity respectively. 'Earner' includes an employee on unpaid parental leave.

The weekly compensation payable by ACC is 80% of the claimant's weekly earnings, as assessed using a prescribed formula.

Rehabilitation

The IPRC Act imposes certain responsibilities on ACC, the claimant, and the employer in relation to rehabilitating an injured person.

HEALTH AND SAFETY

ACC must provide the claimant with the necessary rehabilitation, while claimants must take some initiative and cooperate with ACC to achieve the rehabilitation goals.

Employers have obligations regarding vocational rehabilitation. These apply when ACC decides it is reasonably practicable to return the claimant to their pre-injury employment with the same employer. If ACC decides a claimant should go back to work it will notify the employer in writing. The employer must then take all practicable steps to help the claimant to achieve the vocational rehabilitation goals.

The duty on employers to help rehabilitate injured employees applies to both work-related and non-work-related injuries.

In terms of helping with rehabilitation, ACC recommends that employers should:

- maintain contact with injured employees who are absent from work
- keep an injured employee's job open while that person is rehabilitating
- assist the injured employee and their ACC case manager with the person's return-to-work plan
- arrange the employee's work during rehabilitation so that they do not have to carry out tasks that would be difficult for them to do because of their injury
- offer the injured employee alternative work if they are incapable of returning to their previous job
- allowing the injured employee to work less hours, if necessary
- provide recovering employees with a supportive working environment.

ACC may be able to help employers to rehabilitate injured employees, for eg by topping up their pay if they work reduced hours, assessing whether modifications need to be made to the workplace to accommodate the employee, and helping employers to make the necessary changes to their workplace.

Employer claims reports

Employer claims reports show employers what claims for work injuries have been made by their employees. Employers automatically receive claims reports if there has been claims activity. The reports provide three types of information for the report period:

- claim numbers, including how many have been registered by treatment providers, how many of those have been accepted by ACC, how many claims have been opened, and how many have been finalised and closed
- claim costs (excluding medical fees from doctors and physiotherapists) listed by service costs associated with rehabilitation of injured employees, and total costs of weekly compensation for lost earnings of injured employees
- registered claim types listed by gradual process claims covering injuries that develop over time, serious injuries, fatal injuries, and all other injuries.

Claims reports are sent monthly and 6-monthly. You can request additional reports at any time by contacting ACC on 0800 222 993.

PRIVACY

Privacy legislation protects the privacy of anyone who comes into contact with your organisation. It affects the information you're allowed to hold about people and how you store and use that information.

Employers, marketers, and business owners, in particular, must understand what they can and can't do with this information. Failing to comply can have serious consequences, including liability for damages if your failure harms someone.

Understanding your rights and duties when dealing with private information

The Privacy Act 1993 applies to anyone your organisation may have information about – clients, business partners, staff, and anyone else your organisation comes into contact with.

The Act applies to 'personal information'. That means anything about a person – their name, address, employment record, or information about their health and personal life. Videos and tape recordings are also covered. In short, any information that is about an identifiable person is covered.

You have to have a good reason for holding personal information about a person, you have to make sure they know what information you have, and you have to take reasonable steps to ensure it is accurate.

Does the Act apply to you?

Yes, almost certainly. The Act applies to almost all organisations. It covers all businesses operating in New Zealand, from sole traders to multinationals. There are a very few organisations the Act doesn't apply to – such as the Governor-General, courts, royal commissions, MPs on parliamentary business, and news media organisations during news-gathering activities.

You also need to understand that you are liable for the actions of your staff and any other organisation acting on your behalf.

How should you deal with information about people?

The Privacy Act is based on 12 'information privacy principles'. These principles mean:

- You should only collect as much personal information about people as you need to carry out your business.
- In general, you should collect information about a person directly from that person. However, there are exceptions – for eg this principle doesn't apply if the information came from a publicly available source such as a newspaper or magazine, or if the person consents to having the information collected from someone else, or if collecting the information from a third party would not harm the interests of the person that the information relates to, or if collecting the information directly from the person is not reasonably practical, or if the information will only be used for statistics or research where the person won't be identified.

PRIVACY

- You should tell the person what information you are collecting about him or her, what you will use the information for, who will store it, and who will use it. You also need to tell the person that he or she can view the information you hold and correct any errors.
- You mustn't gather any information illegally or unfairly or in ways that would unreasonably intrude on anyone's personal affairs.
- You have to take reasonable steps to ensure any information you have isn't lost or misused and is protected from unauthorised access.
- In general, people are entitled to see all of the information you have about them. But there are exceptions, see the section on *Requests to see personal information* below.
- If a person asks you to correct errors in the personal information you have about them, you should do so or append a note explaining the request for a correction.
- You mustn't use personal information about anyone without taking reasonable steps to ensure it is accurate, up-to-date, relevant, and not misleading.
- You mustn't keep personal information about someone for longer than is required to achieve the purpose you gathered it for.
- In general, you can't gather information for one purpose and then use it for another. However, there are exceptions – for eg this principle doesn't apply if the information came from a publicly available source such as a newspaper or magazine, if the person concerned gives consent, or if the information will be used for statistical or research purposes that won't identify the individual involved.

In general, you can't disclose information about a person to any other person or business. However, there are exceptions – you can disclose information to someone else if it was gathered for that specific purpose, if disclosure is required by law, or for any of the reasons given in the point above.

You can only assign unique identifiers (such as employee numbers) in limited circumstances.

Appointing a privacy officer

The Act also requires you to appoint a privacy officer. This person is responsible for:
- educating people in your organisation about the information privacy principles and encouraging them to comply
- dealing with people who want to see what personal information your organisation has about them
- dealing with complaints
- liaising with the Privacy Commissioner (see page 129).

This doesn't mean you have to hire an extra staff member. You can do the job yourself, or appoint another existing staff member. The amount of work involved will vary from one organisation to the next, depending on how big the organisation

121

is, how much personal information it has about people, and how many sites it operates on. Bigger organisations might want to appoint more than one privacy officer.

The Office of the Privacy Commissioner holds regular workshops to train privacy officers. The office also provides fact sheets, a video, and other resources to help privacy officers do their job. Specific enquiries may be discussed with one of the enquiries officers.

To help protect your organisation from any action under the Act, any complaints or enquiries about your business which are privacy-related should first be dealt with by your own privacy officer. The officer should also deal with requests for access and correction to personal information. As well, a privacy officer may consider the way in which your business is presently dealing with such information and suggest improvements.

If your organisation has an internal complaints system, it can be used to deal with Privacy Act complaints too. Obviously, that means the person responsible for the complaints system will have to be appointed as a privacy officer. It's not compulsory to have a complaints system, but it is good business practice and having one will help limit your risks.

Requests to see personal information

In general, a person has a right to see any information you have about them. That means employees have a right to see their personnel records, and clients and customers have the right to see what information you hold about them. Within reason, you have to be helpful to people making requests.

If a person asks to see what information you have about them, your privacy officer should deal with the request. If you don't have a privacy officer you should nominate someone at this point.

The request has to be dealt with as quickly as possible. In general, you can't take longer than 20 working days. The person can ask for their request to be treated as urgent, but they have to give you a good reason.

How should you provide the information?

If the personal information is held in written documents, you can provide the person with a copy of the document, a summary of the document, or let them inspect the document.

If the information is in a video or tape, you can give them a copy or let them come and watch or listen to it at your office.

In general, you should provide the information in the form the person wants it in.

Can you refuse access?

You can refuse to give access to the information for a number of reasons, including:

- you don't have the information or you can't find it
- the information isn't readily retrievable
- providing access would disclose a trade secret or prejudice the commercial position of whoever supplied the information or whoever is the subject of the information (but this exception doesn't apply if disclosure is in the public interest)
- disclosure would involve an unwarranted intrusion in the affairs of another person
- disclosure would breach an obligation of confidentiality to whoever supplied the information (but this exception only applies to certain 'evaluative' information, for example, information used to determine if you should employ someone or award them a contract)
- the request is frivolous or vexatious.

There are other exceptions, but generally they don't apply to business situations.

Note that the reasons listed above may be grounds for refusing access to part, but not all, of the information you have about someone. For example, you may have to release a document with trade secrets deleted, rather than refusing access to the whole document.

Can you transfer the request to another company or organisation?

Yes. If your company doesn't have the information requested, but you believe another organisation does, you can transfer the request. However, you should tell the person who made the request that you are transferring it.

Can you charge for access?

You can't charge for processing a person's request for information about themselves. That means you can't charge for helping them make the request, transferring the request, or deciding whether you will agree to it.

However, you can charge for providing the actual information requested. Your charge can take into account the amount of time and resources involved in providing the information, and any extra costs involved in treating the request as urgent – but the charge must be reasonable. If it isn't, the Privacy Commissioner can set a different charge. Public sector agencies cannot charge at all.

COMPLIANCE AND YOUR BUSINESS

Correcting errors

The person has a right to ask for any errors to be corrected. If your company is not willing to make the corrections the person wants, you have to attach a statement saying what corrections the person sought.

If errors are corrected or a statement is attached, you have to take reasonable steps to inform anyone you've previously provided the personal information to.

You also have to tell the person who has asked for errors to be corrected what action you have taken.

Dealing with complaints

If a person makes a complaint about a privacy matter, your privacy officer should deal with the request. If you don't have a privacy officer, you should nominate someone when the complaint is received.

The privacy officer can then investigate the complaint, come to a conclusion about whether your organisation has breached any of the information privacy principles, and determine what action should be taken. It's a good idea to keep the person who made the complaint well informed and involved in the process. Most complaints can be resolved in-house.

But if the complainant isn't happy, he or she can take the complaint to the Privacy Commissioner (see page 129).

The Privacy Commissioner will decide whether to investigate the complaint and, if an investigation takes place, whether there has been a breach of privacy. Note that the commissioner can require you to attend conferences and give evidence.

If the complainant's privacy has been breached, the commissioner will generally try to achieve a settlement between you and the complainant. This may involve an apology, an assurance the problem won't happen again, and possibly financial compensation.

If no settlement is reached, the commissioner can refer the complaint to the Proceedings Commissioner, who will decide if it should be heard by the Complaints Review Tribunal. The Tribunal can:

- declare that a breach of privacy has occurred
- order you to pay damages
- order you to pay costs
- order you to stop the conduct that breached the complainant's privacy and take steps to put right any loss or damage to that person.

Sometimes a complainant will be happy with an apology or an assurance that the breach of privacy won't happen again.

124

PRIVACY

Dealing with personal information

Market research

The Privacy Act doesn't stop businesses from gathering information about people in their target market. You have the right to ask customers to fill in questionnaires, obtain customer information from other companies or agencies, phone people in a particular area, or take other steps to gather information about people who might be interested in your products or services. What the Act requires is that you tell people what the information is being collected for, how it will be stored and used, who it will be passed to (if anyone), and the fact that they have rights to access and correct the information. The law says you can only use information for the purpose that you disclosed when you collected the information.

Opt-out boxes on questionnaires – such as 'tick here if you do not wish to receive future mailings' – are not obligatory under the Privacy Act, providing that people are told if the information might be used for future mailings. However, opt-out boxes do help put the customer in control of their information and so limit your risk. You should also be aware that selling or sharing mailing lists with other organisations may raise privacy issues.

Case study

Rebecca goes to the appliance section of a large department store to buy a DVD player. She talks to a salesperson about the different brands and decides to buy one. The salesperson tells her she can pay at his desk rather than queuing up at the counter and takes her there so he can print out an invoice. In doing so, he asks Rebecca for her name and address. He doesn't give a reason for requiring this information and Rebecca is suspicious. She says she would rather not waste time with paperwork and takes the machine to the counter instead. Later, she discovers that the staff were on commission and that was why her details were wanted. Rebecca is annoyed she wasn't told and doesn't go back to the store again. Though relatively minor, this appears to breach the principle that she had a right to be told why information was being gathered about her.

COMPLIANCE AND YOUR BUSINESS

If you use security cameras make sure the tapes are stored securely and that you have a policy on who may view them.

Using security cameras?

You can use security cameras. However, as this is considered to be a collection of personal information, you must have good reason. If you wish to use security cameras, you should consider what purpose the cameras are being installed for and whether it is appropriate to inform people that they are operating (perhaps by having a sign displayed).

Case study

A business installed a video surveillance camera in its garage after problems with thefts from employees' cars. The positioning of the camera meant members of the public passing in the street outside the garage were filmed and someone complained. However, under the circumstances, it was found that the camera wasn't unreasonably intrusive. The camera showed no more of the street than was reasonably required for perimeter security, and the business agreed to put up signs advising that a security camera was in operation.

Can you tape phone calls?

In certain circumstances you do have the right to tape a conversation without the knowledge of the other party. However, such telephone calls should be made to you and not by you.

If you make the call, you should get the other person's agreement before taping it. If you don't, there may be issues about whether you are able to use the information you gather.

If customers are aware that you record phone calls and impliedly consent, you can generally use the information for legitimate business purposes.

Be aware that a customer will almost certainly be entitled to have access to telephone recordings of their own conversations, provided the information is readily retrievable. However, if a person asks for access to telephone conversations they weren't involved in, but in which they were discussed, then the legal position isn't straightforward and you should get legal advice.

> **Case study**
>
> A woman had a dispute with her employer. She was later phoned by a fellow worker who asked her what she thought of the boss and what her intentions were. The conversation was recorded without her knowledge and the tape was then given to the employer who used extracts from it when responding to her personal grievance claim. The woman complained to the Privacy Commissioner, who found the collection of information in the circumstances was unfair.

References

You can still do reference checks, as long as you have the permission of your prospective employee. Problems may arise if a former employer gives a bad verbal reference and the person complains that they did not give permission for you to contact that employer or authorise that employer to give them a reference.

If you are planning to contact a former employer about someone you are thinking of hiring, you should get clear authority (preferably in writing) from the prospective employee.

If you are approached by another company to give a reference for one of your current or former staff, you should get authority from the staff member before giving a reference.

The same approach applies to credit references – you shouldn't give out information about a person without their consent. You must also bear in mind that all information that you give during a reference check must be accurate and true. False representations made during a reference check could breach the Fair Trading Act.

In all cases, you should keep a file copy of the authorisation so you can prove you were entitled to give out information.

COMPLIANCE AND YOUR BUSINESS

> **Case study**
>
> A woman applied for a position within a Government department and provided her CV and a written reference from a former employer. The application form asked the woman to nominate referees, and she understood that this meant only those nominated would be contacted. She didn't get the job and later found out her former employer who had provided the written reference had been contacted and had provided further comments. She hadn't listed that employer's name on the application form and she believed his comments were wrong. The woman tried to resolve the matter directly but eventually complained to the Privacy Commissioner. The Commissioner found the woman had not authorised the contact and the department also hadn't advised applicants of its policy of following up written references. The department apologised to the woman and agreed to pay her $1,000 compensation. It also revised its application forms and reviewed its recruitment policies and manuals.

It's a good idea to inform staff about the nature of email and to have a protocol for email use.

What about emails?

In return for allowing employees to use the email and internet system for personal use, you may wish to have a monitoring system to check that unauthorised or prohibited material is not being sent or received. Formulating a policy and informing staff is a good way to limit your risks.

Many people assume that an email is like a letter. In fact, it's like a postcard and staff can be mortified to know that email communications are not secure and can be read by others within and outside the organisation. It's also useful to have some way of capturing and recording 'electronic footprints'. These may help you deal with complaints received about unauthorised access to electronic files you hold. It can assist the Office of the Privacy Commissioner if a complaint is received and can act as a safeguard of the personal information you hold, as well as a deterrent to those thinking about accessing information without authority.

If you plan to collect details about visitors to your websites, you should say so, and should explain why you are collecting information and what it is going to be used for. The purpose of collection must be lawful and under the Act you must ensure such information is protected by reasonable security safeguards.

The Privacy Commissioner

The Office of the Privacy Commissioner was established in 1991 to investigate complaints and promote the information privacy principles. There is a team of investigating officers and an enquiries team which takes written and telephone enquiries.

The law says the Commissioner must consider the protection of human rights and social interests that compete with privacy, including the free flow of information and the recognition of the right of government and business to achieve their objectives efficiently.

The Privacy Commissioner may allow businesses to collect, use, or disclose certain information even though that would otherwise breach privacy. Special circumstances must exist so that the public interest outweighs the interference with privacy.

The Commissioner can also issue codes of practice which give exemptions to the information privacy principles. The Health Information Privacy Code 1994 is the most extensive code issued so far, modifying all 12 information privacy principles into 12 rules which apply to the health sector.

The Privacy Commissioner is a watchdog. Besides reporting on proposed laws and policies, the Commissioner can make public statements and monitor information-matching programmes. This involves Government departments comparing personal information held on people with information held by other departments. The Privacy Act says notice must be given to the person before any action can be taken on the basis of a successful match.

COMPLIANCE AND YOUR BUSINESS

> ### Checklist for complying with the Privacy Act
>
> You need to consider:
> - appointing a Privacy Officer
> - how you will deal with complaints about privacy
> - how you collect and store customer and employee details
> - your policies on the use of security cameras and tape recording phone calls
> - your policies on email and internet use
> - getting authorisations for obtaining or giving out references or other personal information.
>
> Regarding personal information, you should:
> - ensure such information is stored securely and records are locked away when not in use
> - develop a confidentiality policy
> - not leave records where someone can look at them or steal them
> - keep records protected in covers, folders, or boxes
> - have a procedure that identifies sensitive records and make sure staff know they are sensitive
> - have a 'clear-desk' policy – put records away promptly
> - do not take records home
> - if records are taken from their normal place, make a note of who took them, when they were taken, and when they were returned.

Protected Disclosures Act 2000

This law is more commonly known as the 'Whistleblowers Act'. It is designed to protect employees and contractors who want to 'blow the whistle' on something wrong within your company or organisation.

The Act protects the 'whistleblower'. So long as they follow the procedures set out in the Act, they can't be sacked or disciplined for telling others about the wrongdoing.

However, the Act only applies to 'serious wrongdoing'. That means things like crimes or threats to public health or safety, or to the environment.

The Act spells out who they can tell. Unless there's a good reason, in the first instance they have to tell someone in your organisation about the wrongdoing. But in certain circumstances they can tell someone outside, such as the police.

What do you need to do?

While it isn't compulsory, it's a good idea to set up procedures for staff to report serious wrongdoing.

Public sector organisations such as Government departments have to have an internal disclosure system. This spells out who staff should go to if they know about a serious wrongdoing that needs to be disclosed.

Private companies aren't required to have an internal disclosure system, but it means you'll get to find out about any allegations of serious wrongdoing within your company, and that means you'll have a better chance of dealing with any major issues before they are reported to outside authorities. A system also improves your communications with staff, stakeholders, and the public, and might reduce the incidence of accidents in the workplace.

How should the disclosure be made?

If you have an internal disclosure system, you should tell your staff about it and they should use it to report any serious wrongdoing.

The disclosure system needs to be independent and confidential. That means:

- the person that staff report to about the wrongdoing must be in a position to objectively hear both sides of the argument, from the staff member who makes the complaint and then from anyone alleged to be involved in the wrongdoing – no one should be the judge in their own cause
- the staff member who makes the disclosure has the right to be heard in confidence – their identity shouldn't be revealed to anyone else unless they give their consent in writing, or there is another very good reason such as the need to protect natural justice or public safety.

What if there is no internal disclosure system?

If there is no system, then the employee or contractor can go to the head of your organisation to blow the whistle.

But in some circumstances the employee may also be justified in telling an 'appropriate authority'. They can only do this if:

- the head of the organisation is or may be involved in the serious wrongdoing;
- no action is taken to remedy the wrong within 20 working days of the head of the organisation being told, or
- telling someone else is justified because the matter is extremely urgent or there are other exceptional circumstances.

The Act spells out which authorities the employee can go to:

- the Commissioner of Police
- the Controller and Auditor-General
- the Director of the Serious Fraud Office

Remember: if an employee discloses information under the Act you can't take legal action – either civil or criminal – against them over the disclosure.

COMPLIANCE AND YOUR BUSINESS

- the Inspector-General of Intelligence and Security
- an ombudsman
- the Parliamentary Commissioner for the Environment
- the Police Complaints Authority
- the Solicitor-General
- the State Services Commissioner
- the Health and Disability Commissioner
- the head of any public sector organisation
- a professional disciplinary body (such as the Medical Council or Law Society)

but not:

- a Minister of the Crown
- a Member of Parliament.

Does it matter who is responsible for the wrongdoing?

Under the law, the wrongdoing may be carried out by one person or one element of the organisation acting independently. It may be directed against the organisation or outside the organisation without its knowledge. It could also be carried out by the organisation itself against an employee or contractor, another organisation, the State, or the environment. Action that is taken by one employee against another, or by the organisation against an employee, may give rise to a personal grievance, as defined under the Employment Relations Act 2000.

What if the employee 'discloses' something that is untrue?

Your employee can only use this law to disclose information if:

- it is about serious wrongdoing
- the employee believes it is true or is likely to be true
- the employee wants the wrongdoing investigated
- the employee wants the disclosure protected (ie, they want to be protected from retaliation or any other fallout).

If the employee knows the allegation is untrue or is acting in bad faith, he or she isn't protected by the Act. The employee also has no right to disclose information protected by legal professional privilege.

What protection does the employee have?

Under the Act, if an employee makes a protected disclosure, you can't:

- fire them or retaliate in any other way – otherwise, you'll be liable for a personal grievance claim under the Employment Relations Act and possibly a claim of victimisation under the Human Rights Act 1993

PRIVACY

- reveal their identity to anyone else – unless they give consent in writing or if revealing their identity is necessary to allow proper investigation of the allegation, or would prevent serious risk to public health or safety or to the environment, or is necessary to comply with the principles of natural justice.

Case study

In 1996, the Privacy Commissioner investigated a letter a nurse wrote about a patient and sent to a Member of Parliament.

The nurse first wrote to the Minister of Health expressing concern about the release of a patient from the secure unit of a psychiatric hospital. The letter contained information about the patient, including comments about his earlier behaviour, state of mind, ability to cope with the outside world, and the risk of his release into the community. The nurse also sent a copy of this letter to the Minister of Police and the National Director of Mental Health. Some months later, the nurse sent a copy of the letter to the MP. It was this act that was investigated.

The Privacy Commissioner found that the nurse disclosed the patient's health information to the MP because the nurse considered it necessary to prevent or lessen a serious and imminent threat to public safety. However, the Commissioner said that, while having reasonable grounds to believe that the patient posed a serious and imminent threat to public safety, the nurse did not have reasonable grounds to believe it necessary to disclose this information to an MP to lessen or prevent the threat. The MP was not the appropriate recipient of the information, the Commissioner said, and the nurse had breached the health privacy code by disclosing more health information than was necessary for the purpose.

The nurse disagreed with this and the Privacy Commissioner did not take the matter further. However, the case caused much public discussion and was the main motivation behind the 'Whistleblower's Act'. Note that the law doesn't cover information disclosed to a Minister of the Crown or an MP.

COMPLIANCE AND YOUR BUSINESS

> **Main points on how to comply**
>
> In order to comply with the Act, you need to consider whether there is an internal complaints procedure in place. This is not compulsory but if you don't have one, it's a good idea to create one, for eg by setting up a 'committee' of senior members of your organisation.
>
> The law should also be made clear to your employees in an accessible way. To limit your liability, you should tell them their rights and assure them that information about wrongdoing can be disclosed without them being disciplined or dismissed. It's a good idea to do this during the induction process. Because the Act requires employees to use the internal procedures to resolve concerns first, this gives the organisation a chance to resolve issues before the employee feels the need to disclose the issues outside the organisation.
>
> If an employee sees evidence of serious wrongdoing, he or she should then use the internal disclosure system. If there is no such system, the employee can bring the wrongdoing to the attention of the head of the organisation, or an outside authority.

Trespass Act 1980

If someone comes on to your site and refuses to leave, they may be trespassing. The Trespass Act 1980 covers rights of access onto private property and sets out the penalties for people who trespass.

A person is trespassing if they are warned to leave a site by the occupier but they refuse. Also, if someone has been previously warned to stay off a site and they enter within 2 years of the warning, they are trespassing.

Issue a warning

If you think someone is likely to trespass or you find someone trespassing, you should issue a warning to the person.

The warning – along the lines that you will call the police if he or she enters or doesn't leave – can be made orally or in writing. A written warning should be delivered directly or by registered mail. It is important to keep a record of when and where the notice was delivered, and who delivered it. The warning remains effective for 2 years. This is sometimes wrongly referred to as a 'trespass order', but you don't need a court order to issue a trespass notice, and you don't need to use a particular form of words.

Once the warning has been delivered, the person immediately commits an offence under the Trespass Act if he or she comes onto the property. The person may be removed and can be arrested if he or she persists in entering.

Also, any person found trespassing on a site may be asked to give his or her name and address. It is an offence to provide false information.

Defences

The person has a legal defence if he or she proves that it was necessary to remain on site for their own protection or the protection of someone else, or because of some emergency involving property.

Another common defence against a charge under the Act is that the occupier consented to the person going onto the property. It is important to remember that everybody has implied permission to walk up the path and knock on your door. You then must ask the person to leave and give him or her reasonable time to leave at the most convenient exit before the person becomes a trespasser.

Taking action

You are able to take action against a trespasser if you are an 'occupier' of the land. Therefore, the protection under the Act applies not just to owners of property but also to tenants and licensees (a 'licensee' is a person who has permission to be on the land).

You may choose to prosecute people who trespass on your site. Under the Act, a person guilty of trespass is liable to a fine of up to $1,000, or 3 months' imprisonment.

However, because of the costs involved, this is unlikely to be a sensible option unless the trespasser has caused substantial damage and you want compensation. A lawyer will advise you of the merits of your case.

Depending on your particular situation, there may be other avenues that you can take. For example, you may be able to take action under the Harassment Act 1998.

The Trespass Act has proved useful for those wishing to prevent protest groups remaining on a site. You must tell the group to leave, and if they fail to do so, the police or security personnel can forcibly remove the protestors. This use of the Act has replaced the earlier procedure of court orders being obtained.

Case study

A woman was part of a protest group that entered a Wellington bank. They were asked to leave by the police but refused to do so and were arrested and charged with trespass. The woman protestor appealed against her conviction on the grounds that her implied licence to enter the bank had not been revoked. However, the court held that the police sergeant was authorised by the bank manager to revoke her implied licence to enter the bank and the appeal was dismissed.

COMPLIANCE AND YOUR BUSINESS

When asking for information you hold about employees or customers, the police have no power above those of an ordinary citizen to get such details, unless they have a search warrant for documents.

Powers of entry and inquiry – police, council officers, and Government departments

Occasionally police, council officers, or other officials may come to your office or site asking to speak to an employee or to enter for some purpose.

Also, from time to time, police, Government departments, or agencies may require details of information held by you about employees or customers.

The New Zealand Bill of Rights Act 1990 gives everyone the right to be protected against unreasonable search or seizure of person, property, or correspondence. However, it is also an offence to refuse to cooperate with some Government departments or officers who ask for documents or the right to enter your premises. If someone seeks to enter your premises to search for documents or to question people, you should ask them to wait while you seek further advice.

Police

The police have implied authority to come to your office reception or site office and ask to speak to any employee or enter the site further.

Either you or your employee are entitled to decline unless the police:

- have a search warrant for that particular office or site
- have an arrest warrant for the employee
- have good cause to suspect the employee has, on the office or site premises, committed an offence punishable by imprisonment
- are 'freshly pursuing' an employee whom they have good cause to suspect committed an offence by failing to stop, reckless or dangerous driving, or driving under the influence of alcohol.

Case study

The police obtained a search warrant and entered a business to gather information to determine whether a crime had been committed. The police later released confidential and sensitive commercial information obtained in the search to a competitor of the business. The police claimed that the information was not confidential and, even if it was, its release was in the public interest.

However, the court found that the information obtained by police should be regarded as confidential and all information disclosed by police was commercial in nature. The public interest defence could not be invoked because the information was not disclosed to prevent a crime or a threat to natural security. This case highlighted the care with which information obtained from businesses, even under warrant, needed to be treated. Damages were awarded.

Government departments or agencies

All employment relationships have implied obligations of confidence. However, some Government departments and agencies have the statutory authority to require you to disclose information held about employees or customers, without stating their reason for needing such information. This authority overrides any contractual obligation of confidentiality and the Privacy Act.

Those with this power include the:
- Department of Work and Income
- Inland Revenue Department
- Customs Department
- Security Intelligence Service
- Commerce Commission.

Occupational health and safety

Health and safety inspectors may enter a place of work for the purpose of carrying out their functions.

A visiting inspector is not required to give notice, except where the visiting time or circumstances may be other than what is 'reasonable' in the circumstances.

Access is therefore available to any place of work during its regular working hours, and where there are no other circumstances which would make the timing of the visit unreasonable.

Inspectors must produce their certificate of appointment to the person in charge.

Council officers

Under the Local Government Act 2002, a council and its officers have a broad power to enter private property (other than a house) to carry out a number of functions.

An authorised enforcement officer may get a warrant to enter property if a breach of a bylaw is suspected. Officers do not need a warrant in order to check whether water supply or drainage works are being misused, to ensure that utility services equipment is safe, to enforce a removal order, or in the case of an emergency.

The Act also allows a council to construct works on private property that are necessary for water supply, trade waste disposal, land drainage, river clearance, stormwater drainage, and sewage.

Before entering any private land, the council must generally give at least 24 hours' notice – except in an emergency. In some cases, the officer has to be accompanied by police.

COMPLIANCE AND YOUR BUSINESS

Under the Resource Management Act 1991 (RMA), an enforcement officer may at all reasonable times enter any place or structure (other than a house) to determine compliance with the Act, a district or regional plan or resource consent, an abatement notice, an enforcement order, or a water-shortage direction. The officer may take samples of water, air, soil or organic matter, or any suspected contaminant.

A warrant to enter and search property can also be issued by the court if there is a reasonable suspicion that a serious offence against the RMA has been committed. This can permit whatever activities are considered necessary for the investigation.

> **Case study**
>
> A council received a complaint about a piggery from a neighbour who suspected that the piggery owner was irrigating her property with pig waste. Under the powers given to enforcement officers under the RMA, a council enforcement officer entered the property one morning at 2.45am to investigate the complaint. The enforcement officer did not find irrigation taking place, although investigations revealed that effluent was being discharged into a natural waterway. The officer took photos of the discharge and surrounding vegetation and took samples of the discharge and samples of the stream water above and below the point of discharge. This evidence was used to charge and convict the piggery owner for discharging a contaminant into a natural waterway without consent, in contravention of the rules of the regional plan.

If you use consultant advisers and have contentious documents that you do not wish to become public, one way to keep control of such documents is to ensure that legal privilege attaches to them.

Legal privilege

Confidential communications between you and your solicitor are protected by legal professional privilege. This right is based on the impossibility of conducting legal business without professional assistance and the need for full and unreserved confidence between you and your legal adviser. There are also other types of privilege that might protect documents that come into existence for the purpose of legal proceedings.

Your communications with your solicitors are privileged if they are made in confidence to them in their professional capacity. Privilege protects not only communications expressly containing legal advice, but also information passed between you aimed at keeping both of you informed. And legal advice is not confined to them telling you the law – it includes advice as to what should prudently be done in the relevant legal context.

Withholding information

The law allows the withholding of information if, and only if:

- it is necessary to 'maintain legal professional privilege' and
- this interest is not outweighed by other public interest considerations.

So, you must ensure that the privilege attaching to documents is 'real'. Merely forwarding a copy of reports to lawyers may not be enough to ensure that legal privilege attaches to them. Consideration must always be given to the content and the purpose for which it was provided.

The test of whether a communication is protected by legal professional privilege is rather broad. Once a solicitor is employed, their job is to ensure that you avoid legal difficulties. Any communication is likely to be privileged if its overall aim is to obtain appropriate legal advice.

Communications between solicitors and other people retained on behalf of your company will be privileged only when that person is effectively standing in your shoes for the purposes of obtaining legal advice on your behalf.

Privilege can be waived or lost under some circumstances if the content of legal advice is disclosed by you to third parties. You should be careful to protect against this happening.

Claiming legal privilege

In deciding whether information is protected under legal privilege, you must consider whether it is 'necessary' to withhold that information in order to 'maintain' legal professional privilege.

A High Court decision on legal privilege noted that:

The essential question in any consideration of whether or not a document is privileged is, was it brought into existence for the purpose of 'getting or giving confidential legal advice or assistance'?

It is always advisable to discuss the protection of privilege, and other forms of confidential information, with a solicitor.

TAX

Business owners' and managers' reactions to tax can vary – boring, time consuming, confusing – very few managers get excited at the thought of sitting down to put their tax affairs in order.

However, making sure that you comply with your legal tax obligations, both for your business and for your staff, need not be an overwhelming job. When you first start it may seem that there's a lot to learn and a lot to remember, but once you've got your tax systems up and running, it's actually quite straightforward.

Complying with your tax obligations doesn't have to be a headache. It's a question of good systems, not rocket science

The secret to keeping your tax situation under control is to set up good systems when you first go into business and to keep your records up to date.

The mistake many businesses make is not stopping to consider their tax obligations until they arise, for eg when their first GST return is due, or an employee needs to be paid and they have to deduct PAYE.

Getting help

Tax is one area of business where it makes sense to get professional help – that is an accountant, tax agent, or lawyer.

While you could probably get your head around the main obligations and do the calculations yourself, tax for a non-accountant is a time-consuming business – time that could be much better spent managing or growing your business, or improving that all-important bottom-line.

An accountant or tax agent will do the job in a fraction of the time you can and because they know all the finer details of the tax legislation will be able to maximise your tax position. They will also be able to give you advice on how your business is doing and how it is projected to grow in the future, invaluable information for managing your business well.

However, it is important to remember that no matter who you get to help with your tax, the final responsibility for complying with your tax obligations rests with you.

You will still need to ensure that you keep comprehensive and up-to-date tax records – if the information you give your accountant isn't complete or correct then they can't produce accurate accounts. You will also need to make sure that you have the money available to pay your tax when it falls due and that you pay it on time.

TAX

> ### Using a tax agent
>
> A tax agent is a person who will help you with your tax returns and other tax matters. In New Zealand any person can set themselves up as a tax agent, they do not need to be a qualified accountant or have any accounts training.
>
> Inland Revenue registers tax agents but registration should not be taken as a sign of competence, only that Inland Revenue will allow the person to act on your behalf for the purpose of completing and filing tax returns.
>
> One of the main benefits of having a tax agent is that you will be granted an extension of time for filing your end-of-year income tax return and will have slightly longer to pay. You can also elect to have all correspondence, returns, and reminders from Inland Revenue sent directly to your agent.

A word of advice

One of the best reasons not to leave getting to grips with your tax until payments are overdue is the penalties.

Penalties attach to all areas of tax. There are penalties for filing returns late and there are penalties if you get it wrong. There are also penalties if you don't pay what you should when you should and what's more you'll be charged interest on what you owe for the amount of time it's outstanding. If matters get serious enough, you may even be prosecuted and criminal penalties may apply.

If you are in the situation where you've let tax matters slip, some leeway is available to you through voluntary disclosure. Voluntary disclosure gives you the opportunity to come clean with Inland Revenue about your tax affairs and put them right, without facing prosecution. There is more information about voluntary disclosure in the *Penalties and interest* section at p179.

Types of tax

This chapter looks at the main tax obligations that arise from being in business which are:

- income tax, including provisional tax, expenses, and depreciation
- GST
- resident and non-resident withholding tax.

It looks at the main tax obligations that arise from employing staff which are:

- PAYE, including allowances and deductions
- fringe benefit taxes
- withholding payments.

It also looks at ACC levies, at penalties and offences under tax legislation, and at the Inland Revenue Department, the services it offers to business owners and managers, and what to expect if the department wants to audit your accounts.

What's that tax?

- **Income tax** is paid by businesses on the profit they make – that is, the amount that's left after business expenses are deducted from sales and income. Income tax returns are filed annually, but most businesses will have to pay instalments throughout the year, called provisional tax. Companies and trusts pay income tax at a 33% rate, while for sole traders and partners in a partnership there are different rates of income tax depending on how much profit you make.
- **GST** stands for goods and services tax and applies to most goods and services supplied in New Zealand. Businesses and self-employed people charge and collect GST on behalf of Inland Revenue, generally at the rate of 12.5%. Charging GST is compulsory for most businesses, but smaller businesses can choose how they account for GST and how often they have to file returns.
- **Resident and non-resident withholding taxes (RWT or NRWT)** are charged on interest earned on investments, dividends paid to shareholders, and royalties. Businesses may have to pay or deduct RWT or NRWT.
- **PAYE** stands for pay as you earn, and is the basic tax taken out of an employee's earnings when they are paid. There are different rates of PAYE depending on how much the employee earns and whether they hold down more than one job. Employers have to account for PAYE deducted at least once a month, sometimes more. In addition to deducting PAYE, employers have ACC levy obligations and may also have to make student loan and child support deductions from their employees' wages.
- **Fringe benefit tax (FBT)** applies to benefits given to employees other than their salary or wages, including motor vehicles for private use, subsidised goods and services, loans, and employer contributions to superannuation, insurance schemes etc. Employers who don't provide fringe benefits can apply for nil status.
- **Withholding payments** (or withholding tax) is deducted by employers from earnings paid to contractors and company directors for certain activities and services.
- **Specified superannuation contributions withholding tax (SSCWT)** is tax that employers pay on contributions they make on behalf of an employee to certain superannuation schemes.

The main tax legislation

- **The Income Tax Act 1994** sets how individuals and businesses will be taxed on the income they earn each year.
- **The Tax Administration Act 1994** sets out the rules for complying with income tax obligations, for eg when returns must be filed and penalties for late returns and payments.
- **The Goods and Services Tax Act 1985** determines how GST will be levied, on what goods and by whom, as well as setting the rules for complying with GST obligations.
- **The Employment Relations Act 2000** establishes an employer's responsibility to keep records showing how wages are calculated.
- **The Injury Prevention, Rehabilitation and Compensation Act 2001** makes the Accident Compensation Corporation (ACC) the sole provider in New Zealand of accident insurance cover for personal injury. Regulations promulgated under the Act set the rates of the various ACC levies.

Am I in business?

Most businesses won't need to ask this question, but if you have any doubts about whether what you're doing (or intend to do) constitutes a business, then you should ask Inland Revenue. They have criteria they apply to decide if an activity or service is a business – the answer will affect the nature and extent of your tax obligations.

You will also need to know what type of business you are running. Different tax rules apply depending on whether you are a sole trader, a partnership, a company, or a trust.

Business type	What it is
Sole trader	A sole trader is a person trading on their own.
Partnership	A partnership is where two or more people join together to run a business.
Company	A company is a formal and legal entity in its own right, separate from its shareholders (or owners).
Trust	A trust is set up under a deed and the trustees administer and manage the trust for the benefit of its beneficiaries.

IRD numbers

No matter what type of business you're running you'll need an IRD number for it. Sole traders can use their personal IRD number or use form IR 595 (individuals) to apply for one. All other types of businesses should use form IR 596 (non-individuals) and will need to attach supporting information.

The tax year

All businesses have a balance date, which falls at the end of their accounting year. For most businesses, the year end (and their balance date) is 31 March.

This is when the final accounts for the year are drawn up, showing how much profit (or loss) the business made during the year. The final accounts are in turn used to calculate the business' final tax obligations for the year and to estimate the interim payments that the business will have to make towards its tax obligations in the following year.

If you want an alternative balance date, you must get written approval from Inland Revenue, but you will need good reason for doing so. The two main reasons that Inland Revenue will accept are:

- where a business is owned by an overseas company and the parent company is required by its own country's legislation to have a different balance date, for eg New Zealand businesses whose parent companies are in Australia are usually granted 30 June balance dates
- where a business is seasonal and wants to align its year-end balance date with the end of its season.

The Inland Revenue Department

As a business owner or manager, your relationship with the Inland Revenue Department will be one of the most important and enduring that you form. The department is responsible for assessing and collecting taxes, developing tax policy, enforcing tax legislation, and for general administration of the tax system. Tax rates are set by the Government.

Inland Revenue offers a range of services to businesses to help them understand and meet their tax obligations. The main ones are:

- Free tax advisory services – for small and medium businesses, including tax advisers who will visit your business and explain the types of taxes you need to know about, the records you need to keep, how to complete and file tax returns, and ways to make meeting your tax obligations easier. There is also a Maori community tax service for Maori small and medium businesses.
- Publications – booklets, summary sheets, and forms on all aspects of business tax obligations, including a guide for first-time employers and *Smart Business*, a useful introduction to business taxes and record-keeping.
- Toll-free numbers for tax enquiries.

TAX

- INFOexpress – a 7-day-a-week, automated telephone service for getting tax information, and ordering forms and booklets.
- *www.ird.govt.nz* – a website containing information, forms, booklets, and helpful tax year calendars with the due dates for businesses' tax returns and payments. You can also request services and file some of your returns online.
- Free newsletters to keep you up to date with tax changes.

Inland Revenue Department phone numbers

Remember to have your IRD number handy when you call any of these numbers.

0800 numbers

General enquiries or requesting a visit from an adviser	0800 377 774
Income tax	0800 377 774
Employer issues	0800 377 772
GST	0800 377 776
Overdue tax and returns	0800 377 771

INFOexpress

Forms and stationery	0800 257 773
Tax packs	0800 257 772
Other services	0800 257 777

What businesses must do

Inland Revenue has summarised what businesses must do to meet their tax obligations under legislation.

You must:

- correctly determine the amount of tax you have to pay
- deduct or withhold the correct amount of tax from payments or receipts
- pay tax on time
- keep all necessary tax information and maintain all necessary accounts or balances
- disclose all information that Inland Revenue requires, in a timely and useful way
- cooperate with Inland Revenue as required by law
- comply with other specific tax obligations.

From *IR 740 Business Taxes – An Overview,* Inland Revenue Department, April 2002.

COMPLIANCE AND YOUR BUSINESS

The information IRD holds about you and your business is subject to the Privacy Act. For more information about the Act and your rights under it see the chapter 3, *Privacy*.

> ### Tax and privacy
>
> Businesses are required by law to give Inland Revenue accurate information (and to keep it up to date) and may be charged penalties if they don't. Inland Revenue shares this information with other agencies both in New Zealand and overseas, the main ones being Work and Income New Zealand, the Department of Courts, The Ministry of Education, and the Accident Compensation Corporation.

Record-keeping

Every person who runs a business in New Zealand must keep thorough and accurate records — you are required to do this by law.

With respect to tax, you need to keep sufficient records to show the business' income and expenses, to confirm your accounts, to calculate your various tax liabilities, and to show the business' assets and liabilities.

This includes records generated as part of your day-to-day business, such as invoices, bank statements, and receipts, and records that you will need to create such as cashbooks, logbooks, and ledgers. It also includes any working papers that you use to calculate your tax position. If your accounting system is complex or computer-based you will need to keep an explanation of how it works.

Businesses that employ staff have additional record-keeping requirements to do with wages, fringe benefits, and contributions to superannuation funds. There are also tax-related record requirements for businesses with investments and for certain types of companies.

Sole traders, partners, and business owners will need to keep their personal records, as will any other person who is claiming a portion of their personal outgoings as business expenses.

A checklist of the main types of records you will need to keep is given below.

TAX

Records checklist suggested by IRD

For business income
- books of account, including cashbooks, petty cash books, journals, and ledgers
- receipts and invoices issued, including normal and tax invoices, EFTPOS receipts, credit card vouchers, and cash register tape
- credit and debit notes
- bank statements and records, including deposit slips and books, and cheque books
- worksheets showing tax return calculations
- other documents needed to confirm account entries.

For business expenses
- books of account, including cashbooks, petty cash books, journals, and ledgers
- invoices issued to you for purchases made for the business
- receipts received for purchases made for the business, including cash sale dockets and till receipts
- bank statements and cheque butts
- credit card vouchers and statements
- depreciation calculations
- details of travel expenses
- details of entertainment expenses
- motor vehicle logbooks
- utility bills, for eg for telephone and power
- legal documents, such as sale and purchase or lease agreements
- interest and dividend statements.

For business assets and liabilities
- lists of debtors and creditors
- stocktake records and statements of year-end trading stock
- a fixed asset register
- year-end profit and loss statements and balance sheets

For employers
- employees' wage records, including wage books, pay sheets, or payrolls
- records of account to Inland Revenue, including employer deductions payment forms, PAYE payment receipts, and employer monthly schedules
- employees' fringe benefit tax records and returns
- details of contributions to specified superannuation funds and SSCWT paid.

If you use your private motor vehicle for business purposes you need to keep a copy of all bills and receipts for the car, along with a logbook to record details of business trips.

149

COMPLIANCE AND YOUR BUSINESS

Tax records
- tax returns, including income tax, GST, and fringe benefit tax returns
- ACC invoices and receipts
- any working papers that have been used to calculate the business's tax position.

Personal records
- personal bank account records, including cheque and deposit books, and bank statements
- utility and telephone bills
- petrol and car maintenance receipts.

For partnerships
- the partnership agreement.

For companies
- the certificate of incorporation
- minute books.

For trusts
- the trust deed.

Make sure you keep a back-up of computerised tax records. Your computer failing will not remove your legal obligation to produce the records.

Storing records

Your records need to be stored in a logical manner, so that they are accessible if Inland Revenue asks to see them and can easily be used to verify your tax calculations.

Records should be kept in English and stored in New Zealand, unless you get approval from Inland Revenue to record them in another language or store them elsewhere. Applications to keep records in Maori are generally approved, provided certain conditions are met.

Inland Revenue allows certain categories of records to be stored electronically, for eg on laser discs or microfilms, provided the original data can be reproduced on a paper if needed. There are conditions attaching to electronic storage, so you should check with Inland Revenue before destroying any hard copy records.

If you keep your financial accounts on computer, you will still need to keep copies of your source documents to verify the accounts.

How long you need to keep your records

Business records (and the personal records of people who own a business) need to be kept for at least 7 years from the end of the tax year they relate to. This applies even if your business stops operating – you still need to hold on to the records.

TAX

It also applies to documents that have been filed with Inland Revenue electronically – you have to keep a hard copy for 7 years. One exception is the employer's monthly schedules, which you do not have to keep a copy of, although you do have to keep the documents the schedule was produced from.

In some circumstances, you can apply to Inland Revenue to be able to destroy your records after a shorter time, usually 4 years. On the other hand, Inland Revenue may require you to keep your records for an additional 3 years (10 years in total), if it is likely that your business will be audited in the near future.

Tax responsibilities for businesses

If you own or manage a business you will have to account to Inland Revenue for income tax. The majority of businesses will also have to account for GST, and some businesses will also account for resident and non-resident withholding tax.

If you employ staff you must account for PAYE, withholding payments, and other deductions from their wages, as well as for ACC levies and fringe benefit tax.

> ### Recent developments
> At the time this book was published, the Government was proposing changing tax legislation to simplify compliance for small businesses. Not all of the proposed measures will be introduced but the more interesting ones include bringing provisional income tax payments and GST into line, and providing assistance to small employers and self-employed people in their first year of business.

Income tax

What is income?

Your business' income is the money that the business earns from the goods and services it provides. The Income Tax Act 1994 does not strictly define what income is but for businesses it is important to remember that it:

- includes invoices that you have issued but have not yet been paid for
- includes sales that you have made but not yet issued invoices for
- includes goods and services provided by a third party as payment for goods or services supplied by your business, provided the third party's goods and services can be given a monetary value
- can include money you receive from the sale of business assets.

Businesses are not taxed on all the income they earn, but can offset their business expenses against it. What's left after expenses have been deducted from business income is called the net profit. Businesses pay tax on their net profit.

Remember: you must keep records, such as copies of bills, invoices, receipts, and logbooks, to substantiate any expenses that you want to claim for.

151

COMPLIANCE AND YOUR BUSINESS

Expenses

Not all business expenses are deductible and Inland Revenue or your tax agent will be able to advise you what you can and cannot claim for.

In general, you can deduct the day-to-day expenses that you incur in running the business. This includes things such as business rents, stationery, telephone, fax and internet costs, wages and other benefits provided to employees, ACC levies, stock, travel, and some entertainment expenses.

You can also deduct a portion of your personal expenses if you run your business from home or sometimes use your personal car for business trips.

One of the main types of expenses that are not deductible are the costs of buying or maintaining assets, such as computers or machinery, that will be used as part of your business. You can however, claim depreciation on the value of these assets as a deductible expense.

Claiming a deduction for depreciation is mandatory, although businesses can choose not to depreciate individual assets. To claim depreciation, you will need to keep a fixed asset register recording what each asset is, when you bought it, the depreciation you have claimed on it, and how much it cost.

There are different methods and rates of depreciation and Inland Revenue produces a comprehensive guide to help businesses work out how much assets can be depreciated each year.

Personal drawings are another expense that in general cannot be deducted. Any drawings made from a business by its owners or employees should be included as part of the business' total income for the purposes of calculating net profit. One exception is where shareholder-employees make drawings from a company during the year and these are treated as a salary for income tax purposes. The salary is deductible.

Filing your income tax returns

A the end of the tax year you must make sure your accounts are up to date, so you know what your business' net profit was for the year. You then have to calculate what tax is due on this profit and let Inland Revenue know by filing a tax return. If your business makes a loss you don't have to pay any income tax, but you still need to fill in and file a tax return.

There are different income tax return forms to use, depending on whether your business is a sole trader, partnership, company, or trust.

Tax returns for standard 31 March balance dates must be filed with Inland Revenue by 7 July in the same year.

Businesses that have non-standard balance dates must file their returns by:
- 7 July for balance dates between 1 October and 31 March
- the seventh day of the fourth month after the balance date, for balance dates between 1 April and 30 September. For example, a company with a balance date of 3 May must file its return by 7 September.

Businesses using a registered tax agent don't have to file their income tax return until 31 March of the following year, giving your tax agent a full year to complete it.

152

TAX

Returns must be accompanied by a copy of your financial records for the year. Rather than sending in a full copy of your accounts you can fill in Inland Revenue summary sheets and attach these instead. However, you must still prepare and keep a copy of your full accounts for the year in case Inland Revenue wants to see them.

Tax rates

How income tax is calculated and the rate that it is charged at varies depending on whether a business is a sole trader, partnership, company, or trust.

Tax rates are set by the Government and can change from time to time. IRD has published the following summary of tax rates as a guide for businesses.

How income tax is calculated	Income tax rate
Sole trader The owner or manager is personally entitled to all profits, but is also responsible for all business taxes and debts. Sole traders can take drawings from the business whenever they like, but these drawings are not deductible and form part of the business's net profit.	Sole traders pay income tax at individual rates as follows: ■ For income up to and including $38,000 – 19.5 cents in the dollar. ■ For income over $38,000 and up to $60,000 – 33 cents in the dollar. ■ For income over $60,000 – 39 cents in the dollar.
Partnership The partnership itself does not pay income tax. At the end of each year, it distributes all of the partnership's net profit to the partners who pay tax on their own share. Sometimes partners work under contracts of service. In this case, they are treated like an employee and paid a salary, with PAYE deducted from it.	Partners pay income tax at individual rates as above.

COMPLIANCE AND YOUR BUSINESS

How income tax is calculated	Income tax rate
Company Any profit made belongs to the company, which must pay tax on it. The company can distribute money to shareholders and employees in various ways, which affects how tax is paid.	The company pays income tax on profits at a flat rate of 33 cents in the dollar.
■ Shareholder-employees can take drawings from the company, which at the end of the year is calculated as a salary that the shareholders pay income tax on.	■ The drawings are treated as a salary and are deductible from the company's income. Shareholder-employees pay PAYE on their salary at individual rates as above.
■ Shareholder-employees can be paid a salary with PAYE deducted. The salaries are a business expense of the company.	■ Shareholder-employees pay PAYE at individual rates as above. Their salaries are deductible from the company's income.
■ The company can pay dividends to shareholders out of the profit once tax has been paid.	■ Flat rate of 33 cents in the dollar applies to all profits.
Trusts The trust's income is divided into two main types.	■ Beneficiaries pay income tax on income received from the trust at individual rates as above.
■ Beneficiary income – income that is paid to a beneficiary of the trust either in or within 6 months after the income year.	■ Trustee income – taxed at a flat rate of 33 cents in the dollar.
■ Trustee income – income that is not paid to a beneficiary of the trust either in or within 6 months after the income year.	■ Special rules exist to prevent tax advantages being obtained from distributing income to minor beneficiaries.

Tax credits

Sometimes businesses may have already paid tax at source on some of their business income, for eg through PAYE or resident withholding tax. These amounts are deducted from the amount of income tax due as tax credits.

Imputation credits

Dividends to shareholders are paid from a company's net profit after income tax has been deducted. Companies can attach imputation credits to dividends so that shareholders can claim a tax credit on them in their income tax returns. This ensures that income tax does not get paid twice.

Companies must deduct resident withholding tax at the rate of 33% from any part of a dividend that does not have an imputation credit attached.

Paying your tax

Although tax returns are not filed until after the end of a business' financial year, most businesses pay instalments towards their year-end tax bill during the year. These instalments are called provisional tax payments.

A business will have to pay provisional tax if its residual income tax for the previous year was $2,500 or more – this means the amount of income tax that was left to pay after any tax rebates and credits have been allowed for.

Because provisional tax is calculated from the previous year's income tax, businesses do not start to pay it until they are in their second year of business. This does not mean that the first year of business is tax-free.

Businesses that don't pay provisional tax when they are liable to, will be charged penalties and interest. See *Penalties and interest* section at p179 for more information.

Paying tax in your first year

Income tax for your first year in business is paid in one lump sum rather than instalments. The payment is due by 7 February in the following year if you have a 31 March balance date. This time is extended if you have a tax agent until 7 April. By this stage, most businesses (if they made a profit in their first year) will also be paying provisional tax towards their current year's income tax bill. This can be quite tough for new businesses, and the best way to avoid getting into difficulties is to put money aside towards your tax bill as it comes in, even in your first year.

Example

Jane starts her business in August 2003 and is using a standard balance date, so her first financial year will end on 31 March 2004. Jane makes a profit in her first year and her residual income tax is $5,900. This must be paid by 7 February 2005, or 7 April 2005 if she decides to use a tax agent. Because her residual income tax exceeded $2,500, Jane is liable for provisional income tax from 1 April 2004, and her first instalment will be due on 7 July 2004.

COMPLIANCE AND YOUR BUSINESS

If you estimate your residual income tax for the year will be less than $2,500, you can elect not to pay provisional tax. But if your estimate is wrong and your residual income tax exceeds $2,500, you may be charged penalties.

Estimating your provisional tax

Business owners and managers (or their tax agents) are responsible for estimating what their provisional tax payments should be. There are two ways of doing this:

- The 'standard' or 'up-lift' option – provisional tax is worked out by adding 5% to your residual income tax for the previous year.
- The estimation option – you estimate how much income you have earned so far in the year and how much tax you should pay on it. You must take reasonable care to get the estimation right, although you can re-estimate as many times as you like during the year. Inland Revenue will help you if you are having difficulty making the calculation.

Paying provisional tax

Provisional tax is paid in three instalments. For a standard balance date of 31 March these are:

- 7 July
- 7 November
- 7 March.

For other balance dates, provisional tax is due on the seventh day of every fourth month after the balance date. For example, if your balance date is 31 October your provisional tax instalments will be due on 7 February, 7 June, and 7 October.

Your provisional tax payments are offset against your final tax bill for the year. You will then either have to pay the balance or will be eligible for a refund. If you still have tax to pay, if you have a 31 March balance date it must be paid by 7 February in the following year, or 7 April if you use a tax agent.

If you use the standard option to estimate your provisional tax, you will not be charged interest if you have a lot of tax to pay at the end of the year. If you use the estimation method you may be charged a shortfall penalty if you get your provisional tax calculations very wrong.

If you over-pay your provisional tax (ie your final tax bill is less than the sum of your provisional tax instalments) you can request a refund at the end of the financial year and in some circumstances, Inland Revenue will pay interest on the amount over-paid.

TAX

> ### Recent developments
>
> The Government has recently passed legislation allowing businesses to pay their provisional tax instalments through a tax pool.
>
> Tax pools are where businesses pool their provisional tax payments with those of other businesses. They are generally run by commercial intermediaries and aim to smooth out the risks of estimating provisional tax liabilities, by offsetting one business' over-estimation against another's under-estimation.

Goods and services tax

Goods and services tax (GST) applies to most goods and services supplied in New Zealand, including secondhand goods. Goods and services that attract GST are called taxable supplies.

Businesses and self-employed people become GST registered, and charge and collect GST on behalf of Inland Revenue at the rate of 12.5%. GST is generally added on top of the price charged by the business for their goods or services.

Businesses must also, at regular intervals, account to and pay Inland Revenue the GST they have charged.

Against the amount of GST due to be paid to Inland Revenue, businesses can offset GST that they have paid on goods or services purchased to run the business – this is called claiming an input tax credit.

Becoming GST-registered

If your business' turnover is, or is expected to be, over $40,000 a year, it is compulsory to become registered with Inland Revenue to charge for and collect GST. This includes overseas businesses if they supply goods or services within New Zealand.

It is important when calculating your business' turnover to take into account grants, subsidies, and the value of bartered or exchanged goods or services, as well as sales and income.

You apply to become GST registered by filling out an IR 360 GST registration form. You must apply within 21 days of becoming eligible or you may be charged penalties. Once you are registered, you will be allocated a GST number.

If your turnover is less than $40,000 a year you can still choose to become registered for GST. This may be worth your while, if, for eg you buy lots of supplies that include GST as part of your business.

Businesses that are GST-registered must keep full records of all the GST they charge for and must keep those records for 7 years.

157

COMPLIANCE AND YOUR BUSINESS

> ### Exempt activities and supplies
>
> Some activities, such as those of an individual working for a wage or being a company director, do not attract GST. Some supplies also do not attract GST. Examples are interest received, bank charges, financial services, and letting certain types of property.
>
> Other supplies are zero-rated, which means that GST is charged at 0%. Examples are duty free and exported goods.

Exports and imports

The New Zealand Customs Service levies GST on imported goods, provided they are valued at over $400. GST paid on imported goods can be claimed as an input tax credit in the usual way.

Exported goods and services provided to a purchaser who is outside New Zealand are zero-rated, which means that GST is charged on them at 0%.

Tax invoices

GST-registered businesses must issue tax invoices for all goods and services they supply to other GST-registered people or businesses, and must keep a copy of the invoice for their records. If they don't, the purchaser can request one, and the business must issue an invoice within 28 days or it will commit an offence.

The exception is where the total price to be paid for goods or services is $50 or less including GST, in which case an invoice is not needed. However, it may still be a good idea to issue one in order to verify your accounts.

If you have to issue a copy of an invoice the fact it is a copy must be clearly marked on it.

What an invoice should contain varies, depending on how much it is for, but they should always be in New Zealand dollars.

> ## What your tax invoices must contain
>
> For supplies worth over $1,000 (including GST):
> - the words 'tax invoice' in a prominent place
> - the name (or trade name) and GST number of the supplier
> - the name and address of the person receiving the goods or services
> - the date the invoice was issued
> - a description of the goods and services supplied
> - the quantity, volume, or hours of the goods or services supplied, and
> - the amount charged for the supply, the GST, and the total amount charged including GST, or
> - the total price charged for the supply, with a statement that GST is included.
>
> For supplies worth between $50 and $1,000 (including GST) you still need to issue an invoice but you do not have to include the recipient's name or the quantity of the goods and services supplied.

GST-registered businesses also have to make sure that they receive invoices whenever they buy anything for the business if the price is over $50 (including GST). You must have an invoice in order to claim a tax credit in your GST return. If the price was under $50 you must have some other record to verify what you bought and how much you paid.

Accounting for GST

Although being GST-registered is compulsory for most businesses, there is some flexibility about how you account for GST to Inland Revenue.

The three ways of accounting for GST are:
- the invoice basis
- the payments (or cash) basis
- the hybrid basis.

Businesses choose which system they want to use when they become GST-registered. If you do not choose you will be put on the invoice basis by default. You can change the basis you use by writing to Inland Revenue.

Ways to account for GST

Invoice basis

You account for GST in the period in which you:
- issue or receive an invoice, or
- receive or make a payment – whichever is earlier.

This means you may be accounting for GST before you actually pay for or receive payment for goods and services.

Payments basis

You account for GST in the period in which you make or receive payment. This basis is only available to smaller businesses, where the taxable value of the business' supplies was $1.3m or less in the past year and is not expected to exceed this in the next year.

Hybrid basis

You account for GST on your sales using the invoice basis and claim GST on your purchases using the payments basis. Any business can choose to use this basis.

Taxable periods

Businesses also have a choice about how often they account for GST. This is called the taxable period and there are one-month, 2-month, and 6-month taxable periods. Generally, all GST taxable periods end on the last day of the month.

Businesses must account to Inland Revenue for all GST paid and received or invoiced within the taxable period.

There are criteria for each taxable period and if you want to change the period you use you will have to apply to Inland Revenue in writing. Most businesses are given the 2-month period by default.

GST taxable periods

- *One month* – any business can choose to account for GST every month but this period must be used by businesses whose sales of taxable supplies are likely to be more than $24 m in any 12 months.
- *Two months* – the taxable period that is given by default. There are two categories (the taxable periods in each category end in different months) and businesses can choose which one they want.
- *Six months* – this option is generally only available to businesses whose sales of taxable supplies did not exceed $250,000 in the past 12 months and are not expected to do so in the next 12. However, Inland Revenue may allow larger businesses to use this taxable period if the business has a proven track record of accounting for GST.

Filing GST returns

Depending on which period your business uses, you will have to file a GST return with Inland Revenue by the last working day of the month following when your taxable period ends – this is called the due date.

Once you are registered for GST, Inland Revenue will automatically send you your GST returns before the end of each taxable period. The returns will have the due date printed on them.

You calculate your GST by adding up all the GST you've received (or charged for if you're using the invoice or hybrid basis) and deducting all the GST you've paid (or been charged for if you're using the invoice basis).

GST return dates

Taxable period	Period ends	Due date for filing return and making payment
One-month	The last day of every month	The last working day of the following month.
Two-month	**Category A** ■ 31 January ■ 30 March ■ 31 May ■ 31 July ■ 30 September ■ 30 November	The last working day of the following month. If the month ends on a weekend or public holiday your return will be due on the last working day before.
	Category B ■ 28 February ■ 30 April ■ 30 June ■ 31 August ■ 31 October ■ 31 December	The only exception is returns that are due at the end of December (ie for taxable periods ending on 30 November), when the due date is extended until 15 January of the next year.
Six-month	■ 31 March ■ 30 September	The last working day of the following month.

If you are GST-registered, you must complete and file a return in every taxable period, even it is a nil return with no tax to pay or to refund. You are obliged to do this until your business stops all taxable activities, in which case you must let Inland Revenue know within 21 days.

If you fail to file a GST return in any taxable period, Inland Revenue will make a default assessment of how much GST you should pay, but you will still have to file the overdue return and will be charged penalties if you have GST to pay.

COMPLIANCE AND YOUR BUSINESS

Paying GST

It is important to remember that the due date on your GST return is for both filing the return and paying the GST. If you don't pay your GST or pay late you will be charged penalties and interest. See the *Penalties and interest*, p179 for more information.

In some months, you may have paid more GST on goods and services purchased for your business than you have charged for, and you will be entitled to a refund. Generally, Inland Revenue will pay the refund to you, although in some circumstances they may withhold it, for eg if you owe another type of tax or they are not happy with some part of your return and want more information.

GST case study

John runs a part-time bicycle repair business. It is only a small business but because his past year's turnover was $51,000, he is GST-registered. John has elected to use the invoice basis, which means that he must account to Inland Revenue for GST in the same month that he issues or receives an invoice, whether or not the invoice has been paid. He has also chosen a one-month taxable period.

In May, John completed a major repair job on a bicycle, which he charged $500 for, plus GST of $62.50. He has issued an invoice for this job but has not yet been paid. He also fixed a puncture, for which he was paid $11.25 (including GST). However, he also received a bill from the bicycle-part supply company for $150 plus GST of $18.75. He has yet to pay this.

John must send Inland Revenue his GST return by 30 June. His calculations for how much GST he owes look like this:

Invoices issued or payments received	GST charged
$562.50	$62.50
$11.25	$1.25

Invoices paid	GST claimed
$168.75	$18.75

Total GST charged less GST claimed = $63.75 - $18.75 = $45.00

For May, John has $45.00 GST to pay to Inland Revenue and he must make the payment by 30 June or he will be charged penalties and interest.

TAX

Resident withholding tax

Some businesses may have to pay resident withholding tax (RWT) on their investments. Others may have to account for it on interest that they pay to investors or dividends that they pay to shareholders.

Paying RWT

If your company receives interest on money that it has in the bank or invested, then RWT will probably be deducted from the interest before it is paid.

Interest is income, and RWT should be paid on it at the highest income tax rate that your business pays or you will receive an end-of-year tax bill.

If you don't tell your bank your business's IRD number, RWT will be charged at the no-declaration rate of 39%. If you do tell them, you will be taxed at the default rate of 19% unless you elect to be taxed at a higher rate.

Deducting RWT

Businesses will have to deduct and account for RWT on:
- interest payments of over $5,000 paid to certain investors
- any parts of dividends paid to shareholders that do not have imputation credits attached.

If either of these situations applies to your business, you will need to register with Inland Revenue as a payer for RWT. Inland Revenue will be able to advise you on how to calculate, deduct, and pay the RWT collected.

RWT paid during the year can be claimed as a tax credit by businesses in their end-of-year income tax returns.

Non-resident withholding tax (NRWT)

Non-resident withholding income is any interest, dividends, and royalties that are paid to someone who is not a New Zealand resident for tax purposes.

If your business pays non-resident withholding income to any person, then you must deduct NRWT at the same time as you make the payment. You must also register with Inland Revenue who will give you more information about accounting for and paying this tax.

Tax responsibilities for employers

Making the decision to take on an extra pair of hands can bring with it a host of tax obligations for businesses and one of the first things you will have to do is register with Inland Revenue as an employer.

As an employer, you will have to make regular returns and payments to Inland Revenue for PAYE and other deductions that you make from employee's wages.

163

COMPLIANCE AND YOUR BUSINESS

Once you've filed your first returns, Inland Revenue will helpfully send you pre-printed return forms and there is also the facility to file some of your returns online. You may also have to account for fringe benefit taxes and withholding payments.

> ### Checklist for wage records
>
> Making PAYE and other deductions from your employees' wages brings with it record-keeping responsibilities. There is more information on keeping wage records in chapter 1, *Employment*, but the main information you need to make sure you include is:
>
> - the total gross earnings, including taxable allowances
> - the amount of PAYE deducted
> - child support deductions
> - student loan deductions
> - specified superannuation contribution withholding tax (SSCWT) deductions
> - non-taxable allowances
> - the net wage.
>
> You will also need to keep all your employees' tax code declarations, and records of the payments you make to Inland Revenue, including pay sheets and PAYE payment receipts.
>
> Records must be kept in New Zealand for 7 years.
>
> One exception is if you file your employer monthly schedule (IR 348) online. In this case, you don't need to keep a copy but you do need to keep copies of the wage records it was generated from.

Remember: it is illegal to treat someone as self-employed to avoid deducting tax.

Employee or self-employed?

The distinction between employees and self-employed workers (such as contractors and consultants) is an important one for businesses. Businesses are responsible for the tax and accident compensation deductions of their employees but self-employed people handle their own.

It can be quite clear which category staff fall into but if you have any doubts chapter 1, *Employment* looks at the factors that the courts (and Inland Revenue) will look at to decide.

> ### At a glance – employers' tax obligations
>
> Employers must:
> - register as an employer with Inland Revenue
> - ensure staff fill in a tax code declaration
> - calculate and deduct PAYE from employees' wages
> - make child support deductions from employees' wages
> - make student loan deductions from employees' wages
> - pay fringe benefit tax on any non-cash benefits given to employees
> - calculate and deduct specified superannuation contribution withholding tax (SSCWT) from contributions made on behalf of employees to certain superannuation funds
> - calculate and deduct withholding tax on withholding payments made to some contractors and company directors
> - pay all deductions (including PAYE) from employees' wages to Inland Revenue by the due dates
> - complete and file an employer monthly schedule
> - maintain accurate wage and other tax records, and store them for 7 years.

PAYE

PAYE stands for pay as you earn and is the basic tax that employers deduct from all employees' earnings.

PAYE is deducted each time an employee is paid. It is deducted from most types of income that an employee earns as a result of having a job including:

- wages and salaries
- overtime pay
- back pay
- holiday pay and pay for statutory holidays
- long-service leave pay
- bonuses and gratuities
- taxable allowances
- redundancy and retirement payments
- shareholder-employee salaries
- salaries to partners in a partnership.

Money deducted by employers as PAYE is held in trust for the Crown, and employers have a legal duty to deduct and pay the correct amounts. You will be charged penalties and interest and may face prosecution if you don't – there is more information on this in *Penalties and interest* at p179.

COMPLIANCE AND YOUR BUSINESS

Allowances and PAYE

Allowances are payments made to staff over and above their normal wages or salary and can be taxable or non-taxable.

Taxable allowances are treated as part of an employee's income and they must pay PAYE on them. Common taxable allowances include:

- conditions allowance
- responsibility allowance
- qualification allowance
- holiday pay
- bonuses, gratuities, and back pay.

Non-taxable allowances are payments made to compensate staff for expenses or wear and tear they have incurred on their employer's behalf while working. They are not subject to PAYE. Common non-taxable allowances are:

- tool allowance
- laundry allowance
- meal allowance
- motor vehicle mileage reimbursement
- some travel allowances.

If an employee doesn't give you an IR 330 or it is incomplete, then you are obliged to deduct PAYE at a higher, no-declaration rate, until they do.

PAYE tax codes

There are several rates of PAYE, depending on how much an employee earns and what their tax code is. The tax codes are printed on the back of Inland Revenue's tax code declaration (IR 330).

Most employees have one regular job that is their main source of income and use the tax code M (or M SL if they have student loan).

It is the employer's responsibility to make sure that all new employees fill out an IR 330 but it is the employee's responsibility to choose the tax code that is appropriate to their circumstances. They must also fill out a new IR 330 if their circumstances and hence their tax code changes.

Employers must hold on to an employee's IR 330 form for 7 years from the date that the employee's last wages are paid.

Calculating PAYE

Inland Revenue produces PAYE tables showing how much PAYE to deduct for each tax code at each income level. There are weekly and fortnightly PAYE deduction tables (IR340), and 4-weekly and monthly PAYE deduction tables (IR 341).

TAX

Rates of PAYE deductions

PAYE is deducted at the following rates for an employee's primary source of income.

Legal rates:

Taxable income	Deduction rate
$0 to $38,000	19.5%
Above $38,000 but not more than $60,000	33%
More than $60,000	39%

Low income rebates are available in certain circumstances. The application of these rebates changes the effective tax rates for employees earning up to $38,000 to those shown in the table below.

Effective rates:

Taxable income	Deduction rate
$0 to $9,500	15%
Above $9,500 but not more than $38,000	21%
Above $38,000 but not more than $60,000	33%
More than $60,000	39%

PAYE is deducted at the following rates for an employee's secondary sources of income. The rate of deduction is worked out from the employee's total taxable income, including their main source of income and any other secondary sources of income they may have.

Taxable income	Deduction rate
Income from all sources is less than $38,000	21%
Income from all sources is higher than $38,000 but not more than $60,000	33%
Income from all sources is higher than $60,000	39%

PAYE and lump sum payments

Certain lump sum payments have PAYE deducted at a flat rate, irrespective of the employee's tax code. These are:

- back pay, bonuses, gratuities, and other lump sum one-off payments – 22.2%, or 34.2% if the combined payments are more than $38,000
- redundancy and retirement payments – 24%.

Employees can choose to be taxed on these payments at the higher rate of 39% (and avoid having end-of-year tax to pay) if their total income for the year is going to be more than $60,000.

Regular bonuses are treated as wages and are subject to normal PAYE.

Accounting for and paying PAYE

There are two main types of forms that employers have to file with Inland Revenue in order to account for PAYE:
- an employer monthly schedule
- an employer deductions form.

Employer monthly schedule

The employer monthly schedule (IR 348) contains details of your employees' gross wages for the month and the deductions (PAYE, child support, and student loan) you have made from them. The form must be completed for:
- employees on wages or salaries
- shareholder-employees
- contractors receiving withholding payments.

Each staff member's details are shown separately on the form, including their IRD number and tax code. You will have to fill in this information on the first schedule you file, but after that Inland Revenue will send you pre-printed forms each month. You will still have to fill in the personal details of new employees or staff who have left during the return period.

The date on which you have to file your monthly schedules will depend on whether you are a small or large employer.

- Small employers are those whose gross PAYE and specified superannuation contributions withholding tax (SSCWT) deductions are less than $100,000 each year. Small employers must file their schedule on the 20th day of the month following the month the schedule relates to.
- Large employers are those whose gross PAYE and SSCWT deductions were $100,000 or more in the previous year ended 31 March. Large employers must file their schedule on the 5th day of the month following the month the schedule relates to.
- New employers are treated as small employers until their PAYE deductions exceed $100,000 in any one year.

> **Filing online**
>
> Employers can file their employer monthly schedules electronically by using Inland Revenue's online facility.
>
> Large employers must file their employer monthly schedules online, unless they have been granted an exemption. If they don't they will be charged a penalty of $1 per employee per month or $250, whichever is greater.
>
> Small employers have the option of filing electronically or manually.

TAX

Employer deductions

PAYE is paid to Inland Revenue using the employer deduction forms, IR 345 or IR 346 (where an employer is registered to make SSCWT deductions).

The employer deduction forms show the total amount of PAYE, child support, student loan, and SSCWT deductions that you have made each month from all your employees. Inland Revenue will send you the forms each month and you must return them with your payment.

How often you have to file your employer deductions forms (and make payment) depends on whether you are a small or large employer:

- small employers and new employers pay on the 20th day of the month following the month in which the deductions were made
- large employers pay twice a month, on the 5th and 20th days of the month.

If you pay late or don't pay you will be charged penalties and interest.

What employers need to file and when

Employer Registration IR 334

What it covers
Registering with Inland Revenue as an employer

When it has to be filed
Registering with Inland Revenue as an employer

Employer monthly schedule IR 348

What it covers
Details of each employee's:
- name
- IRD number
- tax code

plus, totals for the month of their:
- gross earnings
- PAYE deductions
- withholding tax deductions
- child support deductions
- student loan repayments.

When is has to be filed
- small employers – 20th day of the month
- large employers – 5th day of the month
- new employers – same as small employers until PAYE deductions exceed $100,000.

169

COMPLIANCE AND YOUR BUSINESS

> **Employee deductions IR 345 plus payment or IR 346 plus payment**
>
> **What it covers**
>
> **IR 345** Total deductions made in the period for:
> - PAYE and withholding tax
> - child support
> - student loan repayments.
>
> As above plus SSCWT deductions
>
> **IR 346** As above plus SSCWT deductions
>
> **When it has to be filed**
> - small employers – 20th day of the month
> - large employers – 5th and 20th day of the month
> - new employers – same as small employers until PAYE deductions exceed $100,000.
>
> As above
>
> **Fringe Benefit Tax IR 422, IR 421, IR 420**
>
> **What it covers**
> FBT payable for the return period
>
> **When it has to be filed**
> - IR 422: 31 May
> - IR 421: same date as company's end-of-year income tax is due
> - IR 420: 20 July, 20 October, 20 January, 31 May.

if a contractor or employee is GST-registered, withholding tax is calculated on the amount charged before GST is added.

Withholding taxes

Withholding taxes (or withholding payments as they are commonly known) are deducted from payments made to some contractors and company directors.

Not all payments to contractors have withholding taxes deducted – Inland Revenue produces schedules of the types of work and contracts that do.

If a type of work is not listed in the schedule, you do not have to deduct withholding taxes – the contractor will be responsible for any tax to be paid. It is also important to remember that companies do not pay withholding taxes, even if the business or activity they offer is listed in the schedules.

Withholding tax is a form of PAYE. It is deducted at a flat rate, although the rates vary according to the type of business or activity. The amount to be deducted is set out in the PAYE tables and the back of the tax code declaration form (IR 330).

Employers should record withholding tax deductions they make in their employer monthly schedules (IR 348) and employer deduction forms (IR 345 and IR 346). Withholding tax deductions should be paid to Inland Revenue at the same time as PAYE deductions.

Contractors and employees who are liable to pay withholding tax must fill out an IR 330 – if they don't or it is incomplete then you must deduct withholding tax at a higher, no-declaration rate until they do.

TAX

Important points to note are:
- withholding tax deductions do not include an ACC levy and self-employed people will be invoiced for their ACC levies independently
- employers should not make deductions for student loans or child support when making withholding tax deductions.

Exempt payments

Workers can apply to Inland Revenue for a certificate of exemption so that withholding tax is not deducted from the payments they receive.

Certificates only apply for one year and employers must check that they are valid and relate to the type of work the contractor or employee is doing.

Tax exempt payments that the employer makes and the exemption certificate number should be recorded, but exempt payments do not have to be included in an employer's monthly schedule.

ACC levies

In New Zealand, insurance cover for personal injury caused by an accident is provided by the Accident Compensation Corporation (ACC).

ACC cover applies to injuries that happen both within and outside the workplace and is funded through levies that are paid by:
- employers and self-employed people to cover work-related injuries
- employees and other earners to cover non-work injuries
- motor vehicle owners and users (through a portion of the cost of registration fees and petrol sales) to cover injuries from motor vehicle accidents
- the Government, for injuries to people not in the paid workforce.

The level of each type of levy is set by regulation and may alter from year to year.

Employers' levies

Employers pay levies to ACC to provide cover for injuries that happen to themselves and their staff at work or that are work related.

As an employer you are legally obliged to give ACC information about your employees and about the nature of your business. In practice, ACC receives this information from Inland Revenue.

ACC will automatically calculate your levies and send you invoices for them. What your levy is will depend on you business industry code.

ACC also offers a scheme where employers can reduce the levies they pay by demonstrating good workplace safety practices.

> ### Business industry descriptions
>
> Employers, self-employed people, and other businesses must choose a business industry code that best describes their business or trading activities. ACC produces lists of codes covering most industries, services, and activities.
>
> Businesses will be asked to specify their code:
> - as part of their application to become GST-registered
> - when completing their annual income tax returns.
>
> Both Inland Revenue and ACC use the codes. One of the main uses is for calculation of ACC levies that employers and self-employed people must pay – the levies vary depending on the type of activities that businesses are involved in. This is in recognition of the fact that some industries, such as forestry, are more prone to work-related injuries than others, such as office work.

Employers' ACC levies for the year are payable in advance. They are calculated from the business' payroll for the previous year, although employers have the option of providing a more accurate estimate of what the year's payroll is likely to be. The levy is recalculated at the end of the year, when actual payroll figures are available and a new invoice for the balance is sent to the employer.

Employers also pay residual claims levies, which fund the ongoing cost of cover for work-related injuries that happened before 1 July 1999. This levy also varies, depending on what your business industry code is.

Making deductions for employees

All employees pay an ACC levy to cover them for injuries that happen outside of work. This levy is included in the PAYE deductions that employers make – it is called the earner levy. Inland Revenue collects the levy on behalf of ACC.

> ### What does the ACC earner levy cover?
>
> The ACC levy deducted from employees' wages is made up of three parts:
> - the earner levy – which provides cover for non-work injuries
> - the earners' account residual levy – which pays the ongoing cost of cover for non-work injuries sustained between 1 April 1992 and 30 June 1999
> - a levy to fund the Department of Labour's costs in administering the Health and Safety in Employment Act 1992.

TAX

The earner levy is charged at a flat rate of $1.20 (including GST) per hundred dollars earned but there is no need for employers to make a separate calculation – the levy is included as part of the deduction rates shown in the PAYE tables.

ACC levies are charged on most income that is subject to PAYE. The main exceptions are:

- earnings over the earnings threshold
- payments to employees for the first week of work injury
- withholding payments
- redundancy payments
- retirement payments
- student allowances
- tax-free allowances
- jury and witness fees
- various pensions and benefits paid by the Department of Work and Income
- certain other pensions.

ACC is only charged on earnings up to a certain level, called the earnings threshold. The earnings threshold tends to increase slightly in each tax year – for the 2003/2004 tax year it was $88,728. Earnings over the threshold amount are only subject to PAYE and this is reflected in the PAYE tables.

Levies for self-employed people

People who are self-employed, such as sole traders and company directors, pay a combined ACC levy covering:

- an earners' levy for non-work personal injuries
- a self-employed work account levy for work-related personal injuries.

The work-related part of the levy varies depending on the nature of the self-employed person's business and their business industry code.

ACC sends self-employed people invoices for their levies each year. These levies are calculated from information about the self-employed person's income, which Inland Revenue supplies to ACC.

Self-employed people also have the option of nominating an alternative level of weekly compensation (from what they would be entitled to under the standard ACC scheme) that they wish to receive if they have an accident, and paying an additional premium for it.

COMPLIANCE AND YOUR BUSINESS

> ### ACC, income tax, and GST
>
> **Income tax**
>
> The following ACC levies are deductible as expenses from your business income:
> - employer levies
> - employees' wages (including the ACC levies)
> - self-employed people's levies.
>
> **GST**
> - ACC employer- and self-employed levies include GST and you can claim this as a tax credit in your periodic GST returns
> - You cannot claim the GST on the earner levies that you deduct for employees as part of their PAYE).

Deductions

In addition to PAYE and withholding taxes, there are three main deductions which employers must make from their employees' wages. These are:
- child support payments
- student loan deductions
- specified superannuation contributions withholding tax (SSCWT).

Paying deductions

Any deductions that an employer makes for one of these purposes must be paid to Inland Revenue at the same time as PAYE deductions are paid. This is the 20th day of the month for small employers and new employers, and the 5th and 20th day of the month for large employers.

The employer deduction forms (IR 345 and IR 346), which employers file when paying their PAYE, include spaces to record total deductions the employer has made for child support, student loans, and SSCWT during the month.

The employer monthly schedule includes space to record the individual deductions for child support and student loans that have been made from each employee's earnings.

Child support payments

Inland Revenue assesses and collects child support payments from parents who do not live with their children. The collected payments are paid directly to the parent who looks after the children, unless that parent receives a benefit, in which case the collected payments are paid to the Government.

TAX

Inland Revenue will send you a notice (CS 503) letting you know if you have to deduct child support from an employee's earnings. The notice will state:
- the employee's name and IRD number
- when the deductions should start and the frequency
- the amount to be deducted.

Information about child support is strictly confidential and employers must not disclose it, except:
- if Inland Revenue asks for information
- if the information has to be given for the purposes of running the business, including for completing the payroll.

It is an offence to disclose the information in circumstances other than these and the penalty is a fine of up to $15,000 for a first offence.

Child support payments are the first deductions that must be made from an employee's earnings once PAYE has been deducted. They take precedence over all other deductions.

However, 60% of an employee's net earnings are protected for child support purposes. This means that child support payments can take up to, but not more than 40% of what is left of an employee's earnings after PAYE has been deducted. Inland Revenue will take this into account when they let you know how much to deduct, but employers should be aware of this limit if an employee's earnings are reduced for any reason in a pay period.

Variations to child support payments

If for any reason you cannot deduct the full amount of child support from an employee's wages in any pay period, you must let Inland Revenue know by completing a variation schedule (IR 348). If you don't do this, Inland Revenue will assume that you have underpaid and may charge you penalties.

You should also complete the schedule if you've paid more than usual.

Student loan repayments

Employees only have to make repayments on their student loans if they earn over a certain amount, called the repayment threshold. This is currently $15,964 a year or $307 a week.

It is the employee's responsibility to let their employer know if they have a student loan and they expect to earn over the threshold. They should do this by choosing a student loan tax code (with an SL suffix) on their tax code declaration form (IR 330).

Student loan repayments are deducted at the rate of 10% of an employee's income over the threshold – the amounts are set out in the PAYE tables.

Deductions are also made from any lump sums payments the employee receives and from redundancy payments. They are not made from payments subject to withholding tax or certain other types of payments.

> ### Self-employed people and student loans
>
> Self-employed people repay their student loans at the rate of 10 cents for every dollar of income they earn over the income threshold.
>
> Inland Revenue calculates how much your student loan repayment is at the same time that they calculate how much end-of-year income tax you have to pay.
>
> If your end-of-year repayment is more than $1,000, you will have to make interim repayments during the following year. The interim repayment dates are:
> - 7 July
> - 7 November
> - 7 March.

Specified superannuation contributions withholding tax (SSCWT)

Employers must deduct SSCWT on specified superannuation contributions – this is any contribution that an employer makes to a superannuation fund for an employee's benefit.

SSCWT applies to employer contributions under most superannuation schemes. It does not apply to employee contributions that an employer deducts from wages on an employee's behalf.

SSCWT is deducted at 33% unless the employer and employee agree to:
- deduct it at the higher rate of 39%, or
- treat the contribution as part of the employee's earnings and tax it at their personal tax rate.

Deductions must be made at the same time as the contribution is paid.

> ### Changes in the pipeline
>
> There is a legislative amendment before Parliament that will allow SSCWT to be withheld at a rate of 21% for employees earning less than $38,000 a year. This amendment is expected to be passed into law in early 2004 and will have effect from 1 April 2004. The Government is also considering introducing a further SSCWT rate of 15% for employees earning less than $9,500 a year.

TAX

Fringe benefit tax

Fringe benefits are non-cash benefits given to staff and shareholder-employees on top of their wages and salaries. They include:

- use of a motor vehicle outside of work
- low-interest loans
- free, subsidised, or discounted goods
- contributions an employer makes to illness, accident, or death benefit funds
- contributions an employer makes to some life, accident, or health insurance policies
- contributions an employer makes to pensions
- contributions an employer makes to superannuation schemes to which SSCWT does not apply.

Fringe benefits are subject to fringe benefit tax (FBT), which employers must file returns for and pay to Inland Revenue. Unlike PAYE, FBT is not deducted from employees' earnings, but is paid by the employer in addition to the benefit provided.

Fringe benefit tax payments are deductible for income tax purposes.

Important points – FBT

- cash benefits, such as cash bonuses, are treated as part of the employee's earnings and are subject to PAYE not FBT
- employers pay tax on benefits provided to employee or shareholder-employees, even if the benefits are provided by another person
- the benefits must be received as a result of the staff member's employment – so, for eg if a staff member got discounted goods because the company was running a general promotion on the goods, there would be no need to collect FBT
- employers who do not provide fringe benefits must let Inland Revenue know this, so they do not have to file FBT returns.

Calculating FBT

FBT is charged on the total taxable value of the benefits provided. The taxable value is what the employee would have paid for the benefit in normal circumstances, less anything they have actually paid. For example, if an employer sells an employee goods for $10, when the normal price in the shops is $20, the total taxable value for FBT purposes is $10.

Employers have two options for calculating FBT:
- a flat rate of 64%
- a multi-rate calculation, with two options of rates – 49% or 64%.

177

COMPLIANCE AND YOUR BUSINESS

There are also special rules for calculating FBT payable on motor vehicles, as this is most businesses biggest FBT expense.

Inland Revenue produces a guide on calculating FBT and will send this to you when you register as an employer, if you indicate that you will be providing fringe benefits.

FBT and motor vehicles

Motor vehicles are the biggest fringe benefit that most businesses supply to employees and there are special rules for calculating FBT on them. Not all business motor vehicles used by employees are liable for FBT – only those that are available for the employee's private use and enjoyment. This includes travel to and from work.

When calculating FBT on motor vehicles, allowances are made for times when the vehicle is being used for work and for when it is unavailable to the employee.

Record-keeping and FBT

If you provide fringe benefits, you must keep sufficient records so that Inland Revenue can verify the fringe benefits provided and their taxable value. Records should include details of the recipient, the occasion, and the amount paid.

Accounting for and paying FBT

How often you have to account to Inland Revenue for FBT depends on whether you are a small or large employer. The test is the same as for PAYE – small employers are those whose gross deductions from employees' earnings are less than $100,000 each year, large employers are those whose deductions are more than $100,000.

Small employers only need to file a FBT return once a year. The return form they use depends on their balance date.

- FBT annual liable return (IR 422) is used by small employers. The return is due on 31 May.
- Small employers that pay fringe benefits to shareholder-employees are required to use the FBT income year return (IR 421). The return covers the same period as the company's accounting year and is due on the same date that the company must pay its end-of-year income tax.

TAX

Large employers must file FBT quarterly returns (IR 420). They have four return periods and four due dates.

Return period	Due date
1 April to 30 June	20 July
1 July to 30 September	20 October
1 October to 31 December	20 January
1 January to 31 March	31 May

If you don't file your return on time, Inland Revenue will estimate how much FBT you should pay and will send you a notice of assessment.

FBT payments are due on the same date that the return must be filed by. You should enclose your payment with the return. If you don't pay on time you will be charged penalties and interest.

Penalties and interest

When it comes to tax the message is this – do it right and do it on time.

If you fail to meet any of your tax obligations, including filing your returns on time, calculating your tax correctly, or making payments when they are due, you will be charged penalties and interest.

In most cases this is not discretionary – Inland Revenue will charge you, even if you are only a day late, and will not be interested in hearing your excuses. You may also be charged shortfall penalties or face criminal charges.

Arrangements

In some circumstances, if you are having difficulty paying your tax by the due date, Inland Revenue will enter into an arrangement with you to pay it by instalment. Penalties and interest on the outstanding tax will still be charged, but may be reduced.

Penalties for filing returns late

If you don't file your end-of-year income tax return on time, you will be charged a penalty of between $50 and $500, depending on your income. If you use a tax agent and your agent fails to file your return on time you will still be personally liable – the failure to file may be an issue between you and your agent, but will not interest Inland Revenue.

Employers who don't file their employer monthly schedules on time will be charged $250.

Penalties for paying tax late

Inland Revenue uses standard penalties for taxes that are paid after their due dates. These penalties apply to all types of taxes, but not to student loan or child support payments.

Penalties are applied as follows.

- an initial penalty of 1% is charged on the day after the due date
- a further 4% penalty is charged if there is still any amount of tax (or penalties) unpaid 7 days after the due date
- A further 1% penalty is charged for every month that the tax and other penalties remain outstanding – this penalty is incremental, which means that it is added onto the penalties already charged.

Child support payments that are late or unpaid are charged penalties at the rate of 10% when they are initially overdue plus 2% for each month that they remain outstanding. Student loan repayments that are late or unpaid are charged penalties at the rate of 2% of the deficient amount, with a further 2% for each month the amount payable remains outstanding.

Shortfall penalties

Inland Revenue charges shortfall penalties on:

- tax that is underpaid (or not paid)
- defaults in an employer's obligations such as deducting PAYE.

Shortfall penalties are calculated as a percentage of the outstanding tax and the rate varies, depending on the degree of fault by the taxpayer. There are five levels of fault:

- lack of reasonable care – 20%
- unacceptable interpretation of the law – 20%
- gross carelessness – 40%
- adopting an abusive tax position – 100%
- evasion – 150%.

Shortfall penalties are generally only charged for purposeful breaches. They would not be charged where the underpayment was due to a genuine mistake or error, or where a taxpayer had received bad advice from a professional advisor.

Interest

Inland Revenue both charges and pays interest for under- and over-payments of tax – this is called use-of-money interest. The interest is calculated from the day after the original due date for any payment and is based on current short-term deposit and borrowing rates.

Use-of-money interest – current rates

Underpaid tax	11.93%
Overpaid tax	4.83%

Criminal penalties

In certain circumstances, not complying with your tax obligations will mean you have committed a criminal offence and Inland Revenue may choose to prosecute you. If convicted, you may be fined substantial amounts (up to $50,000 for some offences) and could be imprisoned.

Some of the offences are absolute liability offences, which means there is no defence – so the fact that you forgot or did not know you had a certain tax obligation doesn't matter, you will still have committed an offence.

Some examples of absolute liability offences are:

- failing to keep the books and documents required by law
- not providing the required accurate and true information to Inland Revenue, including tax returns and forms
- not registering for GST when you should.

Other classes of offences include:

- knowledge offences, such as knowingly not deducting or withholding tax, or not accounting to Inland Revenue for it
- evasion and similar offences
- offences in relation to court orders
- obstruction
- aiding and abetting.

Coming clean with Inland Revenue

If you make a mistake on a tax return or realise that you have failed to comply with one of your tax obligations, you should tell Inland Revenue about it as soon as possible.

Telling Inland Revenue about a tax lapse before they find out about it is called voluntary disclosure and has the benefits that:

- you will not be prosecuted
- any shortfall penalties will be reduced by 75%
- your name and the offence will not be published.

You can make a voluntary disclosure at any time but if you do it after being told that you will be audited or investigated, the shortfall penalties will only be reduced by 40%.

Audits

All businesses can expect to be audited at some time – Inland Revenue aims to audit business taxpayers at least once every 5 years. An audit is where Inland Revenue checks your tax records to ensure that they are accurate and support the returns you have filed, and that you are fulfilling all of your tax obligations.

Audits are generally carried out at a business' premises and may go into greater or lesser depth, depending on how accurate your records initially appear to be, your tax history, the industry you are involved in, your business' profitability, and whether you are paying reasonable amounts of tax.

Businesses that are being audited should make sure they have all of their tax records and supporting documents on hand and that the appropriate people are available to answer the auditor's questions. Inland Revenue has extremely wide information-gathering powers and can request copies of any written information your business holds. It is an offence not to supply the information, unless it is covered by legal professional privilege.

If Inland Revenue finds tax issues during an audit, you will be sent an amended assessment of tax and will have pay any outstanding tax and possibly penalties and interest. Sometimes the reverse happens and an audit reveals that you have been overpaying tax. In these circumstances, Inland Revenue will refund the overpaid tax together with use-of-money interest.

PROPERTY

Location, location, location – the three most common words in house buying apply equally well to commercial and industrial property.

You don't want to lease a premises to start up your panelbeating business only to find that such a use doesn't comply with planning laws in the area, or buy a building to make widgits in what was built without consents which could make you liable for hefty fines.

Whether leasing, buying, or building from scratch you need to know what property compliance costs you'll face.

COMPLIANCE AND YOUR BUSINESS

It pays to understand your obligations as a building owner

Whether constructing a new building or altering an existing one, it pays to know at the outset what your legal responsibilities as a building owner are.

The Building Act 1991 applies to all building work in New Zealand. Under the Act, the Building Regulations contain the mandatory New Zealand Building Code setting the standard for the work carried out and the approvals process. Planning approvals are handled separately under the Resource Management Act.

Proposed changes to the Building Act are in part due to the 'leaky building crisis' and attempt to provide more stringent regulation of the building industry, including a licensing regime for builders. It should be noted that the proposed Bill is very much in a draft form at this stage and indications are that it will probably undergo significant redrafting before it is passed.

The Building Act 1991

The Building Act 1991 requires owners to:
- apply to the council for a project information memorandum (PIM) and building consent before starting a new building or alterations – do this before beginning demolition or work on the site
- notify the council when you want to change the use of the building – for example from residential villa to restaurant – where that change of use will require alterations to building in order to bring it into compliance with the Building Code
- tell the council when work is completed so a code compliance certificate stating that all work complies with the New Zealand Building Code can be issued
- keep the building in a safe and sanitary condition at all times – most commercial and industrial buildings will require a compliance schedule and annual warrant of fitness.

PROPERTY

> **Warning**
>
> One proposed change in the new Building Bill is to set out fines for offences such as doing or permitting building work without a consent, failing to carry out maintenance required by a compliance schedule, or failing to display a building warrant of fitness where required. The new Bill also proposes to introduce an infringement notice system for other less fundamental offences. These offences will be defined at a later date. An infringement notice is an automatic fine with limited appeal rights and will be issued by territorial authorities (city or district councils).

Building approval

Once you've sorted out what you want to build and have prepared sketch plans you need to get a project information memorandum (PIM) from your local territorial authority. The PIM is usually issued before the building consent. You need to provide detailed information – from the intended use of the building, its location and external dimensions, through to provision for vehicular access and stormwater. In turn, the council will tell you any information relevant to your building project such as the likelihood of flooding or subsidence and what other authorisations you may need such as resource consents under the Resource Management Act.

After obtaining a PIM, you go can ahead and get plans and specifications done which show how the building work will be done and that it will comply with the Building Code.

The next step is applying for building consent. Under the proposed Building Bill, applications for building consent on major projects must include the name of a licensed building practitioner who will be involved in carrying out or supervising the work. However, this change is not due to take effect until 1 July 2009. Also under the proposed regime, certifiers who issue consent will follow the whole job through to final inspection and all territorial authorities will have to be accredited for issuing consents. This change will take effect when the Bill is expected to be passed in mid 2004.

You can save on council charges and prevent hassles later on by including in your consent application any special arrangements you have made for inspection during construction, such as checking by a qualified engineer. It is also wise at this stage to reach an understanding with your council/certifier on whether producer statements are acceptable. Producer statements are usually issued by a recognised specialist such as an architect to that show certain aspects of the project comply with the Building Code – but they don't have to be accepted by the council.

You are required to notify the council when building work is completed. A final inspection is usually made by the council to ensure the work meets the required

You can choose either the council or an accredited private building certifier to check your building plans and inspect construction.

consents and building standards. This will result in the issue of either a code compliance certificate or a notice to fix. In the case of a notice to fix, you will have to put things right before the council can sign off the work as complete. If a notice is not acted on, the council or private certifier can have the work completed at your expense.

Another proposed change is that if no code compliance certificate has been applied for, the authority that issued the consent must decide, within 2 years of the issue of that consent, whether or not to grant a code compliance certificate. Previously, there was no requirement to complete this process within a prescribed period – meaning some owners never bothered applying for a code compliance certificate.

The code compliance certificate is worth having because it shows future buyers of the building that the work is legal and means the value of any building work will be reflected in the property valuation. Without building consent and a code of compliance certificate you risk jeopardising your insurance. And there are stiff penalties – up to $200,000 – for building illegally if the building is dangerous or insanitary, or even for allowing public use of a building where a code compliance certificate has not been obtained.

As the new building owner you will be liable to fix any illegal work. It's a good idea to get any illegal work inspected by an accredited private building consultant. Work in place before the Act came into full force in 1993 has the right to exist unless it's dangerous or insanitary. But after that it's a different story. In cases where a new owner ignores a notice to fix work that isn't code compliant, the council can order the building not to be used, prosecute the new owner up to $20,000 a day, or even order the building to be demolished if it is extremely dangerous (although this is rare).

You can apply to the Building Industry Authority for a binding ruling when you disagree with a council over whether any building work complies with the Building Code to the required extent. Whilst under the new Bill, the Building Industry Authority will be dissolved, the new regulatory body will still perform this role.

Abatal v Waitakere City Council (2002)

The largest single fine under the Building Act confirmed by the High Court relates to the construction of a large greenhouse – 5,400m^2 in size – which was built in Auckland without a building consent. Abatal Ltd was ordered to pay $20,000 and its director James Pike an additional $5,000. The company appealed. In upholding the District Court decision, Justice Chambers said 'in circumstances such as these, there is a real risk that fines, unless substantial, have no deterrent effect at all and instead come to be considered, by business people in particular, as no more than licence fees.'

PROPERTY

Warrants of fitness

Any commercial or industrial building containing systems such as lifts, air conditioning services, or fire-safety devices must have a compliance schedule issued by a territorial authority. These schedules list the safety features and essential services of the building that have to be maintained and inspected by independent qualified experts. Frequency of inspection depends on the compliance schedule. And you can go further than what it states. For example, in 2003 the Building Industry Authority introduced new rules for monitoring the cause of Legionnaires' disease in commercial buildings. It is not a retrospective requirement (so doesn't apply to existing buildings) but the BIA suggested all building owners adopt the new testing regime for existing air conditioning cooling towers.

The building owner or supervisor must obtain a warrant of fitness annually, stating the compliance schedule has been fully complied with during the previous year. An owner, and anyone acting on the owner's behalf in signing the warrant of fitness, is liable for any false statements made. The building owner still has responsibility for the warrant of fitness whether or not the building is tenanted by others. However, if you delegate responsibility to a tenant under a lease, your tenant could also be liable for any Building Act breach.

The owner must ask an accredited independently qualified person to inspect and report upon the building. All their written reports and related material have to be kept by the building supervisor for at least 2 years.

Upgrading the compliance schedule of existing buildings is only required when the building is altered or there is a change of use – say from a warehouse to a retail outlet. While work of this size will involve professionals such as architects and engineers, you'll want a broad understanding from the council of what is involved. The upgrading required may include providing fire escapes, access for people with disabilities, and sanitary facilities.

Workplace obligations

As building owner you're responsible for maintaining your building to a standard that ensures it is safe for anyone using it – staff or visitors. You can't contract out of the responsibility even when hiring a property manager to supervise the building for you.

The Building Act covers only the physical aspects of building work. Managing people within buildings comes under the Health and Safety in Employment Act, and also the Occupier's Liability Act and the Fire Safety and Evacuation of Buildings Regulations. It is a good idea to have a policy and procedures manual setting out how you're going to achieve compliance with these laws.

The Health and Safety in Employment Act covers those who control a place of work. A key concept is that you have to take 'all practicable steps' to ensure the

A copy of the warrant of fitness has to be displayed publicly in your building and updated annually.

COMPLIANCE AND YOUR BUSINESS

health and safety of employees and other people in and around places or work. So you can't just turn a blind eye. You're expected to have a system for actively identifying and managing hazards in your building. If you have such a system and an unforseeable hazard injures someone, then you are less likely to be liable. Fines under the Act have gone up – for most offences the maximum fine increased from $50,000 to $250,000.

See chapter 2, *Health and Safety,* for more information on your obligations under the Health and Safety in Employment Act.

The Occupier's Liability Act regulates the responsibility of building occupiers – either as the owner or lessee – for injury and damage caused to people while on their property. The Act imposes a 'common duty of care' on occupiers to ensure visitors are safe when using the premises. For example, visitors shouldn't run the risk of breaking their ankle by tripping on torn carpet you've neglected to repair. And say an employer authorises an employee's friends to join the office for a social occasion and construction work is being carried out in the office – the onus is on the employer to ensure visitors are warned of any hazards that poses. You can be fined up to $10,000 under health and safety laws for failing to warn authorised visitors of work-related hazards that are out of the ordinary. You may not be liable if a visitor is injured due to faulty repairs or work undertaken by a contractor. Your liability can also be reduced if the visitor is partly responsible – such as if they ignore your large warning signs.

In 1969, the death of seven elderly residents in a Karori resthome fire sparked a Commission of Inquiry leading to the enactment of the Fire Safety Evacuation of Building Regulations. These require building owners to have a standard evacuation procedure approved by the Fire Service and for automatic sprinklers and alarms in institutions holding more than 20 people. The evacuation procedure has to be displayed at all times. The regulations also state requirements for fire escapes and installation and maintenance of fire-fighting equipment. As building owner you have to liaise with your local Fire Service for the approval of evacuation schemes and the holding of practice evacuations. Penalties under the regulations are up to a $200 fine and a further $20 a day for every day during which the offence continues.

Other workplace obligations include dealing with hazardous substances on a property under the new Hazardous Substances and New Zealand Organisms (HSNO) regime. This law replaced a multitude of previous laws and pulls together the management of hazardous substances into one Act.

See chapter 6, *Environment,* for more information on the HSNO regime.

PROPERTY

> ### Hutt City Council v Molenaar (2000)
> In this case, the defendant pleaded guilty to six charges under the Building Act relating to deficiencies in fire precautions in the building and defective operation of the lifts. A fine of $15,000 was imposed, plus an additional $6,250 for continuing offences, totalling $21,250. The continuing offences included $25 per day for 181 days when safety work remained outstanding plus $25 per day for 69 days when there was no lift certificate.

Energy efficiency

Statutory compliance for energy efficiency comes under the Building Act 1991 and Energy Efficiency and Conservation Act 2000 when building or altering a commercial building. It requires insulation in walls and around hot water cylinders and sets maximum energy levels for artificial lighting. There are currently no requirements for energy efficiency under the annual warrants of fitness though there has been plenty of talk about it.

As emission charges are put in place and energy costs continue to rise, there are increasing commercial incentives for building owners and occupiers to voluntarily include energy efficiency systems in new and existing buildings. A quarter of New Zealand's energy use is consumed in or by buildings. It is estimated energy efficient buildings can produce gains in worker productivity and reduced absenteeism by around 5-to-15% – not bad when you consider a 3% gain in productivity over a building's life could pay for a whole new building.

The Energy Efficiency and Conservation Authority (EECA) has an energy audit grant scheme that pays up to half of the cost of an energy audit (maximum $10,000). It has also released a set of best practice guidelines for incorporating energy efficiency into the design of commercial buildings.

Leasing

Let's face it, small to medium businesses are most likely to lease rather than buy their work premises, particularly when starting out. Traps in leasing are much the same as for buying a commercial property – and then some. The lease is a contract enforceable under the Property Law Act 1952 and the Land Transfer Act 1952 so aim for one as flexible as possible. You're in business to grow and you don't want to be locked into space that no longer meets your needs. On the other hand, you don't want to be turfed out without warning by the landlord and lose all the goodwill in your thriving business.

Remember: You can get a subsidised energy audit done of your commercial building. Auckland's Waitakere Hospital did one of its new hospital design prior to construction and energy savings of up to 20% ($145,000) a year were identified.

Director guarantees

You may be required as the company director to provide a guarantee of all of the tenant's obligations in the lease, including financial, to the landlord, especially if you're a start-up business. Most people don't realise that by signing a personal guarantee they put their family home up for grabs if things go wrong. Instead, you can offer a bank guarantee covering 3-4 months' rent which the landlord holds. Try to limit the amount guaranteed and for how long – say 2 years – by which time you'll have proven you're a model tenant.

And remember if you're sub-leasing some space and obtaining a guarantee from your sub-tenant, financial guarantees are only worth as much as the person offering them. Getting unpaid rent from a bankrupt isn't easy so look for another form of financial bond.

Assignment and sub-letting

When you want to shift out of the building before your lease expires, if your lease allows you can either assign the lease or sub-let to a new tenant, usually to a party approved by the landlord. As a condition of agreeing to assignment of the lease, a landlord will often require the new tenant to sign a deed of covenant making them liable for all the lease terms. Without this deed of covenant, the landlord is restricted to recovering obligations that 'touch and concern the land' only – such as rent, rates, and repairs. Even with this deed there can be ongoing liability for the previous tenant. The law requires the landlord to chase the new tenant for any unpaid rent. But if they are unable to recover the money from them, the landlord can come back to you providing it is still during the existing term of your lease. You can get around this by including a clause in the original lease that if you do assign the lease to a new tenant you're no longer liable.

Sub-letting is a different kettle of fish because even if you move out of the building you are still directly liable to the landlord for rent and other lease obligations. The new tenant is directly liable to you.

Rent issues

The whole basis for your rights of occupancy are set out in the lease. It will cover how much rent you pay, how often the rent is reviewed, rights of renewal, any right to terminate early, assignment of the lease, and what operating expenses you pay. If you're a retailer in a shopping centre the lease is also likely to state whether the landlord has the right to relocate your business within the mall.

You can negotiate how often rent reviews occur and by what method – whether it is linked to the consumer price index, a fixed percentage annually, or as is more common in retail, a base rent plus a percentage of turnover (make sure it is not a percentage of every sale). Watch out for rachet clauses, which as the name implies are not always good for tenants. Rachet clauses prevent the rent ever going down below a specified amount – usually what it was at the date of review or when the lease was first taken out regardless of whether rents elsewhere have dropped dramatically.

In a typical commercial lease the landlord has to send out a notice of review to tell you they want to up the rent. You have a specific time, say 28 days in which to respond to that notice or the new rent is deemed to be fixed from the time of the notice – a use it or lose it clause. Respond in time and you can negotiate on any rent increase and if the lease allows take the matter to arbitration if you fail to agree.

Diarise the dates when renewal notices are to be given. A typical lease will say that if you want to renew the lease, you have to give notice in writing to the landlord no later than 3 months before the lease expires. By failing to do this within the specified time you run the risk of the landlord not granting a new lease. This can be a major headache particularly when you have developed a business with goodwill relating to the site itself, such as a petrol station. But there is an out – if you fail to give notice in time you have the right under the Property Law Act to apply to the court for an order directing the landlord to renew the lease, providing you do so within 3 months of your lease expiring.

Outgoings and maintenance obligations

Typically as a commercial tenant you are responsible for the operating expenses and internal maintenance of the building. Outgoings include such things as rubbish collection, service contract charges for lifts and air-conditioning, and management expenses. As a single tenant in a building you can be expected to pay for everything. The landlord is usually responsible for structural and exterior repairs.

Insurance is often paid for by the tenant but usually taken out by the landlord. You'll want to ensure the cover is adequate and that your interest as tenant is noted on the landlord's policy. Some Wellington building owners in particular have had difficulty getting full earthquake insurance and there have been large increases in premiums worldwide since September 11.

The person primarily liable for rates and water charges under the local government laws is no longer the tenant, it is now the building owner. However, leases usually require tenants to pay the rates.

Leasing checklist

- Find out if you have to pay fit-out costs when you move in and what condition you have to leave the premises in (eg are you required to completely strip the premises or to recarpet or paint before you go?).
- Obtain a budget of outgoings and ask whether any significant outgoings are expected.

COMPLIANCE AND YOUR BUSINESS

While building owners are legally responsible under the Building Act for maintaining the building and annual warrants of fitness, tenants can take on this liabilty if this is negotiated into the lease.

- Ask if there is a sinking fund (a kitty for large maintenance) and who holds the sinking fund in a commercial building, what it is to be used for, and how much you have to pay.
- State in your lease that the landlord has to regularly maintain the building's exterior common areas in the building, grounds, and carparks to a certain standard or it can reflect badly on your business. You may also want to include a clause allowing you to check any specifications for structural repairs so it doesn't lead to any shoddy work you could be culpable for as an employer.
- Check you have the right of use for your particular business under your lease, eg before setting up your panelbeating shop in a new industrial unit. You'll also need to check the district plan or regional plan to see if you require resource consents for that use.
- A title search will show any covenants on the title preventing certain uses but it won't tell you whether your business is a permitted use under the district plan or regional plan. This will be shown on a LIM.
- In unit title (or strata) developments a body corporate runs the building. Check the body corporate records to see if the rules restrict what type of business is conducted there, for eg no late-night discos. And watch out your lease doesn't allow a rival business – say another lunch bar – opening up right next door to you.

Modern Merchants Ltd v Gillard & ors (1997)

The South Mall Shopping Centre in south Auckland was subdivided into 26 unit titles by a new owner. As required under the Unit Titles Act, each unit was assigned a unit entitlement based on relative value. As a result the lessee was liable for 7.62% of the centre's expenses and outgoings. But the lease had a variable rent provision requiring the retailer to pay a percentage of the centre's outgoings based on the ratio of floor space the leased premises bore to the centre's total lettable floor space. On this basis, the lessee had to pay 11.989% of the rates and insurances and 8.6% of all other outgoings. Understandably, the lessee wanted to pay the smaller amount. The landlord won the case in court and on later appeal. The appeal was dismissed on the grounds that, despite the change in ownership structure, the lessor had to be viewed as the owner of the whole centre and the variable rent clause was not affected by the unit titles' provision.

Signage

Fancy your business name in neon lights on top of the building you're leasing? It's not quite that easy. You have to negotiate signage rights and naming rights to the building in your lease – and naming rights are worth a lot of money.

You also have Resource Management Act issues and local bylaws to consider. Rules for signage can be restrictive in residential streets, on industrial estates and heritage buildings, and they vary between councils. For example, Auckland City deals with signage under bylaws while other councils do so under the District Plan, and some do both. These planning rules include the sign's location, whether it protrudes from the building envelope, whether it is securely attached, and how brightly lit it can be. There can even be rules restricting colour and content.

There may also be body corporate rules relating to signage in a unit title development or covenants on the title. And while you may want to 'stop traffic' with your business sign you need Transit New Zealand approval for signs adjacent to state highways.

Ernst & Young v Kiwi Property Holdings Ltd (2003)

Accountancy firm Ernst & Young took its landlord, Kiwi Property Holdings, to court to stop the name of a new tenant, IBM NZ, going on top of the Majestic Centre in Wellington. Opposition from local residents had stopped the centre getting a name in bright lights on the roof under its original resource consent. But Ernst & Young included rights in its lease to approve any new name for the building and to have first offer on naming rights. Ten years on Kiwi offered signage at the top of the building to IBM after getting a non-notified resource consent which ignored the conditions of its previous consent. Kiwi argued that naming and signage rights were different – and they are. However, Ernst & Young contended giving IBM signage rights was effectively the same as naming rights in this case because the public was likely to start calling the building the IBM Centre. It produced experts who said the $70,000 per year IBM agreed to pay for signage rights was more than most naming rights in Wellington. Justice Paterson ordered a permanent injunction stopping the IBM signs going up.

COMPLIANCE AND YOUR BUSINESS

Buying and selling a commercial property

A commercial property is likely to be your most significant asset. You must consider whether the building complies with the Building Code under the Building Act. You also have to meet legal undertakings and watch out for pitfalls in the sale and purchase agreement.

Firstly, think about the most appropriate property ownership structure – a partnership, a joint venture, a trust, a sole trader, or a loss attributing qualifying company (LAQC) – to ensure it is tax efficient. And remember, if you're getting a mortgage the banks may want to have some say in how you use the property and may even want to approve tenants if you're sub-letting.

Title searches

Find the right location to operate your business and then search the property's records before signing the contract. It's far easier to get a vendor to fix any problems or renegotiate your price before you buy than chasing them afterwards.

The title and deposit plans are held by Land Information New Zealand (LINZ). These record who owns the property, any mortgages, and any other restrictions which may limit what you can build and do with it, such as covenants (eg a right to stop you building in a certain area) and encumbrances (eg a sewer line). The title may also be subject to easements such as rights-of-way or drainage rights. Find out the terms and conditions of these easements. For example, with a right-of-way you'll want to find out how many property owners have the right to use this and what obligations users have to maintain it. The deposit plan shows what buildings are legally on that property. Once you've walked over the property make sure the buildings and the deposit plan match – or start asking the vendor questions as to why they don't.

Check that the boundary is as stated on the title. This may require a survey. There have been cases where buildings have encroached onto neighbouring properties. When this occurs you have to go to the time and expense of creating an easement – the right to occupy that strip of land on another title – and compensate the other owner for that right.

Ensure on your title you have legal access to your property and sufficient parking for your intended use. An Auckland motelier had a thriving business with truck drivers because they could park their big vehicles easily overnight on land next to the motel. But the land was on a separate title and its owner decided to build on it. The motelier's turnover halved because he had no legal right to that parking and the truckies went elsewhere.

If you're borrowing significantly for the purchase, a lender will require a valuation report from a registered valuer to show you're not paying above market value.

Get a Land Information Memorandum (LIM) from your local authority. This is a report on the property from their records. Information provided includes among

A building consultant's report or an engineer's report can also be useful to give you peace of mind the building isn't about to fall down or subside into the creek below.

other things whether proper building consents were obtained and met for additions or alterations to the building, potential erosion, payment of rates, or whether public works such as road widening is to take place in the area. The LIM also shows if the council has any outstanding requisitions or notifications over the property that require action and will come with the land if you buy and they are not satisfied within a prescribed period. These are the responsibility of the building owner.

A LIM may be required by the bank if you're taking out a mortgage – and it can save a lot of hassles later on. Say your building has a multi-fuel burner installed without building consent. Even if it was correctly installed, lack of the necessary consents can result in your insurance being invalidated if the burner causes a fire on the property.

You can make the purchase conditional on being satisfied with all of these reports and enquiries.

Zoning and property use

The LIM report will also show zoning in the area you propose to buy. It's pointless buying a warehouse in a residential area where industrial activity is not permitted by the local council, unless there is already a resource consent in place authorising this use. Environmental impacts of activities are controlled by the Resource Management Act through the requirement for resource consents, but you also have to take into consideration permitted activities included in your local regional or district plan.

As an example, Auckland city has a range of business zones for commercial and industrial activity across the Auckland isthmus. For instance, business 1 and 2 zones provide for small- to medium-scale local businesses near residential zones, while the business 3 zone allows for existing areas of intensive activity outside of the central business district, such as Newmarket and Otahuhu.

You have to comply with the zoning rules unless you have existing use rights or resource consents. When zoning changes around your property you have the right to continue as you were, providing the use was legal when it was established and the effects are the same or similar in character, intensity, and scale as those that existed before the District Plan or rule was notified. These existing use rights are hard to confirm and easy to lose – you have to be careful not to extinguish the rights because they usually allow you to do things you can't do now as of right. They can be restrictive if you're wanting to expand your business or for any potential purchaser who may be forced into applying for new resource consents if they want to do things differently.

It can be time consuming and expensive – into the tens of thousands of dollars – to try to vary resource consents and if you're in breach you could risk enforcement action by the territorial authority.

For certain business uses, such as a restaurant or liquor outlet, you will need permits to meet health and food safety regulations and also require a liquor licence under the Sale of Liquor Act 1989. If buying an existing business you need to check the permits. You don't want to buy a restaurant seating 80 people and then find the permit allows only 40 seats and your turnover is halved. Or that the council never gave permission for those dinky little tables and chairs out on the street.

Owners rule

The Kitchener Group has set up a comprehensive development code administered by an incorporated owners' association for development of business-zoned land on Auckland's North Shore. Each building owner in the development becomes an association member. The code regulates uses, architectural and landscaping design, signage, and even the care and maintenance of vacant lots. No grotty workshops or flashing neon signs here and a bunch of businesses – from panelbeaters to boat builders – are banned. Office, light manufacturing, and distribution companies are welcome, providing they follow the rules. Transgressors face hefty fines from the owners' association.

Subdivided land

New Zealand has five common forms of land titles – freehold, leasehold, unit title, strata, and cross-lease. Freehold owners have free reign on their property while on a leasehold title you pay a rent to occupy land owned by someone else.

Unit title is becoming more common for commercial and industrial property. Under unit title, you have control over the unit you buy as if it was freehold and there are areas within the building such as the foyer which are common property and owned by the body corporate. All of the unit holders are members of the body corporate. Where ownership of an office building is shared, difficulties can arise through problems with the definition of rights over common parts of the building such as stairways and lifts. The Unit Titles Act governs what body corporates can do. As rules do vary between body corporates, check the body corporate rules before you buy. Also check out the body corporate records to find out about any issues simmering beneath the surface such as arguments over who is going to pay for a leaking roof, by asking the body corporate manager for permission to look at the meeting minutes. Pre-purchase you will be issued a section 36 certificate which outlines what levies and insurance have been and are to be paid.

Cross-leasing was originally used as a way for developers to get around restrictive town planing rules and build more on the same amount of land. Increasingly through, cross-lease title owners are seen as having only limited rights.

All cross-lease owners are tenants in common in ownership of the head title. This means when doing any building alterations you need permission from the other cross-lease owners to do so. If you don't get permission, you could create a defective title that will cause headaches when you want to sell. The standard cross-lease form contains provisions that aren't found in most commercial leases – restrictions like what colour you can paint your building or who you sub-let to. In the past, cross-lease owners have tended to act as if they had freehold title and ignored any of these covenants, but it is now becoming more common for the other cross-lease owners to take legal action to enforce them.

Treaty of Waitangi claims

Treaty of Waitangi claims are generally not an issue for the average punter but it pays to be aware of them. Before purchase you need to check there are no treaty claims made on the land. The title shows if there is a memorial that former State-owned enterprise land may be used to redress treaty issues. The same can happen with former Crown land such as schools or police stations.

If you have purchased land and it ultimately ends up being used for treaty claims you will get compensated as if it was an acquisition under the Public Works Act. It's a commercial judgement you have to make and the price you pay will want to reflect that uncertainty. Bear in mind it can take years, decades even, for treaty claims to be settled.

Owners are compensated at market value if the land is acquired but this doesn't take into account business goodwill that may be related to the site or moving costs.

Under the claims process, claimants submit a claim to the Waitangi Tribunal. The Tribunal groups together related registered claims to hear at the same time, after they have been researched by a number of parties. Hearings are held before the Tribunal and a report issued. If the claimants and the Crown agree to negotiate, it can take some time to reach a settlement. And there can be a whole series of outcomes including return of the land, money paid as compensation, or a public apology. The claimants can withdraw their claim at any stage or decide to skip the whole process and negotiate directly with the Crown. The Tribunal can refer a claim to mediation. It can also turn claims down if they are deemed to be trivial, frivolous, or vexatious.

Overseas Investment Commission approval

The Overseas Investment Commission (OIC) oversees the Government's policy on foreign direct investment as set out in the Overseas Investment Regulations. Some $398 million worth of New Zealand land, including 35,555 net hectares of freehold land, was approved for sale to overseas people in the year ending 2002 – the lowest figures since 1993.

COMPLIANCE AND YOUR BUSINESS

You will need to apply for the OIC's approval if you're an overseas-owned company purchasing:

- a building or property worth more than $50 million
- land over 5 hectares and/or worth more than $10 million
- any land on most offshore islands
- coastal property
- 'sensitive' land over 4 hectares on or adjoining a reserve, conservation land, historic or heritage areas, or lakes.

There are a number of exemptions including companies which are essentially New Zealand-controlled despite more than 25% overseas ownership, or life insurance and superannuation schemes which are investing for the benefit of policy-holders, where more than 75% of the policy-holders are New Zealand residents.

The OIC has the power to determine land applications providing they don't involve sensitive land. However, it doesn't take much to cause land to qualify as 'sensitive' and thereby requiring ministerial consent. And remember it is adjoining properties that can be sensitive rather than your own. This is not always obvious by a title search. For example, a historic place or wahi tapu area may be entered into the historic places register established under the Historic Places Act. Land will also be sensitive where there is a current application or proposal to make an entry into that register.

It can take longer than you think to prepare the information required for approval before it is submitted to the OIC, particularly when you're buying more than one property. The OIC's current statistics on approval state the average turnaround is 2 working days or 2 weeks for ministerial decisions.

The OIC has an ongoing monitoring role to ensure any conditions of approval are being met by the purchaser. Under the Overseas Investment Act 1973, the High Court has the authority to sell property and prosecute anyone not complying with these conditions.

If you need to apply for OIC approval, you will have to supply a host of information – from details on your business entity and ultimate beneficial owners through to your proposed use of the land. When buying more than one property you need a summary schedule setting out total hectares – simply attaching titles is insufficient. Also include certificates on adjoining land. The OIC has set out key concepts each application should include to demonstrate the 'benefits' of investment. For details visit *www.oic.govt.nz*.

PROPERTY

Buyer beware

One of the better known legal maxims is 'caveat emptor', or let the buyer beware. What it means is the purchaser needs to check out what they're buying is worth the money and the seller has no responsibility. But there are a couple of pieces of legislation that mean the vendor in a real estate deal can't get away that lightly – the Contractual Remedies Act and the Fair Trading Act.

Under the Contractual Remedies Act, a vendor can't include a provision in a contract that the purchaser buys wholly on the basis of their own judgement. A court can ignore such a provision after taking into account all the circumstances, including the relative bargaining strengths of the parties and whether they had a solicitor.

The Fair Trading Act prohibits deceptive or misleading conduct in trade, so you can be liable if a real estate agent makes deceptive or misleading respresentations on your behalf. Let's say the real estate agent advertised your property as having a stupendous harbour view, knowing all the time a proposed development was underway next door that would block out the view. In this scenario, both the vendor and the agent can be liable to the purchaser.

Your standard sale and purchase agreement for real estate has a number of vendor warranties and undertakings which, if wrongfully given, can lead to a damages claim or even allow the purchaser to cancel the contract. Check that these have not been deleted by the vendor or amended in the sale and purchase agreement before your sign. vendor warranties include statements:

- as to whether the vendor has received any notices or demands relating to the property such as a letter from the local council demanding various works be done
- about the fact that no work has been carried out on the property without the required building consent
- that the building has a current warrant of fitness.

The warranties are even more extensive when it is a cross-lease or unit title property up for sale.

If you're the owner of a tenanted property you should check tenant payments are up-to-date before you sell. Otherwise you could lose your right to receive these payments.

> ### Murdoch v Chiplin (1991)
>
> This case involves a private house sale where illegal work was discovered, but it also applies to commercial properties. In 1991, a Timaru couple bought a house where the previous owner had made various alterations and additions. These included putting a steel beam in the basement, building an additional room with a pot belly stove installed in it, and the installation of a shower. About a month after the new owners moved in, water leaked through the roof during heavy rain. Further investigation showed the steel beam in the basement had been installed without necessary building permits and was deemed dangerous by the council. The sagging beam made the floor slope and doors hard to open. The court found there had been a breach of the sale and purchase agreement and the defendants had to buy back the house at the same purchase price and pay the plaintiff's court costs, even though this meant selling a house subsequently bought elsewhere.

Buying a company with existing properties

The first thing to do when buying a company with existing properties is to check out all the details of the titles, including whether they are freehold or leasehold and any tenant arrangements. Get all this information in writing. You'll also want to check for any breach or non-compliance with legislation relating to fire safety, health and safety, or building work (a LIM is useful for this). And where the company is a tenant in a building, look for any breach of the lease conditions and whether the lease can be assigned.

Transferring consents

You should also make sure that the activity being carried out on the site is in fact covered by the necessary resource consents. You can go to the council and get a copy of the resource consents if these are not provided by the vendor. You may need to transfer over some of these existing consents. Land use consents run with the land.

Other types of consents don't run with the land (such as for your factory discharging into the air) and these need to be transferred. Some regional councils may have restrictions on transfers, particularly for water discharge. If you don't get the consents transferred you have no lawful base for continuing that activity. You could be breaching the Resource Management Act – and in the worst case scenario end up being closed down.

Site contamination

Another trap to watch out for when purchasing an existing business is whether any of the properties involved have site contamination. A site can become contaminated when hazardous substances are spilt or dumped, either accidentally or during normal business because of poor operational practices. As well as causing sickness in people on the site, the presence of these substances can limit your use of the land, and substantially reduce the land value. Information on contaminated sites is held by regional and local councils but there is no requirement in New Zealand for landowners to disclose site contamination to their council and therefore not all contamination is registered.

There are certain flags you can watch out that may indicate the presence of contamination, eg any industrial property where the previous use was related to gas works, service stations, dry cleaning, timber treatment, or even an orchard. Where you suspect there may be trouble it pays to get an environmental audit. To prevent liability for any contamination you can put warranties to this effect in your lease or purchase agreement. Under the Resource Management Act you are not liable for any historical contamination – this relates to contamination that took place prior to 1991 when the Act came in.

See chapter 6, *Environment* for more information on Resource Management Act.

Contamination clean-up

The Pinesong Resort, overlooking Auckland's Manukau Harbour, was originally developed from horticultural land to include accommmodation, a conference centre, and golfcourse. It has since been redeveloped by Metlifecare into a retirement village. While in horticultural use, a timber processing business used a gully on the Green Bay site to deposit more than 55,000 tonnes of timber preservative, contaminated wood waste, and chemicals. Detection of this contamination effectively halted plans in the early 1990s to redevelop the site into a retirement village. Costs for removing all contaminated fill to meet health regulations made development uneconomic and the property was significantly devalued.

However, further collaboration between developers, the property owners, and regulators turned up a range of five options – from leaving the contamination in situ and retaining a low intensity conference use with restrictions on use of infilled areas, through to complete removal of the contaminants and refilling of the site for unrestricted use. The middle ground was chosen. Selective removal of hotspots, on-site treatment, encapsulation of moderately contaminated fill, and selective monitoring provided environmental protection above the bottom line guidance criteria and made it economic to proceed with the development.

Due diligence checklist

- Have you obtained details of all the property owned by the company, including copies of title deeds?
- Are chattels, fixtures, and fittings included in the sale? Look at the age, state of repair, valuation and suitability of all the fixed assets and any chattels, plant, fixtures, and fittings.
- Have you obtained details of all leases and tenancies? Ensure the lease is able to be assigned to you.
- Do you need a LIM to check on building work, etc?
- Are there any issues that may impact on your ability to compete effectively in the marketplace such as compliance systems, quality assurance standards, or ability to obtain insurance?
- Is it unit title property? If yes, then check the body corporate records.
- Have you checked warranties by the vendor as to rent, ownership, and repair of plant/assets/fixtures and fittings and compliance with statutory obligations?
- Is any of the land 'sensitive land' or does any of the land adjoin such land, such as an historic area or wahi tapu area?
- Will you need OIC approval?
- Have you obtained details on any past disputes between the company and neighbours, landlords, tenants, or local authorities in respect of the land?
- Have you got copies of the compliance schedule and warrant of fitness as required under the Building Act?
- Is there any impending change in circumstances that may impact on the viability of the business you're acquiring (eg regulatory change, zoning change, change in technology)? Look for any planning application notices by your neighbours or modification of any planning permission.

ENVIRONMENT

All businesses need to comply with New Zealand's environmental laws and regulations. New Zealand's environmental laws set high standards for protecting the environment from adverse effects, and failing to comply with them is potentially very serious. The Hazardous Substances and New Organisms Act 1996 (HSNO) allows fines up to $500,000 (plus $50,000 a day) – and amendments being considered in late 2003 will substantially increase fines in respect of breaches relating to new organisms.

Business obligations under the environmental laws

The Resource Management Act (RMA) and the Hazardous Substances and New Organisms Act 1996 (the HSNO Act) are the principal environmental laws affecting businesses. Other environmental laws with compliance issues you may need to be aware of include the Ozone Protection Act 1996, the Historic Places Act 1993 and the Antiquities Act 1975.

Resource Management Act 1991 (RMA)

If you're planning a business activity that will have environmental effects on land, air, or water, you will most likely need a resource consent before you can proceed. A resource consent is a permission, issued in most cases by a local or regional council, to undertake an activity that might otherwise be in breach of a district or regional plan (see district and regional plans box).

When do you need a resource consent?

Resource consents are required for all manner of activities, from extensions to buildings to major infrastructural developments. While the latter may not affect a small business, you still need to be aware of any requirements a local authority may have in order for a resource consent not to be necessary. Rules within district or regional plans 'trigger' the need for a resource consent – for instance you may be able to build to a certain height without a resource consent, but should you want to exceed the height restriction, a resource consent will be required.

Five types of resource consent are granted under the RMA:

- land use consent (required if you plan to build, modify or demolish structures; excavate; disturb habitats of plants and animals; or deposit anything on land or to undertake an activity)
- subdivision consent (most subdivision proposals require permission)
- coastal permit (any activity that does not comply with a regional coastal plan requires a coastal permit)
- water permit (for using and diverting water other than for domestic or reasonable stock watering purposes)
- discharge permit (required if you plan to discharge water or contaminants into water or land).

Whether or not you need a resource consent depends on how the activity you are proposing has been categorised in a regional or district plan.

If your activity is a **permitted activity** you won't need a resource consent as long as you comply with the performance standards established in a district or regional plan. A permitted activity could be running a retail shop in a business zone, or running a home business in a residential area. However, if you plan to make renovations or changes that are in breach of a permitted activity's performance standards, the activity will fall into one of the following categories.

A **controlled activity** is one which requires a resource consent and which a council has reserved the right to control. A council cannot refuse the consent, but it will give careful consideration to particular matters and you will be required meet any conditions the council attaches to the consent.

A **restricted discretionary activity** requires a resource consent. A council can turn down the consent application, or require conditions to be met, but only on issues it has identified in a plan. For example, a council may restrict its discretion to particular categories of effects such as traffic generation, amenity, and lighting spill.

A **discretionary activity** is an activity for which resource consent is required and the council has not limited those matters it can consider when assessing an application. For example, service stations are a discretionary activity in the business zones of Auckland City and the criteria outlined in the District Plan include: traffic generation, access, noise, and the protection and maintenance of amenity values.

A **non-complying activity** is an activity that contravenes a rule in a district plan, and has not been described as either a discretionary activity or a restricted discretionary activity (see above). To be granted a resource consent for a non-complying activity, you must convince a council that the adverse effects on the environment will be minor, or that granting the consent will not be contrary to the objectives and policies of the district plan. Unless these 'thresholds' are met, the council must decline your application.

A **prohibited activity** is just that and no resource consent can be granted. The only way a prohibited activity can be authorised is by changing the district plan.

Your obligations

Under the RMA, your business will be required to comply with the provisions of the district and/or regional plan operating in your area (see overview below). If you have been granted a resource consent (permission) from a district or regional council to carry out an activity, you will need to comply with any conditions that apply.

When you're planning a new business or expanding an existing operation to take on a new activity, you must first find out if the district or regional plan (in some cases both) for your area allows you to do what you have in mind. If the plan does not provide express permission to carry out the activity, or you cannot meet one or more of the performance standards in the plan, you need to apply for a resource consent.

The Resource Management Act (RMA) – an overview

The goal of the RMA is to ensure New Zealand's land, air, and water (including coastal waters) resources are sustainably managed so that they are available to be used or enjoyed in the future by our kids, grandkids, and the generations beyond.

Why do we need the RMA? Most human activities have an effect on the environment, and sometimes these effects harm things we take for granted, like the air we breathe, the water we drink or swim in, or the ecosystems that native plants and animals depend on. The RMA works by managing the effects of activities such as noise or pollution, rather than with particular types of activities. It provides a framework for ensuring any adverse environmental effects of our activities are 'avoided, remedied, or mitigated'. It provides principles for resource management planning and decision-making on issues affecting how and where we live.

Administration of the RMA is carried out by 12 regional councils and 70 city and district councils. In addition, there are four unitary authorities that do the work of both regional and district councils.

In addition to the above, the Department of Conservation and the Minister of Conservation have a role under the RMA to oversee the management of the coastal environment. The Minister approves the New Zealand Coastal Policy Statement, regional coastal plans, and, of most interest to businesses, applications for activities with significant or irreversible effects on the coastal environment (such as structures or reclamations). The Ministry for the Environment and the Minister of the Environment also have a role. The Ministry is principally concerned with setting policy, while the Minister can 'call in' major projects, in which case the Minister acts as the district or regional council.

ENVIRONMENT

Regional and district plans

Communities (which includes the business community) and individuals are encouraged by the RMA to involve themselves in the resource management planning process by contributing to community decisions on such things as providing playgrounds, where business activities should be located, or land development.

District and regional plans are long-term (10-year) planning documents which take account of community wishes and will include rules that may affect where you can locate your business, or rules aimed at ensuring your business does not adversely affect the environment or your neighbours. Rules cover such things as noise control; discharges to air, land, or water; parking; subdivision; and land development. Plans will also identify sites with important historic, cultural, or natural characteristics that warrant protection.

Regional councils prepare regional policy statements and regional plans. City and district councils prepare district plans. These documents, produced with input from the public, describe:

- the environmental issues present in a district or region
- goals for sustainable management of the environment
- environmental objectives and policies, and the methods that will be used to achieve those goals.

A regional policy statement provides overall direction for managing environmental issues in a region. A regional plan establishes policies and rules regarding the management of particular aspects of the environment (eg air, land, water, and the coast). A district plan establishes policies and rules for the way land is used in your area, and must be consistent with regional policies and plans. These in turn must 'give effect' to any national policy statement produced under the RMA (while the Ministry for the Environment is producing a policy statement on biodiversity, currently the only national policy statement is the New Zealand Coastal Policy Statement).

The district plan is the document of most direct interest to small businesses as it contains information that will let you know if what you have planned can be carried out as of right, or if you need a resource consent.

Do you need a consent?

Don't rush out and buy property or go ahead with your proposed activity without first establishing whether you need a resource consent. This could be disastrous if you later discover that you in fact do need council permission – you also risk severe penalties under the RMA. Consulting the district or regional plan and talking with council planning staff are necessary first steps to work out whether or not you need

COMPLIANCE AND YOUR BUSINESS

a resource consent. Council plans are available at all libraries, and are also usually found on council websites.

Choice of location and the nature of the activity will affect whether or not you need a resource consent. As outlined earlier, councils treat some activities as 'permitted activities' which don't require a consent, though conditions in district and regional plans (which might cover such things as signage, parking, and so on) will need to be met.

> ### Location, location, location
>
> You can expect a smoother ride along the RMA compliance trail by locating your business appropriately as some activities are better suited for particular areas than others. For instance, certain businesses such as medical centres and dairies are more likely to be allowed within residential areas than a panelbeating workshop, and may even be deemed 'permitted activities'.
>
> On the other hand, if you plan to gut and extend a house and turn it into to a surgery or shop, you may still need a consent. You can't expect to be allowed to set up a panelbeating workshop within or next to a residential area as of right – clearly, it would be wiser to set up in an area zoned for light industrial activity. However, if you did want to go ahead in a residential area, you'll have to apply for a resource consent and convince the council that you can 'avoid, remedy, or mitigate' the potential effects on the environment and your neighbourhood.

Applying for a resource consent

Applying for a resource consent can be a time-consuming and potentially costly exercise. It is essential that you factor in sufficient time for the application process, particularly if you need to consult with people affected by the proposal. Before lodging your application you will need to:

- thoroughly scope your venture to identify all potential issues
- identify the type of resource consent you require – in some cases you may need more than one consent
- discuss the proposal with council officers
- prepare an assessment of environmental effects
- consult with anyone who may be affected by your proposal.

In your application you are legally required to:

- detail the type of resource consent you need
- provide a description of the proposed activity and where you will carry it out
- list other resource consents that are necessary for the activity and whether or not you have applied for them

- provide an assessment of environmental effects
- provide any other information required by a plan or associated regulations.

Assessment of environmental effects

The assessment of environmental effects is one of the most crucial parts of your application as this is where you get down to explaining the nitty gritty of the proposed activity, any effects it may have, and how you will mitigate those effects. The assessment is mandatory – without it council will require further information or even reject your application. If it's a large or complex application, you may need input from a range of professionals – engineers, planners, ecologists, and so on.

The assessment of environmental effects must include the following information:

- a list of possible alternative locations or methods for undertaking the activity if significant environmental effects are likely
- an assessment of the actual or potential effects on the environment of the proposed activity
- an assessment of any risks to the environment if hazardous substances or installations are to be used
- the nature of any discharge, the sensitivity of the receiving environment to adverse effects, and any possible alternative discharge methods
- a description of the mitigation measures (including safeguards and contingency plans where relevant) to be undertaken to help prevent or reduce the actual or potential effects
- an identification of those persons interested in or affected by the proposal, the consultation undertaken, if any, and response to the views of those consulted
- how the monitoring of any effects will be carried out and by whom.

The assessment of environmental effects must also consider:

- any effect on those in the neighbourhood and, where relevant, the wider community including any socio-economic and cultural effects
- any physical effect on the locality, including any landscape and visual effects
- any effect on ecosystems, including effects on plants or animals and any physical disturbance of habitats in the vicinity
- any effect on natural and physical resources with aesthetic, recreational, scientific, historical, spiritual, cultural, or other special value for present or future generations
- any discharge of contaminants into the environment, including any unreasonable noise and options for the treatment and disposal of contaminants
- any risk to the neighbourhood, the wider community, or the environment through natural hazards or the use of hazardous substances or hazardous installations.

The Ministry for the Environment's guide to preparing assessments of environmental effects (quote reference ME308) can be downloaded from the

Ministry's website: *http://www.mfe.govt.nz/publications/rma/basic-aee-prep-guide-mar99.html*.

Getting good advice

The RMA is a legal and practical maze and you will need sound advice from an early stage to ensure that you comply with the resource consent application process. Council staff can help you identify the type of resource consent(s) you need and other issues worth considering, such as whom you may need to consult with. Most councils publish guidelines to the resource consent process, and have made these available on their websites.

Be cautious in the early stages about how you present the details of your proposed activity in your application to the council. You don't want to risk creating a negative impression which may affect the outcome of your application. Informal advice you receive from council officers should not be relied on as the final word.

Seeking advice from your lawyer or an independent environmental consultant can be helpful or indeed necessary, especially for larger, more complex proposals. Environmental consultants are familiar with council planning requirements and staff and their involvement will make the process flow smoother. You may find it useful to engage a lawyer or planning consultant to informally sound the council out on what you plan to do, if necessary on a confidential 'no-names' basis.

As well as assisting with informal and formal negotiations, a planning consultant can help ensure that you have thoroughly scoped your proposal and provide technical advice. The consultant can also manage other aspects of the application process such as consultations with affected parties (see below), and preparation of the assessment of environmental effects and the resource consent application.

The Environment Waikato website has useful advice on independent consultants: *www.ew.govt.nz/resourceconsents/enviroconsultant.htm#Heading2*.

Consultation

Consulting with people who are going to be adversely affected by your proposal is not mandatory under the RMA, but it is nonetheless good practice. Having written agreement from all adversely affected parties will save you time and money, and will go a long way toward ensuring your application is granted, especially if the council treats your proposal as a 'non-notified' application (see *Lodging your Application* below).

Only those who will be adversely affected by your proposal (in many cases these will be your neighbours) need to be consulted, not those who are simply interested parties. Council staff or your planning consultant will be able to provide advice on who to consult. Any consultation must occur before your resource consent application is lodged.

ENVIRONMENT

> **What is consultation?**
>
> General principles for consultation, outlined by the Environment Court, include the following:
> - consultation must be about a proposal, not a fait accompli
> - you must listen to what others have to say and consider their responses
> - the consultation process must be genuine, not a sham
> - you must keep an open mind and be prepared to change your mind, or even begin anew
> - you must also provide sufficient information and time to enable those consulted to adequately consider the proposal.

Meeting people on the site to discuss your proposal is a good idea. Even if you can't satisfactorily resolve all issues, you will at least know what might come up if the application reaches a hearing stage, and have covered them in your assessment of environmental effects.

Your application will be helped considerably if you can get written consent from adversely affected parties. They must sign any plans and fill out a standard consent form, available from the council.

COMPLIANCE AND YOUR BUSINESS

> ### Consulting with Iwi
>
> For the uninitiated, iwi consultation may seem a daunting prospect. The same principles for consultation described above apply, but with iwi there is a particular need to handle consultations sensitively and in a culturally appropriate manner.
>
> It's a good idea to get advice from the council and/or a planning consultant on who to approach, and how to make the approach. Most councils employ an iwi liaison officer and keep a register of iwi with an interest in the region. The manner of the consultation will depend on the scale of your proposal, its effects, and the places affected.
>
> Some general advice is offered here:
>
> - Ideally you need people working for you who are well versed in iwi protocol – a consultant planner will have experience in this area and may know iwi representatives.
> - Allow sufficient time. Some iwi are not well resourced and may have a number of resource consent applications to deal with at any one time. Iwi trustees may only meet once a month so you need to be realistic about how quickly they will deal with your proposal.
> - Always send senior people to any meetings with iwi – you will most likely be meeting with senior kaumatua and it will be insulting to them if you send a lower level manager.
> - Ask where iwi representatives would like to meet rather than assume they will meet somewhere that suits you.
> - Expect to provide a koha (gift) towards the time the iwi spends considering your application. This is quite legitimate as there is no Government funding for consultation and in some cases iwi have hundreds of resource consent hopefuls wanting their signoff on applications. For larger applications, iwi may request that a formal cultural assessment is undertaken, which you pay for.

Lodging your application

Once you have gathered all relevant information, prepared the assessment of environmental effects, and consulted with adversely affected people, you are ready to lodge your application. Councils have standard application forms for applicants to use.

Once the application has been lodged, you should be ready to respond quickly to requests for further information or to attend technical meetings. Ensure your advisors are present at these meetings. Where applications involve significant adverse effects, a council may decide to prepare its own report (using its own council experts or external experts).

An important decision that the council must make within 10 days (excluding time for more information) is whether or not to publicly notify the application and hold a public hearing. Most applications (well over 90%) aren't publicly notified and are decided by council officers.

The RMA provides that an application must be notified unless:

- the application is for a controlled activity
- the council is satisfied that the adverse affects of the activity on the environment will be minor
- all persons who, in the opinion of the consent authority, may be adversely affected by the activity have given their written approval.

Applications for restricted discretionary activities also may not be notified if a rule in a plan expressly provides that notification is not required.

If your application is not publicly notified, third parties cannot make a submission, nor can they appeal the decision to the Environment Court (see *Appeals* below). A council's decision on whether or not to notify an application can be judicially reviewed by the High Court.

Public hearings

If an application is publicly notified, a public hearing must be held no later than 25 working days after your application has been lodged (excluding time for dealing with requests for further information). Public submissions will be called (anyone can make a submission), and you may have to attend a pre-hearing meeting at which issues or disputes are discussed. If matters can be satisfactorily resolved at this meeting, a public hearing may not be necessary.

The hearing will be conducted by a planning committee made up of publicly elected representatives and/or independent commissioners. They will consider a report and recommendations from council officers and submissions from the applicant and the public. After hearing evidence, the committee will make a decision, including conditions that must be met if the application is approved.

At the hearing:

- your lawyer and/or professional advisor should be present along with any witnesses, and prepared witness statements will be required
- you, your advisors, and witnesses should be prepared to answer questions about the effects of your proposed activity, and to address the recommending officer's report and concerns raised by public submissions.

Under the RMA, councils may extend all timeframes up to a maximum doubling of the period.

Appeals

You, as applicant, or anyone who has made a submission on your application, can appeal the council's decision to the Environment Court. Appeals must be lodged within 15 days of receipt of the council's decision.

An Environment Court hearing is a fresh hearing in which the merits of the application are considered from scratch. Appealing to the Environment Court is a serious and expensive undertaking – legal advice is essential before you proceed. New evidence may need to be prepared, and you will also find yourself pitted against the council, who will defend its decision with its own lawyers and witnesses.

Drafting the appeal by a lawyer can cost around $1,500, with the hearing costs on top of that. You also risk having costs awarded against you if you lose.

If a submitter appeals a decision, you have no choice but to defend the council's decision. In many instances you cannot require the decision-maker to support you, and it can effectively mean it is up to you to defend the council decision.

The law allows mediation to take place before the hearing to see if mutually acceptable outcomes can be reached, thus avoiding the hearing and associated costs.

If you're not satisfied with the Environment Court decision you can appeal the decision to the High Court, but only on points of law. Few resource consent applications go to the next stage – the Court of Appeal.

Further information on the Environment Court can be found at *http://www.courts.govt.nz/environment/index.html*. The Environmental Defence Society provides detailed information about lodging an appeal on its website: *http://www.rmaguide.org.nz/rma/court/lodgingappeal.cfm*.

Complying with your resource consent

Consents outline what you are allowed to do; where the activity is to be carried out; any restrictions on volume, rate or quantity (of effluent discharges, for eg); when the consent period ends; and other compliance conditions. These could involve the posting of a performance bond, meeting performance standards, monitoring (eg water quality or ecological monitoring), contingency plans for emergencies, providing compliance reports to the council, and provision of parking etc.

You can begin exercising your consent after the 15-day appeal period expires provided no appeals are lodged (see *Appeals* above). Non-notified applications become operative on the date specified in the consent. You will be asked to advise the council when you begin the activity.

Not complying with your consent risks enforcement action by the council and liability for any costs associated with enforcement. Council inspectors can enter your property at any time to ensure you are complying with conditions.

Renewing your consent

No automatic right of renewal exists for your resource consent. Under the RMA you must apply for a renewal no later than 6 months before the consent expires. You may continue to operate under the original consent until the application for a new consent has been determined (including any appeals against that decision). If you apply for a renewal between 3 and 6 months before expiry, councils have discretion whether to allow you to continue to operate under the original consent. These timeframes mean that it is prudent to start work on a renewal application well ahead of the expiry date. Missing the statutory date for renewal applications is serious matter, as you may need to cease business until the renewal application (including possible appeals) is determined, or a new application is heard.

> **Some compliance techniques**
>
> It's important to maintain a reliable diary system to remind you when compliance reports are due or when you need to begin working on a renewal application. You will probably already be using a computer diary system with 'pop-up' reminders for tax payments and other important tasks, so it shouldn't be difficult to add consent compliance reminders to that system.
>
> This task could be delegated to a staff member (perhaps the person responsible for paying wages, or if the business is large enough, you could employ a compliance manager). A compliance manual or checklist – it doesn't need to be long – is a useful tool for ensuring staff are aware of their compliance responsibilities.

Breaching conditions

Breaching the terms of a resource consent is a criminal offence with potentially serious ramifications. You should be upfront with the council if you discover you are breaching consent conditions as this approach will help minimise the consequences for your business. The penalties imposed will depend on the scale of the offence.

When a breach occurs you must take immediate steps to rectify the situation. Secondly, you should draft a letter to the council (with help from your lawyer) detailing the breach, the steps you have taken, and the timeframe for correcting the situation.

Three levels of enforcement are available under the RMA. At the lower end of the scale is an **infringement notice**, which is similar to an instant fine for speeding. Infringement notices are issued for minor offences – like breaching a condition of a resource consent where the breach does not result in significant adverse environmental effects. Fines range from $300 to $1,000.

COMPLIANCE AND YOUR BUSINESS

At a far more serious level, district or regional councils can serve you with an **abatement notice** directing you to take particular actions or to cease doing something that is affecting the environment. Not complying with an abatement notice is a criminal offence and you risk being prosecuted. You can object to an abatement notice by appealing to the Environment Court, but you must still comply with the notice.

For serious ongoing breaches, the Environment Court can serve you with an **enforcement order**. Anyone, including a trade competitor, can apply for an enforcement order. Again, it is an offence not to comply with the order. Not complying with an enforcement order leaves you open to the full force of the RMA – a fine up to $200,000 plus penalties of up to $10,000 for every day the offence continues after the order was served.

In addition to abatement notices and enforcement orders, the RMA also provides for monetary penalties for breaches of the Act or a resource consent (and very rare prison terms).

Hazardous Substances and New Organisms Act 1996 (the HSNO Act)

This section focuses primarily on the hazardous substances aspects of the Hazardous Substances and New Organisms Act 1996 (the HSNO Act) as it is unlikely small businesses will be involved in the introduction of new organisms to New Zealand. Given that literally thousands of hazardous substances are used, stored, or sold by businesses today, compliance requirements are discussed here in general terms.

The HSNO Act imposes strict penalties and liabilities for offences against the Act so it is very important, in what is a highly complex area to manage, that you ensure that its requirements are complied with. Penalties under the HSNO Act are even more significant in dollar terms than those under the RMA, and include a prison term not exceeding 3 months or fines not exceeding $500,000 and $50,000 for every day the offence continued.

ENVIRONMENT

About the HSNO Act

The purpose of the HSNO Act is to protect the environment and the health and safety of people and communities, by preventing or managing the adverse effects of hazardous substances and new organisms. Like the RMA, the HSNO Act repealed a number of earlier laws such as the Dangerous Goods Act 1974 and the Toxic Substances Act 1979 and consolidated them into a single Act. The Act created a new agency, the Environmental Risk Management Authority (ERMA), which is responsible for running an assessment and regulatory approvals process.

Anyone planning to introduce a hazardous substance or new organism not already legally present in New Zealand must get permission from ERMA. Of most direct interest to users of this book, the HSNO Act covers all aspects of hazardous substances management, from importation and manufacturing to handling, transportation, and storage.

Transitional arrangements

The hazardous substances parts of HSNO came into force on 1 July 2001. However, because of the sheer number of hazardous substances that need to be transferred from the old legislation to the new Act, a transitional period is currently in effect.

The transitional arrangements apply to all hazardous substances approved under previous legislation before 1 April 1999. All substances introduced since then are approved and controlled by the new legislation. The transitional period is expected to take 3-5 years to complete.

What is a hazardous substance?

A hazardous substance is defined as anything with one or more of the following properties:

- explosiveness
- flammability
- ability to accelerate a fire
- toxicity to humans
- ability to corrode human tissue or metal
- toxicity to the environment
- capacity to develop one or more of the above properties on contact with air or water.

Regulations published at the end of the transition period will set thresholds for each of these properties.

217

The Act does not apply to radioactive, ozone depleting, and infectious substances, which are covered by other Acts. Nor does it cover most manufactured articles containing hazardous substances (except explosives, eg fireworks) as they are unlikely to exceed threshold levels.

What is a new organism?

A new organism includes micro-organisms, reproductive cells, fish, plants, insects, genetically modified organisms (including plants or animals that could become a food product), and species not currently in New Zealand. New organisms also include organisms held in containment – such as zoo animals. The HSNO Act regulates the introduction of new organisms to New Zealand. The Act does not cover organisms already present in New Zealand before 29 July 1998, humans, or genetically modified foods in processed forms.

Applying for approval to introduce a new organism

Few if any small businesses, such as retailers, are likely to seek to directly introduce or develop new organisms. Garden centres, for eg, rely on seed importers such as Yates to ensure compliance with regulations covering the introduction of new plants. The HSNO Act contains a schedule of prohibited organisms that pose particular threats to New Zealand. Pet shop owners and animal breeders should be aware of this list, which includes animals such as snakes. The Biosecurity Act 1993 and associated regulations also prohibits specified organisms from entering the country.

The ERMA New Zealand website has detailed information about the new organisms application process: *www.ermanz.govt.nz*.

Planning to introduce a hazardous substance?

If you are planning to introduce, manufacture, or develop a new hazardous substance you will need to apply to ERMA for approval. ERMA maintains a register (also available on its website) if you need to check if a substance has already been approved. The application process is rigorous and requires thorough documentation about the substance.

For more information about applications see the ERMA New Zealand website.

Features of the HSNO hazardous substances control regime

- Hazardous substances are classified by the HSNO Act according to their hazardous properties – flammability, explosiveness, toxicity, corrosiveness, oxidising ability, and toxicity to the environment – an approach in line with the international globally harmonised system (GHS) for hazard classification.
- The Act controls are performance-based – unlike the prescriptive approach of the old legislation, it provides flexibility to adopt new technologies to meet performance standards.

- The Act controls cover the entire 'life cycle' of hazardous substances: safe packaging, how they are identified (in labelling, documentation, advertising, and worker safety information), emergency management, tracking systems to locate highly hazardous substances, competency of people handling highly hazardous substances, and disposal.
- A 'test certification' regime replaces the old system of licences and permits. These certificates certify that systems, equipment, or people are complying with hazardous substances controls.
- Codes of Practice, assessed and approved by ERMA, are promoted as a means of ensuring compliance with the HSNO Act. They will include assessing and approving existing codes being used by industry to deal with hazardous substances.

An overview of your responsibilities
- You must comply with ERMA-required controls for each 'approved' substance you deal with.
- Manufacturers, importers, and suppliers have particular responsibilities for ensuring products they bring to New Zealand are approved by ERMA, that they comply with packaging controls, and are supplied with required identification, workplace safety documentation, and disposal information.
- Users must ensure they have the correct documentation and certification for each substance, including labelling, workplace safety documentation, and records and tracking information for highly hazardous substances.
- Approved handlers may be required for handling some substances (such as explosives and highly poisonous substances).
- Packaging must comply with packaging rules. You must ensure that packaging isn't damaged, the substance can't escape, and that labelling offering safety, disposal, and other information isn't damaged.
- You must dispose of hazardous substances according to information supplied with each product, bearing in mind also the trade waste disposal requirements.
- You must be prepared to deal with emergencies. This might involve preparation of emergency plans, making sure labelling allows easy identification of a substance in an emergency, and having appropriate equipment for dealing with spills or fires. Where large quantities are involved, site design should ensure any spills are contained.
- When transporting hazardous substances you must comply with safety controls specific to each substance, meet requirements for vehicle signage, ensure labels aren't damaged and that all documentation is on hand, have emergency plans in place, and ensure that competency requirements for approved handlers have been met.

COMPLIANCE AND YOUR BUSINESS

- If you are a retailer handling or storing small quantities of low hazard substances for sale, your main responsibilities are keeping potential ignition sources away from the material, and ensuring labels are not damaged when they are stacked or stored. Special requirements must be met for the sale of fireworks and ammunition.

Hazardous substances under transition arrangements

Until the transfer of hazardous substances to the HSNO Act is completed and new regulations are released, toxic substances, pesticides, and dangerous goods are controlled by the same provisions of the various Acts and Regulations that applied before July 2001.

Toxic substances

Toxic substances are handled, stored, or used by a wide range of small businesses, including pharmacies, surgeries, vet clinics, and shops. Enforcement of the transitional regime is the responsibility of ERMA, however pursuant to the toxic substances regulations, the Minister for the Environment, in consultation with the Minister of Health has some responsibilities.

During the transition period you will need to comply with the toxic substances controls that applied under the Toxic Substances Act 1979 and associated regulations. These controls are based on categories of toxic substances (deadly poisons, dangerous poisons, standard poisons, and hazardous substances). All toxic substances and people handling them must be licensed by ERMA. Other controls include:

- all poisonous or harmful substances must be stored and transported in appropriately labelled, impervious resealable containers
- poisons and other harmful substances must be stored as specified for each substance – deadly or dangerous poisons must be locked up
- if a spill occurs, affected premises or vehicles must be isolated and decontaminated
- a Medical Officer of Health has powers to demand information and confiscate substances which are believed to be in breach of the Act
- an accurate record is to be kept of all toxic and harmful substances – employees must be properly trained in handling toxic substances, and educated about the requirements of the Act.

Pesticides

Pesticides regulations affect a wide range of people, including anyone who imports, sells, or uses pesticides. During the transitional period, pesticides are controlled by the provisions of the former Pesticides Act and its associated regulations. Only pesticides registered and licensed by the Pesticides Board can be used or sold.

ENVIRONMENT

Anyone using pesticides (eg spraying contractors) must be approved by ERMA. Other controls include:

- warranties – at the time of sale pesticides must be in accordance with the particulars on labels
- in case of spills, material safety data sheets describing the properties of all chemicals must be kept on site and carried when pesticides are transported
- you must meet all obligations under pesticide regulations covering advertising, labelling, and selling in bulk.

Dangerous goods

Dangerous goods include substances such as gases (eg methane or acetylene), flammable liquids (eg fuel oil), and flammable and oxidising substances. During the transition period dangerous goods are controlled by the provisions of the former Dangerous Goods Act 1974 and associated regulations. City and district councils are responsible for administering the controls.

If you are storing or using dangerous goods your premises may need to be licensed and the goods stored in approved and labelled containers depending on the quantity you store or use. If dangerous goods are stored contrary to the controls, the person who stored them, the owner of the goods, and the occupier of the premises are all potentially liable. The onus is on you to ensure that employees and contractors comply as required.

Accidents involving dangerous goods or incidents that create a threat of explosion or fire must be reported to the council and reasonable steps taken to deal with the threat.

Enforcement

The HSNO Act says everyone involved in hazardous substances and new organisms has a duty to meet the Act's requirements. ERMA's compliance regime places strong emphasis on voluntary measures such as self-responsibility, and complying with codes of practice and industry standards.

Enforcement of hazardous substances control is carried out by a range of agencies:

Local Authorities	Dangerous goods (during the transition period)
	Any enforcement functions transferred by other agencies
OSH, Department of Labour	In any workplace
Ministry of Health	Any workplace, to protect public health

COMPLIANCE AND YOUR BUSINESS

Ministry of Consumer Affairs	Gas systems, installations or appliances
Police, Land Transport Safety Authority	Roads, rail, vehicles
Civil Aviation Authority	Aircraft, airports
New Zealand Customs Service	Border control

You must cooperate with enforcement officers. Under the Act they have broad powers, including the right to enter premises to determine if controls and regulations are being complied with. They are able to issue infringement notices and compliance orders, and collect information and evidence.

Infringement notices, compliance orders, and test certificates

As with the RMA, you can be issued with an infringement notice and fined for minor offences.

Compliance orders are issued for more serious breaches. You will be required to stop doing something or take actions to ensure that you comply with hazardous substances controls, usually within a given timeframe.

Test certificates may be required as a means of verifying that you have met HSNO Act controls and regulations. Certificates can only be issued by test certifiers approved by ERMA.

Offences

You commit an offence if you fail to meet the Act's requirements or controls, or do not comply with a compliance order. It is also an offence not to report new information on the adverse effects of a hazardous substance or new organism.

Liability

Liability is strict in that, to establish liability, the prosecution does not have to prove that you intended to commit an offence. Principals, directors, employers, and employees can all be held responsible for an offence, though a range of defences are available – such as where a principal or employer did not know or could not reasonably be expected to have known about the offence, or took reasonable steps to prevent or stop it, and took all reasonable steps to remedy the situation.

Further advice

ERMA New Zealand has produced a vast amount of information including *Your Guide to the Hazardous Substances and New Organisms Act*. ERMA's website is another useful source of up-to-date information. The Ministry for the Environment's HSNO Act website provides an introduction to the Act and your responsibilities: *www.hsno.govt.nz*. Enforcement agencies and their websites are other useful sources of information.

ENVIRONMENT

Ozone Layer Protection Act 1996

The Ozone Layer Protection Act 1996 and its associated regulations are designed to phase out the use of chemicals that destroy the Earth's protective cover of ozone. The Act implements New Zealand's obligations under the Montreal Protocol, the 1987 global environmental agreement that took aim at a number of man-made chemicals, including chlorofluorocarbons (CFCs), which scientists had shown were responsible for thinning the ozone layer. These chemicals have been widely used as refrigerants, aerosol can propellants, and fumigants.

Most, but not all of these chemicals were phased out in New Zealand by the mid-1990s. Compliance issues for businesses under this Act thus focus on chemicals still to be phased out, the proper disposal of chemicals from old equipment or machinery such as fridges and fire extinguishers, and importing products from countries that have not agreed to the Montreal Protocol.

Key compliance issues that may affect small business include the following:

- It is an offence to import, export, manufacture, sell, or use products containing ozone-depleting chemicals except in circumstances described by the regulations. Exemptions exist for essential uses such as asthma inhalers.
- It is an offence to knowingly release substances controlled by the Act during the installation, servicing, operating, or dismantling of equipment. Businesses carrying out this work or otherwise directly handling ozone-depleting substances may require accreditation.
- Businesses can be required to develop a code of practice or otherwise ensure they are conversant with relevant regulations.
- Products, machinery, or other equipment containing ozone-depleting substances cannot be dumped in a landfill – they must be disposed of by a registered collector.

The following products that use or contain ozone-depleting substances are prohibited:

- aerosols that contain any controlled substance except for methyl bromide
- fire extinguishers
- plastic foam, or any goods that contain plastic foam manufactured using CFCs
- dry-cleaning machines that contain, or are designed to use, any controlled substance as a solvent
- imports from non-complying countries that contain any controlled substances other than HCFCs or methyl bromide
- dehumidifiers, refrigerators, freezers, air conditioners, supermarket display cases, heat pumps, and water coolers that contain CFCs.

COMPLIANCE AND YOUR BUSINESS

Independent audit

If you're taking over premises it's recommended that you have an independent audit carried out to verify that no prohibited ozone-depleting chemicals are present in equipment or machinery – for eg old fire extinguishers. (This audit can also cover products covered by hazardous substances legislation such as PCBs and asbestos.)

This Act is administered by the Ministry of Economic Development. Further information can be found on the Ministry's website, *www.med.govt.nz*, or from the Ministry for the Environment website, *www.mfe.govt.nz*.

Historic heritage:
Historic Places Act 1993
Heritage protection provisions of the RMA
Antiquities Act 1975

Some businesses will be affected by laws protecting New Zealand's historic heritage. This will be the case if you are considering buying a building registered in the Historic Places Trust Register, listed in a district plan, or carrying out work that might affect a historic building or site. In most instances, businesses will need to deal with either a city or district council and/or the New Zealand Historic Places Trust. It is possible also that you may need to consult the Department of Conservation, which manages historic sites on public conservation land).

The RMA and the Historic Places Act 1993 are the two main laws with business compliance implications when it comes to historic heritage and archaeological sites. Related to these Acts is the Antiquities Act 1975, which covers the protection of antiquities, including their sale.

> ### What is Historic heritage?
>
> The RMA defines historic heritage as natural or physical resources that contribute to an understanding and appreciation of New Zealand's history and cultures. Historic heritage is a broad term that includes historic sites, structures, places, and areas; archaeological sites; sites of significance to Maori; and surroundings associated with natural and physical resources. The Historic Places Act further defines an archaeological site as any place in New Zealand associated with human activity that occurred before 1900, pre-1900 shipwrecks, and any place that provides evidence relating to the history of New Zealand.

ENVIRONMENT

Your responsibilities
You are obliged to ensure that your business activity does not in any way damage, modify, or destroy historic heritage unless permission has been granted to do so.

Which jurisdiction?
Both councils and the Historic Places Trust can have responsibility for historic places, and it is possible that consent from both organisations may be required in respect of historic places or items.

City and district councils
Councils list places protected for their heritage values in district plans (see section on *RMA*). These may include notable buildings, whole streets representative of an architectural style or period, or sites significant to Maori. Notable trees also receive protection. Varying levels of protection are offered: a heritage order is the highest level of protection, usually given to significant sites such as Wellington's St James Theatre.

Business activities affecting heritage values will be subject to a range of restrictions – for eg on signage, modifications (such as facades), or demolition work. Activities that affect or may lead to a loss of heritage values may require a resource consent (also see the *RMA* section for a description of the resource consent process).

Historic Places Trust
The Historic Places Trust maintains a register about 6,000 of the country's most important historic places, historic areas, wahi tapu (places sacred to Maori) and wahi tapu areas (groups of wahi tapu). These places are categorised as either Category I or Category II sites. Category I sites have special or outstanding historical or cultural heritage or value, while Category II sites have historical or cultural heritage significance or value. It is possible to modify a registered place, but any work must be authorised by the Trust. The full list of registered historic places is available from Trust offices. The Trust is currently in the process of making this register available on its website: *www.historic.org.nz/Register*.

The Trust's jurisdiction covers all archaeological sites (places associated with human activity that occurred before 1900), whether they are registered or not. It is an offence under the Historic Places Act to damage, modify, or destroy the whole or part of an archaeological site if the person knew, or should have known that it was an archaeological site, without permission from the Trust.

COMPLIANCE AND YOUR BUSINESS

> ## Archaeological sites: do's and don'ts
>
> ### Do
> - cease operations if an archaeological site is uncovered or suspected
> - apply to the Historic Places Trust for authority to resume work on or around an archaeological site
> - provide whatever assistance is required to Trust representatives.
>
> ### Don't
> - damage, modify, or destroy any archaeological site unless permitted to do so by the Trust
> - obstruct Trust representatives from carrying out their functions on a site.

Applying for authority to damage, modify, or destroy an archaeological site

When applying for this authority you will need to provide:

- a description of the activity and the site
- an assessment of any archaeological, Maori, or other relevant values and the effect of the proposal on those values
- a statement as to whether consultation with tangata whenua and any other person likely to be affected has or has not taken place
- the consent of the owner if the owner is not the applicant.

If you're uncertain about a site's archaeological values it will pay to consult the Trust because if you've gone ahead and it turns out you have damaged, modified, or destroyed an archaeological site without authority you are liable for prosecution. Furthermore, if the Trust has reason to believe unauthorised work may be about to occur, it is entitled to carry out an investigation and recover costs – even if the investigation discovers no archaeological site exists.

Conditions

When the Trust grants an authority to damage, modify, or destroy a site you will be required to comply with conditions. One of these may be a requirement to employ a suitably qualified person to carry out an archaeological investigation before work begins – that person must be approved by the Trust.

Fines

Destroying an archaeological site without authority can lead to fines up to $100,000. Damaging or modifying a site risks fines up to $40,000. Breaching the conditions of an authority, or carrying out an archaeological investigation in breach of conditions or without written permission also risks a fine up to $40,000.

Powers of entry

You are required to allow Trust representatives to enter land to carry out investigations into archaeological sites or to locate or inspect any historic place.

Getting advice

Councils and the Historic Places Trust are obvious places for advice about complying with historic heritage laws. Hiring a consultant archaeologist or conservation architect may be warranted, or may be required as part of any work you do.

> **Recent cases**
>
> The Historic Places Trust has taken several successful prosecutions in recent years against those causing damage to archaeological sites. Recent examples include:
> - In 2000, an Auckland property firm was fined $15,000 for partly destroying, damaging, or modifying a historic pa on land that it owned in Northland. One of the firm's contractors had bulldozed a significant part of the pa, estimated to be between 200 and 500 years old.
> - In 2001, a Waikato bottle digger was fined $6,000 plus costs for severely damaging an archaeological site containing bottles and other collectables that dated back to the 19th Century.

Antiquities Act 1975

The discovery of artefacts (or items that may be artefacts) must be reported to the Department of Internal Affairs or the nearest public museum. Artefacts must not be sold or disposed of without the prior permission of Internal Affairs.

Antiquities include a wide range of items, such as things which appear to be more than 60 years old, old books, remains of extinct animals or plants, moa eggs and bones, and parts of old boats, ships, or aircraft. Artefacts are essentially any object related to the pre-European habitation of New Zealand.

Where Maori artefacts are discovered it may also be appropriate to consult with iwi. Antiquities may not be removed from New Zealand without permission from Internal Affairs. Regulations also exist to prevent the sale and purchase of the eggs and bones of moa and other extinct birds.

Managing risk: environmental management systems

An environmental accident involving your business can have far reaching consequences (particularly under the RMA and the HSNO Acts), including the risk of heavy fines, imprisonment, and being ordered to carry out a clean up or other remedial action. In some circumstances, individuals can be criminally liable when a company is convicted – eg under the RMA, directors, managers, and anyone involved in the management of a company face the risk of prosecution. Companies are also liable for the acts of their agents, contractors, and employees, while employees in some instances can also be held criminally liable.

Such risks underscore the need to have a good environmental management system in place to ensure you are complying with the law. Key elements of a sound environmental management programme will usually involve:

- awareness of relevant legislation and controls, including resource consent conditions
- knowledge of industry practice in complying with legislation and controls
- establishing procedures and practices designed to ensure compliance and prevent pollution, including a clear allocation of environment-related functions within a firm
- adequate monitoring and internal reporting of both compliance and incidents
- adequate supervision to ensure reliance upon reporting is justified
- good record keeping
- prompt responses at all levels to environmental incidents.

To effectively and efficiently identify environmental legal risks, you must first identify and understand the context in which you are working. That means asking questions, which will differ depending on the situation you are in. If you're running an established business, questions might include:

- has your company got all necessary resource consents?
- are consent conditions being complied with?
- do you have a programme in place to ensure replacement consents are applied for before the old consents expire?
- do you have all other environmental permits (eg a trade waste discharge permit), and are these being complied with?
- are there activities that may be susceptible to accidental discharge of pollutants, and do you have review systems in place to ensure standards are met?

If you are purchasing a company or asset:

- does the company or asset hold all necessary consents and permits, and are conditions being complied with?
- is there a risk that the site or neighbouring properties may be contaminated as a result of past or current activities?
- what environmental management systems are in place?

ENVIRONMENT

Once you've established the context in which you are operating you need to review existing activities against the requirements of current, new, and proposed legislation. If you are planning new activities, you will need to subject these to the same review, thus ensuring nothing is left to chance when making investment decisions.

Commonsense questions to ask yourself

In order to manage environmental risks and reduce the possibility of an accident and subsequent legal action, you need to carefully think through all that could go wrong at your site. In the event of an environmental incident, you'll need to prove to authorities that you've thought about the risks and done something to address them. That's about getting it onto paper and making sure everyone in the company knows what the policy is. While it's difficult to generalise, some basic commonsense questions you could ask yourself that apply to all businesses include:

- what will give rise to an environmental incident in my business?
- how have I tried to address environmental risks, and how have I documented that I have addressed those risks?
- how have I communicated environmental management risks and safety procedures to managers and staff, and how have I recorded that I communicated this information to them?
- has all equipment being used on the site been properly certified?
- have I ensured that new employees are aware of potential environmental risks and safety procedures?
- when something goes wrong, how will I demonstrate that I've actually thought about potential risks and done something to address them?

Some more specific questions might include:

- does your site look clean and tidy (if it's not, it will be difficult to argue that you're doing everything you're meant to under both environmental and health and safety legislation)?
- do you have safety devices to make sure containers don't overflow?
- have you got bunds to contain spills?
- do you need an air discharge permit or a trade waste permit?
- are there noise issues, and is noise apparent on your boundary?
- what's in that unlabelled bottle that's been sitting around unused for several years?
- does the person delivering things to your site know which areas are no-go zones?
- If the delivery truck is late, is it okay for a consignment to be left outside the roller door until Monday?

MARKETING AND SALES

Why you can say and do absolutely anything you want to.*

Dealing with customers and making sales is at the heart of almost every business. Therefore, it is important to know your legal rights and responsibilities regarding the way your business markets and sells its products or services. Your business will be both a supplier to some businesses or people, and a customer of others – this chapter covers your rights and obligations in both situations.

*Some conditions may apply

COMPLIANCE AND YOUR BUSINESS

Several laws protect consumers

When you market and sell your products or services you need to be aware of your obligations under the Fair Trading Act 1986 and the Consumer Guarantees Act 1993. Some businesses also have obligations under other laws such as the Hire Purchase Act 1971, the Unsolicited Goods and Services Act 1975, the Door to Door Sales Act 1967, and the Layby Sales Act 1971. Advertisers must also comply with the Advertising Standard Authority's codes of practice, the Commerce Act 1986, and applicable intellectual property law.

Most of the time your business' responsibilities as a supplier and rights as a customer are covered by the same laws. However, only consumers acquiring goods and services ordinarily acquired for personal, domestic, or household use are protected by the Consumer Guarantees Act. It does not apply to services or goods supplied to businesses.

A quick guide to the Fair Trading Act

New Zealand consumer protection law includes the Fair Trading Act which prohibits misleading and deceptive conduct and other unfair business practices. It helps to define what you can and cannot say in promotional material and to customers.

You can breach the Fair Trading Act if you don't tell customers about their rights under other consumer laws, such as the Consumer Guarantees Act, the Door to Door Sales Act, and the Unsolicited Goods and Services Act.

The range of conduct prohibited by the Fair Trading Act is very broad. The Act applies to all written and oral information given to customers. It even applies to information that is not disclosed to customers, if keeping silent about the information could mislead or deceive your customers. Even information that is only partly wrong can breach the Act.

You can be liable even if you did not intend to mislead or deceive customers, and even if no one was actually misled. The important question is whether you could or did mislead customers.

It applies to websites, including those hosted overseas that target New Zealand customers.

The Fair Trading Act is enforced by the Commerce Commission. The Commission can bring criminal proceedings against you for breach of some parts of the Act. Maximum fines for criminal conviction are up to $200,000 per offence for a company and $60,000 per offence for an individual. If you breach other parts of the Act, you may be ordered to pay compensation and costs, along with having to pay your own legal costs. Contracts that you enter into in breach of the Act could be altered or made void and you could be ordered to publish an apology to customers. Any courtroom victories against you may be publicised widely. Even when the Commerce Commission settles investigations without going to court it usually issues a media release.

The Commerce Commission places a lot of weight on protecting the customer. It says: 'The courts have said the Act is there to protect everyone, including those who may be gullible, of less than average intelligence or poorly educated. Certain groups, by reason of language difficulties, age or lack of education, may be susceptible to being misled or deceived. If your customers include such people, you must take this into account and be especially careful'.

The Commerce Commission

The Commerce Commission is responsible for enforcing the Fair Trading Act and the Commerce Act, which governs competition between businesses and competitive behaviour. It is also responsible for laws regulating some specific industries such as the dairy industry, telecommunications, and electricity.

The Commission has the power to start its own investigations of businesses and their dealings. It can negotiate settlements with businesses but it cannot impose fines or other punishments itself – it takes the cases to court. The most common problem involving smaller businesses is caused by breaches of the Fair Trading Act, but the Commerce Commission also investigates breaches of the Commerce Act. In some circumstances bigger businesses must deal with the Commission when they want to buy or invest in a competitor.

The Commission has booklets explaining the Acts and Regulations it administers. You can visit them at their website at www.comcom.govt.nz or call 0800 943 600 for more information.

Labelling and safety standards

The Fair Trading Act is used to enforce Regulations on labelling rules that will affect anyone who makes, imports, or sells clothes. These rules determine what should be said on labels about the country of origin, fibre content (ie fabric type), and care (cleaning and ironing).

Some products are also covered by specific safety standards, and these must be considered before you go into production or distribution. These products include toys for infants and babies, bicycles, childrens' nightclothes, and cigarette lighters. The Commerce Commission has fact sheets that spell out the rules on labelling and safety standards.

If your product falls under the definition of a therapeutic product, then the claims you can make about it will be affected by the Ministry of Health's product

COMPLIANCE AND YOUR BUSINESS

rules governing therapeutic products. A therapeutic product is any product that diagnoses, prevents, or treats disease, or alters the shape, structure, size, or weight of the human body.

Depending on what's in it, your product might also be covered by separate food and vitamin rules that affect what you can say in promotional material and packaging. Making claims about the therapeutic value of products or services might also breach the Fair Trading Act if they are misleading or deceptive.

Advertising – what you can and can't say

The Fair Trading Act applies to advertising and other promotional material, such as packaging and in-store material. It even applies to verbal statements you or your staff may make when talking to a customer. Key areas that require careful attention by all businesses include:

- claims about products or services
- price claims and comparisons
- use of fine print
- imitations on stock availability
- promotional issues.

The goods you advertise must be available for sale. Attracting customers by advertising goods and services that you cannot supply is called bait advertising – and it's illegal.

Exceptional circumstances that cause a product to sell out will not necessarily breach the Act. However, you must not offer a product with limited stock at a special price with the intention of attracting customers to buy that product only to suggest, for example, that they buy an alternative, more expensive product. You must supply advertised goods or services at the advertised prices for a reasonable time, or for a set period, and you must have them in reasonable quantities. Websites must be kept up-to-date so you don't promise stock that isn't available or at prices that no longer apply. Any limits on sales, eg 'one per customer', must be stated in the advert.

So what's a 'reasonable quantity' or a 'reasonable time'? They aren't defined in the Act – they are interpreted differently depending on factors such as the type of demand you usually have for the advertised products or services.

If you genuinely can't provide advertised goods, eg because of a late shipment, the Commerce Commission recommends you issue rainchecks and provide the products at a later date.

MARKETING AND SALES

> ### Case study
> **Advertised products must be available**
> In September 2003, BP Oil New Zealand changed its nationwide television advertising campaign following concerns raised by the Commerce Commission. The adverts for BP Ultimate and Low Sulphur Diesel were liable to mislead customers because BP did not disclose that these two products were not readily available in all its outlets. BP Ultimate was only available at 36 North Island service stations while Low Sulphur Diesel was only available in Christchurch.
>
> The Commission said it was essential that businesses were aware of their responsibilities to clearly and accurately represent their goods or services: 'Omitting important information can cause people to be misled, and it is particularly important that all advertising is clear and accurate so that they can make informed choices.'

Any description of the goods and services that you advertise or offer must be accurate. For example, you cannot describe goods as 'duty free' if that type of product does not normally have any import duty. This requirement for accuracy includes any pictures of goods or premises – if you can't see the beach from your motel then don't use a picture of it in your advert. The same rules apply to packaging and can even be applied to the size of the picture of the product used on the package.

Any claims you make about your product and its benefits must be true, including claims made about food products. All claims about performance or quality should be able to be independently verified if possible. As well as having to comply with Food Safety Authority rules on labelling, food, and drink products must be packaged and advertised in a way that does not mislead customers.

Any claims like 'low in fat', 'sugar free' and 'lite', must be true in comparison to other foods of the same type. It is not acceptable to advertise 'low-fat water' because all other water is fat-free. 'Fresh' means the product has not been frozen. There are other rules on claims such as 'pure' and '100%'. Some commonly made mistakes are explained in the Commerce Commission's booklet *Food Labelling, Promotion and Marketing*.

Other image-related claims like 'environmentally friendly', and claims of endorsements and sponsorships must also be true. You should not use advertising to create an image for your product or business that cannot be backed up by facts.

If you quote tests or surveys, you must be able to provide evidence to support your claims. Any in-house test made by you or your suppliers should be able to be independently verified.

COMPLIANCE AND YOUR BUSINESS

Promoters of franchises or home businesses must not make misleading claims about the profitability or risks of a business venture. If challenged you must be able to show the information you based your claim on, such as a record of sales of the business being franchised. Alternatively, any claim that you make about future events must be based on a reasonable belief that you can fulfil the claim. You should also take care to let regular customers know if you alter standard terms and conditions that they might have become used to. A sudden change to terms and conditions could be misleading in some circumstances.

Case study

You can't blame the manufacturer

In May 2003, Agpac Plastics pleaded guilty to breaching the Fair Trading Act and was fined $6,610 including costs in the Auckland District Court. An investigation showed its 'B & A Polythene' product ranged from 196 to 265 microns thick, but was advertised as 250 microns thick.

In sentencing, Judge Moore noted that this was a classic case of why labelling had to be accurate. 'The general public ... rely on labelling for suitability, rather than having the ability to check the accuracy themselves,' he said.

In response to Agpac's submission that it relied on the manufacturer of the product for its representation that the polythene was 250 microns, Judge Moore said that Agpac had made no effort to put in place any quality control mechanisms and this 'was simply not good enough'.

MARKETING AND SALES

> ## Case study
>
> ### It has to work
>
> A company claiming that its Wave Shield mobile phone radiation protection device blocked up to 97% of electromagnetic radiation from the inner ear was permanently prevented from marketing the product and convicted on four breaches of the Fair Trading Act.
>
> The Commerce Commission sought permanent injunctions against Waveshield (New Zealand) Limited to prevent the company from advertising and selling its product. The company was fined $4,000, plus costs with company director Miles Dixon being personally liable for $2,000.
>
> The Commission had obtained expert evidence asserting that these types of devices do not provide any significant protection from electromagnetic radiation from mobile phones. Even if the Wave Shield device was effective, the experts said there was no evidence of health risks associated with mobile phone use.
>
> The Commission was concerned that the company was not only making false and misleading claims about the product, it was promoting the device as having been 'tested' and 'proven'. In sentencing Judge Erber commented that the defendants were acting as 'snake oil merchants'.

Comparative advertising – what you can say about competitors

You are allowed to compare your products with those of your competitors – but you must be able to prove that the comparisons are accurate and true. For example, if you list the price and features of two-litre saloon cars, it would be misleading to compare your fully-featured model to your competitors' basic models. You should be careful about using phrases such as 'best available', 'outperforms all others', 'superior quality'.

You must be quite specific when using comparative pricing in adverts, eg 'Was $599, now $499' or 'Elsewhere up to $30 – our price $24.99'. This is a very common advertising technique but must be used carefully to avoid being misleading.

Comparative price checklist

The Commission suggests you review the following checklist before drawing up a comparative advert.

- **Was $...** Have the goods you're advertising been available for sale in your store at the stated previous price for a reasonable period immediately before this offer?

237

COMPLIANCE AND YOUR BUSINESS

- **Elsewhere $...** Can you prove that identical goods are currently being sold by another trader in your local market for the 'elsewhere' price you're stating in your advert?
- **Recommended Retail Price $...** Can you prove that the RRP is the actual RRP suggested by the manufacturer? If yes, can you prove the item is available for sale at this RRP locally?
- **Worth $...** Can you prove the item is worth the advertised value in the current market?
- **Save $...** Are consumers actually saving that amount? Are you or one of your competitors currently charging the higher price?
- **Sale price $...** Are the goods advertised genuinely reduced from their normal selling price? If advertising a storewide sale, have you got a substantial proportion of your stock at prices that are less than they were before the sale started? Is the reason for the sale genuine? Are you really going out of business? Was there really a fire?

Small print and long words

Remember, the Commission assumes that customers are easily misled and business people must be careful not to exploit them. This makes it risky to use small print, asterixes, or technical terms to justify and explain any claims made in the main part of your advert. Small print cannot be used to modify a claim made in the body of the advert if it changes the nature of the main claim. The Commission tests the overall impression made by the advert and has brought prosecutions over the use of small print and technical terms or jargon.

'Special conditions apply' does not protect you when the conditions are inconsistent with the main message.

Puffery

The Fair Trading Act doesn't prohibit 'puffery' – which means you can make obvious exaggerations that are so obvious they are unlikely to mislead. This lets you make claims that cannot be tested, such as 'The best bar in the world and that's a fact'. Just be careful about making claims that could not realistically be true or can not be measured or tested and could therefore be proven incorrect.

Free gifts, free credit, and free delivery

If you advertise something as free, then it must be truly free. You cannot inflate the price of an item to cover a gift. You cannot offer customers a discount as an alternative to the gift, as this suggests the gift was built into the price. You must also provide gifts and free items automatically without waiting for the customer to ask for them.

The same rules apply to offers of free credit or interest-free terms. The Commerce Commission has said that the terms 'interest free' and 'free credit' have the same meaning.

For example, in interest-free and free-credit promotions, the interest-free or credit-free price must be the same as the cash price. You cannot offer a better deal for cash, as this suggests the interest was built into the price.

The Commission says that to remove any possibility of misleading customers, you should not charge booking fees, compulsory insurance, or other hidden charges on interest-free deals.

You must also be very careful that adverts for interest-free deals include any conditions, such as a minimum purchase of $500, or the fact the offer only applies to existing customers. If you don't say this in the advert you can be punished for attracting customers to your store with misleading information.

Free delivery must also be free. If another customer who picked up the goods would pay a lower price, then delivery isn't free. You cannot inflate the price in expectation of delivery costs. Also, if any conditions apply (eg 'inner city only') you must say so in all adverts.

Advertising Standards Codes

Apart from legal requirements under the Fair Trading Act, you should also be aware of the rules set out in the Advertising Standards Codes, administered by the Advertising Standards Authority (ASA). If one of your adverts breaches these codes, the ASA's members – who include media organisations such as newspapers and TV – cannot run it. So, while breaching the code won't necessarily expose you to court action or fines, it may mean you have to write-off the cost of an advertisement.

The ASA's decisions are often published in newspapers, which could expose you to bad publicity. Defending your advert before the authority also involves legal expenses.

The ASA has 14 Codes of Practice covering advertising to children, comparative advertising, environmental claims, ethics, farm safety, financial advertising, food advertising, gaming and gambling, liquor, people in advertising, road safety, therapeutic advertising, tobacco products, and weight management. For more information about the codes visit the Authority's website at *www.asa.co.nz* or telephone 04-472 7852.

COMPLIANCE AND YOUR BUSINESS

Case studies

Advertising Standards Authority decisions

Energy drinks, therapeutic properties, and children

Bull Rush energy drink advertised itself with the claim 'the combination of B vitamins and taurine boosts vital bodily functions and converts them to energy stimulating recovery…'. The Complaints Board decided this was a therapeutic claim under the ASA's Therapeutic Code. It said the advert should have therefore included a summary telling consumers about the possible side effects of large amounts of the product, adding this was especially important as the cartoon-style advert targeted young people. The board decided the advert did not meet the required high standards of social responsibility. This decision set a precedent, requiring all energy drinks to meet the Therapeutic Code.

Safety helmets for cyclists

Mazda was forced to withdraw all New Zealand screenings of an advert for the Mazda 6 because it included a flashback sequence showing a child riding a bike but not wearing a helmet. The Complaints Board said it is unacceptable to portray cyclists or motorcyclists without safety helmets.

Nature Bee Potentiated Bee Pollen and Hon John Banks

Nature Bee's 30-minute infomercial promoted the values of bee pollen using endorsements from satisfied users. One of these was former MP John Banks. During the infomercial he was identified as 'Nature Bee Hon John Banks' and his endorsement was followed by another from a woman who was also enthusiastic about the product. At the time the advert was shown, John Banks was an owner of Topline International, the company producing Nature Bee Pollen, and the woman was an employee. The Complaints Board unanimously decided that it was potentiallly misleading to include endorsements from an employee and an owner without identifying their relationship with Nature Bee Pollen. It also said a product recommendation by Mr Banks – identified on screen as a former Minister of the Crown – would be likely to be perceived as carrying greater weight than that given by an unknown member of the public.

Direct Marketing Association

The Direct Marketing Association (DMA) also has a code of practice. DMA members may refuse to handle your advertisement or advertising campaign if it does not comply with this code. The DMA defines direct marketing as 'the process by which consumers are offered the opportunity to obtain or purchase goods or services or make charitable donations direct by mail, newspaper or magazine, radio, television, telephone, facsimile, email, internet, or any similar means of communication'. For more information see the DMA's website at *www.dma.co.nz*.

Making a sale

Making a sale is the most important part of any business, but it's important to make sure you don't get so focused on closing the sale that you break the law in the process.

It is important to remember that as a business owner you are responsible for all staff, including contractors, commission-only staff, and sales reps working away from the office. While you might not know exactly how they make a sale, you are still responsible for everything they say and do while making it.

Unless clearly and specifically stated, all prices displayed in New Zealand, in print, on shelves, and on products themselves, must include GST. If you haven't clearly marked products or services as 'GST exclusive', then you don't get to add GST.

Customers are entitled to know all other costs applying to goods and services before they agree to buy. These could include legal fees, administration charges, insurance, and essential accessories. Prosecutions have been made for cellphone dealers who advertise the cost of the phone but not the connection package.

Banned selling practices

Inertia selling

You cannot force people to do business with you. Inertia selling involves sending goods to customers and then billing them if they don't return it. This is covered by the Door to Door Sales Act and the Unsolicited Goods and Services Act. If you send unsolicited goods, it's up to you to get them back at your expense. The recipient gets to keep them if you don't.

Harassment and coercion

It is prohibited by the Fair Trading Act to attempt to sell goods, services or 'any interest in land' through harassment, coercion, or physical violence. You must take care not to use, or let your sales staff use, techniques which could possibly make customer feel harassed or intimidated into making a purchase.

Remember that the Fair Trading Act is usually interpreted in favour of the customer, and courts have special concern for people who may be gullible, of less than average intelligence, or poorly educated. If you or your staff try the hard sell on someone elderly or hard of hearing, for example, you could be breaking the law.

Pyramid selling

The definition of pyramid selling is broad and includes any business that pays you for recruiting staff, customers, or members. Several recent prosecutions have been of New Zealanders who joined and promoted businesses that were introduced from overseas. This is particularly relevant now new maximum penalties have been passed – $200,000 for both companies and individuals. The court can also order payment of the commercial gain earned. If you are interested in any business that pays you for recruiting staff, customers, or members, get it checked out by a lawyer first.

Referral selling

This is the practice of offering potential customers some reward if they provide the names of other people who then buy from you. It is prohibited under the Fair Trading Act because the first customer gets no reward unless the referred people make a purchase. It is not referral selling to offer rewards for names if the offer is made after the first customer paid for their goods and services.

Pro-forma invoicing

This is billing someone for something they did not receive. It is a common scam, but you can also be guilty if you mistakenly issue an invoice for goods or services you did not provide.

MARKETING AND SALES

Case study

Pyramid selling

In 2003, Christchurch-based Infinity Concierge and its operators were fined $38,760 for operating and promoting a pyramid selling scheme in breach of the Fair Trading Act. The fines included costs.

The British-based scheme offered membership costing $3,500 plus GST to an alleged concierge service. It also offered access to a closed buyer group that claimed to receive discounts at various rates from a number of businesses. Members were given the opportunity to earn significant remuneration by the recruitment of new members. This was emphasised throughout the presentations. The Commerce Commission executed a search warrant at one of these invitation-only seminars, then froze Infinity Concierge's bank accounts and placed an injunction preventing it operating or promoting the scheme.

When the matter made it to court, the business was fined $20,000 and the owners were themselves fined between $3,000 and $7,500. The judge said the penalties would have been higher against certain individuals were it not for their dire financial circumstances.

Ministry of Consumer Affairs

The Ministry of Consumer Affairs is responsible for the Consumer Guarantees Act, Door to Door Sales Act, Hire Purchase Act, Layby Sales Act, and the Weights and Measures Act.

The Ministry's Consumer Information Service produces a range of booklets that, while generally written for consumers, can be relevant to businesses. There are also two services that are directly relevant to businesses: the Trading Standards Service and the Energy Safety Service.

The Trading Standards Service has a Trade Measurement section and a Consumer Safety section. Trade Measurement is responsible for checking the accuracy of equipment and goods sold by weight, measure, or number. It also investigates public complaints. Consumer Safety investigates unsafe products and has the power to recommend a mandatory recall to the Minister.

The Energy Safety Service is responsible for ensuring the safe production, distribution, installation, and use of electricity and gas.

The Ministry also publishes a Refund Policy Notice. This large card outlines traders' refund obligations in short, clear sentences and large, clear print. These notices can be displayed in stores to explain the policy to staff and customers. The Refund Policy Notice is available from the Ministry. Contact it via its website at *www.consumer-ministry.govt.nz* or telephone 04-474 2750.

Standing behind your product or service

You have a legal obligation to stand behind the products or services you sell. Along with the Fair Trading Act, there are other laws that protect businesses and individual customers. For example, if you are selling products or services ordinarily acquired for personal, domestic, or household use by consumers, you also have responsibilities under the Consumer Guarantees Act. If you are selling goods ordinarily sold for commercial purposes, or if you are selling to businesses, the Consumer Guarantees Act does not apply but your responsibilities are covered by the Sale of Goods Act.

Your obligations under the Consumer Guarantees Act

The Consumer Guarantees Act sets out your responsibilities to customers buying goods for personal, domestic, or household use. It does not apply to goods normally used commercially, even if they are used at home. These would be covered by the Sale of Goods Act. Goods that could be used either way, like stationery or pens, are likely to be covered by the Consumer Guarantees Act. Others that are ordinarily acquired for personal, domestic, or household use but are in fact acquired for commercial use can be excluded if you agree with the purchaser at the time of the sale.

When you sell goods, the Consumer Guarantees Act automatically guarantees your customers that you have the right to sell the goods and that they match any sample or description that you used to sell them. If you do not agree on the price of the goods with the customer, then the Act guarantees that the price that you charge will be reasonable. It also guarantees that goods can be repaired and that spare parts will be available for a reasonable period of time after the goods are sold.

The Act also guarantees that goods are of 'acceptable quality'. This means that they are fit for the purpose for which those types of goods are usually supplied, they are free from minor defects, and they are safe and durable. Goods must also be of acceptable finish and appearance and they must be free from minor defects.

What's acceptable depends on circumstances like the price and the type of product. For example, a cheap toaster isn't expected to last as long as a top of the range one. It also depends on what the customer is told about the goods and what is said on the product packaging and labelling. For example, second-hand goods and manufacturers' seconds do not have to be of the same standard as new, top quality goods, but must be clearly labelled as 'second-hand' or 'seconds'. Apart from the stated fault, seconds are expected to be of the quality expected of the same goods that are not seconds.

Goods must meet customers' requirements if they tell you their requirements before closing the sale. If a customer comes to your store to see a power tool on special for $19.95, and says they want it to drill masonry, then they are entitled to be told if the drill is fit for that purpose.

Remember that the guarantees provided in the Consumer Guarantees Act apply automatically. They do not need to be recorded in writing or in a contract.

The Consumer Guarantees Act puts similar requirements on services as it does on goods and products. If you are in a service business it is advisable to find out why the customer wants your services and advise them if the service they want is suitable for the job. This may require you to explain technical terms or deal with people who don't understand your trade. For example, if they ask you to paint their roof because it leaks you should explain that a coat of paint won't fix the problem. Otherwise you may become liable for failing to fix the leak.

The Act also guarantees that your services will be given with reasonable skill and care. You should not attempt to provide a service if you can't meet this standard. If you don't agree on a time for completion and on the price at the outset, then the work must be completed in a reasonable time and you must charge a reasonable price. You must be able to justify the time taken and the price charged in relation to other businesses offering the same service in your area in similar circumstances.

The Act applies to free items given away with a purchase, and to goods that are leased or hired. It does not cover auctions or tenders, real estate or goods bought for resale.

The guarantees provided in the Act can't be limited by any other manufacturer's or retailer's guarantee. Just because a manufacturer's or retailer's guarantee has expired, does not mean that the Consumer Guarantees Act does not apply. It is an offence to suggest that the manufacturer's or retailer's guarantee is the only guarantee, or that goods or services are sold without a guarantee. Doing this breaches the Fair Trading Act with a maximum fine of $200,000 for companies or $60,000 for individuals.

You can contract out of your responsibilities under the Consumer Guarantees Act – but only in relation to commercial goods or services, or goods or services sold to businesses. If you want to contract out of the Act it must be done in writing at the time of the agreement to purchase. It is an offence to attempt to contract out of the Act when the goods or services are goods or services ordinarily sold for personal, domestic, or household use. In other words, you cannot make a blanket rule contracting out of your responsibilities under the Act for every sales transaction your business makes.

What to do when a customer complains

If a customer has a complaint they must come to you in a reasonable time and give you an opportunity to put it right. Customers could have up to 6 years to complain from the time the problem appears, but the Ministry of Consumer Affairs recommends they contact you as soon as possible. You will not be liable for problems that develop after the problem was detected.

When a complaint is made under the Consumer Guarantees Act you should be careful to identify whether you are responsible for the problem depending on whether it is a manufacturing or retail fault. Retailers and manufacturers sometimes have different obligations under the Consumer Guarantees Act.

COMPLIANCE AND YOUR BUSINESS

For example, if a customer asks for a lawnmower that is good for cutting grass on uneven ground and a retailer provides a lawnmower that is not suitable for that purpose, then the manufacturer is not liable for breaching the guarantee that the lawnmower is fit for the purpose for which it is supplied. This would be the retailer's responsibility because the retailer made the representation that the lawnmower was fit for that purpose. A retailer will not be liable if spare parts are not available for a product if they did not know that spare parts were unavailable from the manufacturer.

If a customer complains about a minor fault, the Consumer Guarantees Act gives you the right to choose the remedy that you offer to your customer. You can choose between offering repairs or offering an identical replacement. You can also offer a refund of the purchase price if you cannot reasonably be expected to make repairs, eg if the cost of repairs is more than the cost of a new item. Refunds should be paid in the same way as the original sale – you do not have to give a cash refund for a credit card sale.

You may be responsible for paying for repairs if the customer could not bring the problem to you first, eg a car breaks down away from your town.

If you choose to make repairs, you must complete them in a reasonable time, and return the goods to the state they were in before the fault developed. You don't have to make them as good as new. You cannot charge for repairs or for postage if the repairs are made under the Consumer Guarantees Act.

If the fault is substantial then the Act gives the customer the right to choose the remedy. The Act defines a substantial fault as one where the goods are:

- unsafe
- significantly different from the sample or description
- unfit for the particular purpose the customer bought them for and cannot be modified to do the job
- substantially unfit for their normal purpose
- goods that a reasonable customer would not have bought had they been aware the fault would happen.

Remember, faulty goods do not have to be returned in the original packaging.

When there is a substantial fault the customer can choose between rejecting the goods and asking for a refund or replacement, or keeping the goods and asking for a refund of part of the purchase price to reflect the fact that they bought something that was worth less than they thought. Some customers might also be entitled to compensation for damage caused by a defective product. For example, damage to DVDs made by a faulty player.

When there is a serious problem with services the customer can cancel the contract and ask for a refund or refuse to pay. They do not have to give you the chance to remedy the problem.

MARKETING AND SALES

You do not have to provide a refund if a customer changes their mind about their purchase. The Ministry of Consumer Affairs makes a large, clear refund policy sign that many retailers display behind the counter. It is available from the Ministry and contains the wording shown below:

> **REFUND POLICY** We do not have to provide a refund if you have changed your mind about a particular purchase, so please choose carefully. If the goods are faulty we will meet our obligations under the Consumer Guarantees Act to provide a remedy.

It is an offence to display any signage that could mislead customers about their legal rights. You are risking prosecution if you display signs like 'No Refunds', 'No Returns on Sales Goods' or 'For a refund goods must be returned in their original packaging with 30 days'.

You do not have to provide refunds, repairs, or replacements for goods or services you did not provide.

Your obligations under the Sale of Goods Act

The Sale of Goods Act covers goods ordinarily sold for commercial use. It doesn't cover services. You have more power to contract out of your responsibilities under the Sale of Goods Act than you have under the Consumer Guarantees Act.

You still have to ensure the goods are of merchantable quality and are fit for the purpose they were bought for. If the customer tells you they need the goods for a specific use, you are obliged to tell them whether the goods they are considering are suitable for that use.

It's possible to exclude or limit your liability under the Act by specifying that defective goods won't be repaired or replaced, or some parts of defective goods will be repaired while others will not. It is also possible to limit the time you are prepared to guarantee goods. You can choose to exclude liability for damage caused by faulty or defective goods. All exclusions of liability must be clearly agreed before purchase and that agreement should be recorded in writing.

Customers who have purchased faulty goods may be entitled to:

- a full or partial refund
- compensation for loss
- damages for losses caused by the fault.

It is possible for the damages to exceed the value of the product itself. That means it is sensible to contract out of the Sale of Goods Act if you can.

More information on the Disputes Tribunal is available from your local District Court.

Disputes and the Disputes Tribunal

If you cannot come to an agreement with an unhappy customer or supplier, then your customer may take the dispute to another level. Simple disputes can be taken to the Disputes Tribunal. Disputes involving larger sums of money must be taken to court, and you should contact your lawyer.

The Disputes Tribunal is operated by the Ministry of Justice. It is not a court and a lawyer cannot represent you. A referee decides your case rather than a judge. Disputes involving a value less than $7,500 can be heard automatically, while disputes involving a value over $7,500 and up to $12,000 can only be heard with the agreement of both parties.

The Tribunal cannot adjudicate unpaid bills, but it will look at the type of dispute likely to come from faulty goods and services. It can order payments to be made or work to be done, and can also order that a person is not liable for the claim.

The decisions are enforceable by law, and can be appealed. The Disputes Tribunal can make decisions based on the merits and justice of the case, having regard to the law but not being bound to strictly observe it.

If a complaint is made to the Tribunal against you, you will be informed in writing. You can lodge a counter-claim. If the claim is against you and you don't turn up, then it will be heard without you. You can present evidence and bring witnesses to support your case. This could include specialists in your trade or representatives from a trade organisation.

The Commerce Act and you

The Commerce Act prohibits conduct that reduces the level of competition between businesses. It also prohibits restrictive trade practices. As in sport, it is possible to be 'too competitive' and break the rules. Some agreements that you enter into to benefit your business might also breach the Act without you meaning them to.

The Commerce Act has some of the strongest penalties of any business law. For breaches of RTP provisions they include:

- for businesses – a $10 million fine or three times the commercial gain derived from the anti-competitive activity, or 10% of the business' group turnover if the amount of the gain cannot be determined
- for individuals – a $500,000 fine per offence – employees can be personally liable and it is illegal for an employer to indemnify staff for any fines they may be liable to pay for price fixing.

Prohibitions under the Commerce Act

Prohibitions under the Commerce Act include the following:

Resale price maintenance

It is an offence to enforce a minimum retail or reselling price for your products. You can set a recommended retail price, but your customers are perfectly entitled to discount below this if they want to. It is important to make it clear that no one is obliged to sell at or above the recommended price. Refusing to resupply a customer with a product it has discounted will breach the Act.

Price fixing

You cannot make arrangements or agreements with competitors designed to set, maintain or control prices, including agreements about discounts, rebates, allowances, or credit. This applies both to the price of goods you sell, and of goods you buy, in competition. Price fixing doesn't need a formal agreement; a discussion can do equal harm. Sharing information on market share, or on prices if they are not publicly available, can be enough to break the law. Price fixing is illegal regardless of whether it has any effect on competition. There is no defence and very limited exceptions apply.

Misusing a substantial degree of market power

The Act makes it an offence for businesses with a 'substantial degree of market power' to use their market power to restrict competition. This includes using their market power to restrict market entry of a competitor, deter competition in a market, or to eliminate a business from a market.

As at 2003, there is no tested definition of the term, 'substantial degree of market power'. It is expected that court precedents will clarify it, and in the meantime courts will look to the Australian interpretation of the same term.

Working out when competition is too aggressive can be difficult, as it is essential and acceptable for businesses to attract new customers and attempt to increase their market share. Misusing a substantial degree of market power could include:

- refusing to supply a competitor, or only supplying them on unfavourable terms, especially if those terms cannot be justified by factors such as volume, loyalty, transport costs, or credit risk
- requiring your customer to buy more than one product or service if you have market power relating to one of those products
- charging different prices to customers if the price difference cannot be explained by costs and where it is designed to harm competition
- selling a product below cost to drive out competition – note this does not prevent you from discounting slow lines to liquidate cash.

Misusing a substantial degree of market power

The Act also prohibits contracts, arrangements, and understandings with competitors that have the purpose, effect, or likely effect of substantially lessening competition in a market. You do not need market power for an agreement to breach this part of the Act. Practices that could breach this part of the Act include agreeing with a competitor not to compete for each other's business, agreeing on a price that you and your competitor will pay a supplier that you both use, or refusing to supply a client unless they stop dealing with a competitor.

Contacting the Commission

If you believe that you or your business has been affected by anti-competitive behaviour by suppliers or competitors, you should contact the Commerce Commission. The Commission will consider your information and may start an investigation.

Case studies

Commerce Commission decisions under the Commerce Act

Toyota dealers fined for price fixing

Eight Auckland Toyota dealers were fined a total of half a million dollars for price fixing. The price-fixing agreement was made at regular franchise group meetings in May and June 1993, where the dealers admitted they discussed and agreed to set common maximum discounts. Seven of the dealers admitted the price fixing and were ordered to pay penalties of $50,000. The dealers who admitted breaching the Act were Albany Toyota, North Shore Toyota, North Western Toyota, Greenlane Toyota, Derbyshire Toyota, Manukau City Toyota, and Papakura Toyota. Giltrap Toyota did not admit any breach and went to Court, where it was ordered to pay $150,000 for price fixing in breach of the Commerce Act.

> **Fletcher Concrete warned for discounting**
>
> In 2002, the Commission warned Fletcher Concrete that below-cost pricing by Firth risked breaching the Commerce Act. It also said that any business that used their market power to deter or exclude competitors was risking breaching the Act.
>
> The price-cutting was allegedly designed to protect the position of Fletcher Concrete in the cement industry from competition from imported cement. The Commission believed Firth's pricing was designed to send a message to the importers and to the users of imported cement that any future imports would be met with similar deep price-cutting campaigns.
>
> The Commerce Commission said this kind of price-cutting was anti-competitive and was likely to increase prices and reduce services in the long term. From a consumer's perspective, low prices in the short-term may appear attractive. However, if they result in competition being significantly damaged, this may result in a lack of competition and higher prices in the future.

Privacy

If you collect and/or keep information about customers you will have responsibilities under the Privacy Act. Anyone can ask to see the details you have recorded against their name. The information can only be used for the purpose it was gathered for. You cannot sell or give your customer database to another business or person without the permission of the people who gave you their contact details – this includes sharing it with other franchise dealers to develop a chain-wide database, or working with other businesses to develop a database of shopping centre customers.

See chapter 3, *Privacy* for more information on the Privacy Act.

Protecting your brand

Today, more than ever before, many businesses sell ideas or information. Even if your business is making widgets, your designs, packaging, and logo all combine to make your brand. Ideas, information, inventions, designs, and brands are all intellectual property. They are all assets of your business and you should protect them as much as you can.

Protecting ideas

A simple idea that is not put on paper or expressed in any other way cannot be protected except as a trade secret under the law of confidential information. If you have a brilliant idea for a television series involving hidden cameras, home improvement, and celebrities on a tropical island, you have no legal way to stop anyone else using the idea before you do. Put it on paper, because then what you have written down will be protected by copyright.

Different types of protection

There are different types of protection for intellectual property.

Copyright

Copyright automatically covers all original literary, dramatic, musical and artistic works, sound recordings, films, broadcasts, cable programmes, and published editions. Artistic work includes plans, drawings and models, and film covers any moving images including video, DVD, and formats that haven't been invented yet.

Registration of copyright is not required and no formal system for copyright registration exists in New Zealand. A copyright statement is the best way to inform others that a work is protected and consent is required to copy or exploit it. The copyright statement has the © symbol, the name of the copyright holder and the year the work was first published, eg © Brookers 2004.

New Zealand is a signatory to international copyright treaties, so New Zealand copyright works are recognised in most countries overseas. It also means that work that is copyright overseas cannot be used in New Zealand without permission.

Patents

Patents apply to inventions and processes and so cannot be used to protect logos or concepts. Under the Patent Act the invention must be:

- New – an invention is new if a description of the invention has not been published in New Zealand before the patent application was filed. No notice is taken of information published outside New Zealand but not publicly available in New Zealand.
- A 'manner of new manufacture' – this excludes things like products of nature, mathematical formulas, bare principles, schemes or plans, and methods of medical treatment of humans.

A patent gives the inventor a right to exclude others from making, using, or selling the invention or process during the patent term of up to 20 years. In return, the owner must publish a complete description of the invention. You can't have patent protection and keep the invention a secret – that's the deal.

New Zealand patents only apply to New Zealand. To get overseas protection you must file applications in other countries or file an international application under the Patent Co-operation Treaty.

MARKETING AND SALES

Anyone can file an application for a patent, but it is complex legal territory and you should seriously consider using an experienced patent attorney to advise you and deal with the paper work. A poorly worded or submitted application will increase your costs and may not offer the protection you need.

Trade marks

Trade marks are a common type of intellectual property protection used by New Zealand businesses. Trade marks offer legal protection and require registration, but are simple and cheap to apply for.

Trade marks can also cover a wide variety of signs. The Trade Marks Act defines trade marks as: 'any sign or combination of signs, capable of being represented graphically and capable of distinguishing the goods or services of one person from those of another person.'

A 'sign' can be a brand, colour, device, heading, label, letter, name, numeral, signature, smell, sound, taste, ticket, or word, or any combination of these. This is a very broad definition, but that doesn't mean that anything can be trade marked. Some types of names or designs are, in fact, almost impossible to trade mark.

The Trade Marks Act specifically rejects:

- surnames, business, or company names unless they are presented in a unique or unusual way, or incorporated into a trade mark as one of its elements
- trade marks that are the same as or similar to trade marks already registered
- trade marks that are likely to mislead, confuse, or are offensive
- generic terms, like 'soap' for soap products
- superlative terms, like best, super, finest, etc
- descriptive terms, like 'sweet' for ice cream
- place names.

This makes some business and product names better prospects for protection than others. The best prospects are invented words, like Pepsi, Xerox, and Kodak. Unfortunately for business people, invented words by their very nature cannot trigger any recognition, desirability, or an intention to buy from prospective customers, so a good trade mark choice is not necessarily a good marketing choice.

The second-best prospects for a name are words that combine or distort existing recognisable words. Examples include Vodafone, OneSource, or Suju (a takeaway bar selling soup and juice).

Another choice could involve using a recognised word that has no connection to the service or product. This may have some registration issues but can still prompt interest in potential customers. An example is Apple Computers.

Trade marks offer legal protection and are simple and cheap to apply for.

Categories

A registered trade mark does not give you exclusive use of the trade mark. You must register your trade mark in specific classes related to your business sector. There are 45 different classes.

You will have difficulty registering your trade mark in classes that are not related to your business, and you cannot make a registration simply to stop other people using the trade mark. Other businesses may be able to use a trade mark that is similar or identical to your registered trade mark provided the goods or services offered are so different to yours that people are unlikely to be misled or confused.

Protection

Once your trade mark is registered, you have the exclusive right to use it in the class that you registered it in. No one else can use your trade mark or a trade mark that is so similar that it's likely to deceive or cause confusion.

You will also have the right to assign or licence your trade mark to another person or business.

Registering a trade mark

Registering a trade mark is quite simple. You can download the forms from *www.iponz.govt.nz*, call the Intellectual Property Office of New Zealand (IPONZ) and ask for the forms, or apply online. Trade mark protection costs $112.50 per category for 7 years, and, unlike patents, can be renewed indefinitely.

Infringing a trade mark

If you believe someone is using your trade mark or a trade mark that is confusingly similar, the first step is to send them a 'cease and desist' letter written by your lawyer. Avoid the temptation to take direct action or write to them yourself, as you may create additional problems. Remember, they may have registered the trade mark in different categories, so if you drive a truck over their sign you will feel stupid.

Using your registered trade mark without permission breaches the Trade Marks Act and, if the product or service is similar to yours, they may also be guilty of 'passing off', or breaching the Fair Trading Act. A court can impose fines, award damages, and grant an injunction forcing them to stop.

To ensure you are not guilty of breaching an existing trade mark, you should register any logos, brands, and other 'signs' associated with your business. The first step of registration involves checking that the trade mark is not infringing someone else's trade mark.

You can search the IPONZ data base yourself at *www.iponz.govt.nz*, or get IPONZ to conduct a search for a fee. If IPONZ makes the search it will inform you in writing whether your choice infringes existing trade marks.

More information

For more information on copyright, patents, or trade marks, contact IPONZ at *www.iponz.govt.nz* or telephone 0508 447 669. IPONZ is a part of the Ministry of Economic Development.

Cybersquatting

Cybersquatting is the practice of registering an internet domain name with the intention of selling it to another business rather than using it yourself. Typically the domain name will include the name of an established business and it will be registered but not used as a website. Cybersquatting is generally illegal.

If you wish to use a registered domain name that includes the name of your business, but is not already being used for a website, contact an experienced intellectual property lawyer for advice.

It is illegal for another business to set up a website with a name like your business' name and offer a similar service or product. Under New Zealand law this is 'passing off'. It is also prohibited under the Fair Trading Act. Similar laws will apply in other countries.

Parallel importing

Parallel importing is the practice of buying legitimate goods subject to intellectual property rights overseas and importing them for distribution without the consent of the owner of the local intellectual property rights in the goods.

This means other people may be able to import and sell or hire goods that you have the New Zealand copyright or trade marks for. This could include any branded products like sports clothing, books, appliances, software, or music CDs.

Parallel importing has been legal in New Zealand since 1998, but the rules allowing it – the Copyright (Removal of the Prohibition on Parallel Importing) Act 1998 – have since been changed. If your business is involved in distributing branded goods, or if you are considering importing branded goods, then speak to an intellectual property lawyer about your rights.

While somebody may be able to parallel import goods, they must not use your trade marks or infringe your copyright. If the goods have not been made by an authorised manufacturer then they will be pirated or counterfeit and cannot be sold in New Zealand under any conditions.

For more information on parallel importing contact your lawyer or the Ministry for Economic Development at *www.med.govt.nz* or telephone 04-472 0030.

Fakes, forgeries, counterfeits, and piracy

Pirated or counterfeit goods infringe copyright or trade marks and so they cannot be sold in New Zealand.

Piracy is the unauthorised copying of copyright goods, typically videos, DVDs, CDs, and software.

Counterfeiting is the unauthorised manufacture of goods bearing a trade mark, typically branded clothing and footwear.

It is a breach of the Copyright Act to deal in pirated or counterfeit goods. It can also breach the Fair Trading Act to pass off fake goods as the genuine item. Maximum penalties under the Copyright Act are 5 years in prison or a fine of $150,000. Maximum penalties under the Fair Trading Act are a fine of $200,000 per breach for a company, and a fine of $60,000 per breach for a person. Apart from prison, fines, and confiscation, you could also face civil action and claims for damages. Many such cases are settled out of court.

If you are importing or selling branded goods, it is crucial to determine that the goods are authentic. Even if you are parallel importing – bypassing the New Zealand agent – you must ensure the goods are what they seem to be.

If you hold the New Zealand rights for copyright or trade-marked goods, you should lodge protection notices with the New Zealand Customs Service. This will tell Customs that the goods and their trade marks are protected within New Zealand. Customs will then check imports to ensure they do not infringe New Zealand intellectual property rights.

Note that this protection cannot be used as a defence. If you import goods it is your responsibility to ensure they are legitimate. You cannot assume that they are legal just because they passed through Customs.

For more information contact the New Zealand Customs Service at *www.customs.govt.nz*, or telephone 0800 428 786.

MARKETING AND SALES

Case study

Cookie Time protects its packaging

Brothers Michael and Guy Mavell started Cookie Time in 1983, when Michael was 21 and Guy was 19. They started by baking the cookies at home and now make about 44 million cookies every year. It's not hard to make a chocolate chip biscuit, so the Cookie Time point of difference depends as much on packaging and presentation as it does on big chunks of chocolate. For this reason Cookie Time has had several challenges to its brand in New Zealand and overseas, and has fought two court cases to protect its reputation.

The best-known case occurred in 2000, and resulted in a court injunction on rival baker Griffins. It was triggered by Griffins selling chocolate chip biscuits packaged in holiday-themed red and green buckets.

Cookie Time has been selling special Christmas packages since 1985. These were sold directly through commissioned sellers visiting workplaces. Since 1992 Cookie Time had used the same packaging – red 2-litre buckets with a green plastic lid.

In October 2000, Griffins started packaging its own recipe chocolate chip biscuits in a red 2-litre bucket with a green lid. Its label had several features in common with Cookie Time's, including size and shape, colours, photos of cookies along the length of a bottom, and a prominent cartoon character in the middle.

Griffins' buckets were sold directly and through supermarkets. They contained 375g of biscuits compared to 650g for Cookie Time's, and sold for about $5 less than Cookie Time.

Cookie Time wrote to Griffins about the situation, but in the end took it to court. Cookie Time claimed Griffins was passing off and breaching the Fair Trading Act. It also said Cookie Time's brand and reputation were threatened by Griffins' bucket with its lower price and fewer biscuits. Cookie Time successfully applied for an injunction stopping Griffins selling biscuits in the bucket.

CORPORATE GOVERNANCE

Forming a company helps shelter you from liability if your business collapses. Unless you've given personal guarantees, creditors can generally take only the money and assets you've invested in the business. By contrast, sole traders are liable for all the business debts.

But in return for this protection, society imposes standards on those who own and run companies. Most of these standards are set out in the Companies Act 1993 and the Financial Reporting Act 1993. Ignoring them can cost you dearly.

Corporate Governance rules affect all companies – big or small

All companies must have at least one director who has the legal responsibility to run the company or oversee whoever this task is delegated to. This legal duty is part of corporate governance, which also includes duties in relation to financial reporting, management of business risk and even, beyond legal requirements, ethical conduct. If you are a director of a company you need to be aware of your duties under a wide range of legislation.

Under the Companies Act, a company is regarded as a person. It can perform any business or activity, or enter any transaction, subject to general law and its own rules, which it lays out in its constitution. A company can:

- buy and sell assets in its own name
- sue and be sued
- hire and dismiss staff
- pay wages and distribute profits.

Reflecting the importance of the status, the maximum fine is $10,000 if you use a name including the term 'Limited', or its abbreviation, 'Ltd', when this does not apply to a true limited liability company.

Under the Companies Act, companies can have several shareholders or just one. Tens of thousands of single-owner companies in New Zealand have just one director.

Every company must have a registered office, a share register, and at least one director.

New and smaller companies should invest in good governance standards. These need not be complex or involve great expense. However, good governance structures and behaviours should help companies to be successful.

What a share gives you

Under the Companies Act, a share in a company generally gives you rights to vote at meetings of the company, a proportional share of dividends and to the company's surplus assets, in a liquidation. However, these general rights can be negated or modified by the company's constitution.

Shares can be transferred subject to the company's constitution. For example, it is common for company's to include pre-emptive rights in their constitution (under which any shareholder wishing to sell their shares must first offer them to the other shareholders).

Frequently, a company's constitution provides for the directors to approve all share transfer prior to the transfer being recorded in the company's share register.

Failure to keep a share register can cost the company and each director a fine of up to $10,000. A company can use an agent to maintain the register. While a share register can be divided into two or more registers kept in different places, that is not very common (and there are rules about ensuring that the principal share register is kept up to date with all transfers). The principal share register must be in New Zealand.

Companies can issue shares during their trading life, as well as at formation, provided their constitutions allow this, or shareholders approve.

Who has the say in a company?

The Companies Act reserves to shareholders certain fundamental decisions that affect ownership. As a shareholder you appoint directors to manage the company or supervise its managers. You can dismiss directors, too.

Only shareholders can:

- adopt or change the company constitution
- authorise major transactions
- approve amalgamations with another company
- accept proposals that the company be put into liquidation.

Constitution

Your company's constitution, together with the Companies Act 1993, regulates how your company runs. People sometimes talk of a company's memorandum of association and articles of association, or just 'articles'. These were the equivalent of a constitution under the Companies Act 1955, and were compulsory.

A constitution, the new term, became voluntary with the 1993 Act, and many companies have one. When there is no constitution, the Companies Act 1993 sets the rules.

A company can set up or vary a constitution at virtually any time. A court also has the power to vary a constitution – on the application of a director or shareholder.

The Companies Act gives the constitution authority, except where it contravenes or is inconsistent with the Act. Then the Act overrules it.

Major transactions

Under the Companies Act, a major transaction can only be approved by shareholders. A transaction is a major transaction if it:

- entails selling assets of the company or buying assets worth more than half of the value of the company's total assets, or
- will involve the company incurring debts or other obligations worth more than half the value of the company's total assets.

Shareholders' approval must be made by special resolution (see page 273).

Board of directors

The Companies Act 1993 requires a board of directors, or the sole director if there is only one, either to manage a company or direct and supervise its business.

You cannot be a director if you are under 18, if you are an undischarged bankrupt, or if you are prohibited under the provisions of either the Companies Act 1955 or Companies Act 1993. Being subject to a property order under the Protection of Personal and Property Rights Act 1988 also rules you out.

In addition, you must meet any qualifications for directors in the company constitution. This might specify that a person must hold a minimum number of shares in the company before they can be a director.

If you want to resign from a board you must do so in writing. A company can remove you from the board in the following ways:

- the shareholders can vote not to re-elect you at the end of your term
- subject to a company's constitution, the shareholders can also vote you off the board by ordinary resolution.

Board quorum

Unless the constitution of a company provides otherwise the quorum (minimum number for a board meeting) is a majority of directors eg if there are five, three must be present.

Delegation of board power

Subject to any restrictions in the company's constitution, a board can delegate certain of its powers to a committee of directors, to a director, to an employee, or to any other person. Unless the following conditions are met, however, the board is held responsible for the acts of the person with the delegated power:

- the board must believe on reasonable grounds that the person will exercise the power in accordance with the duties imposed on directors by the Companies Act and the constitution
- the board must monitor, by reasonable methods properly used, the exercise of the delegated power.

Director remuneration

Under the Act, unless the constitution says otherwise, directors as a board set their own pay and benefits. However, they must place details of all payments, remuneration, loans etc, in the company's interest register and those voting in favour of the particular remuneration must certify that the particular payment is fair to the company and give their reasons for that opinion. If the relevant procedure is not followed or reasonable grounds did not exist for the belief that the payment was fair to the company, then the director is liable to the company if he or she cannot show that the payment was fair to the company at the time.

The CEO's terms of engagement

The board usually sets the chief executive's salary, and selects and monitor that person's performance.

Indemnification of directors and employees

A company can, subject to having appropriate provisions in its constitution, indemnify directors, and also employees, for liabilities arising from their jobs. There are a variety of exceptions to this including that no indemnity can be given in respect of criminal liability or a breach of the duty to act in good faith.

Good faith: director's credo

As a director, you must act in good faith and in the company's best interests. In law, good faith essentially boils down to a proper motive. You must believe you are acting in the best interests of the company. This might depart from your own personal interests.

Reckless trading

A director also has a duty to ensure the company is not trading in a reckless manner. This means the director cannot agree to, cause or allow the business to be carried on in a manner likely to create a substantial risk of serious loss to the company's creditors.

Also, you cannot agree to the company incurring an obligation, such as a debt, unless at the time you believe on reasonable grounds that the company can meet that obligation or pay that debt when it falls due.

Standard of care

How are we to judge your performance as a director? The Companies Act requires you to act with the care, diligence, and skill that a reasonable director would use in the same circumstances. Note the standard is that of a reasonable director and not of a reasonably skilful director nor of a reasonably careful director.

Legal cases suggest you should keep yourself informed about the company's dealings, make inquiries when relevant, and seek competent advice when prudent. If a court ever analyses how you fulfilled your duties to the company, your ability to rely on reports, statements, and other information supplied by professionals and other parties could be quite important.

The law provides that, as a director, you may rely on company reports, statements, financial data, and other information. You may also rely on expert or professional advice from:

- an employee of the company you believe on reasonable grounds to be reliable and competent in the relevant matter

- a professional adviser or expert you reasonably believe to be competent in the matter
- any other director or committee of directors upon which you did not serve in relation to matters within their authority.

You can rely on the information and advice only if you act in good faith, make proper inquiry where needed, and have no knowledge that your reliance is unwarranted.

Director's interests

As a director you must disclose any interest you have in any transaction or proposed transaction with the company. When you become aware of the interest, make the disclosure immediately. Failure to do so can cost you a fine of up to $10,000. The transaction in which you had an interest can also be set aside in certain circumstances.

How do we define when a director is interested in a transaction of the company? Under the Companies Act, it is when the director:

- is a party to the transaction, or will or may derive a material financial benefit from the transaction
- has a material financial interest in another party to the transaction
- is a director, officer, or trustee of another party to the transaction, or of another person who will or may derive a material financial benefit from the transaction
- is the parent, child, husband, or wife of another party to the transaction or of a person who will or may derive a material financial benefit from the transaction
- is otherwise directly or indirectly materially interested in the transaction.

As a director, if you are a shareholder, director, officer, or trustee of another named firm or person, you must advise your board in writing of the interest, including its monetary value, if this can be measured.

Your company must keep an interests register. If you are a director with an interest in a transaction you must log this in the register. If the company has more than one director, you must also advise the board of your interest.

You may still vote on a transaction, attend a board meeting where it is discussed, and sign a company document related to the transaction. Your company's constitution must allow this, however.

Relevant interest in shares

If a director has a 'relevant interest' in shares of the company you must immediately after acquiring or disposing of the relevant interest disclose this to the board of directors including details of the transaction, and have this recorded in the interests register.

CORPORATE GOVERNANCE

The Companies Act defines the term 'relevant interest' very broadly. In essence if you own shares or can control the voting rights to shares you are regarded as having a 'relevant interest in shares'.

As a director, when you buy or quit a relevant interest in shares issued by the company, you must give the board details immediately, including the transaction price.

When information you have as a director may be relevant to the valuation of the company's shares or securities (such as bonds), or to the valuation of those of a related company, you may buy or quit the shares or securities only if:

- your buying price is at least the fair value of the shares or securities
- your selling price is not more than the fair value of the shares or securities.

'Fair value' is decided on all the information known to the director at the time, or on all information available to the public then.

If you breach these rules, you may have to compensate the person on the other side of the trade.

Among other duties, directors must ensure the Registrar of Companies must be advised within 10 working days of a share issue, or they can be fined up to $10,000 each.

Company information

As a director you have access to much confidential information about the company. You must not give this information to anyone, make use of it yourself, or act on it. Exceptions are:

- when disclosure is for company purposes or is required by the law
- if you are representing a person's interests on the board – you may disclose the information to that person unless the board specifically bars this
- if the board authorises you in advance to disclose information to someone else or allows you to make use of or act on the information – you must enter details of the disclosure, use, or act in the interests register, and the disclosure, use, or act must be unlikely to harm the company.

Directors' meetings

Under the Companies Act, directors meet as a group as frequently as they choose, unless the company constitution specifies the number of meetings to be held.

You have the right as a director to attend all board meetings. If the board tries to shut you out (other than in circumstances permitted by the company's constitution), you can seek an injunction against it.

Unless the company's constitution provides otherwise, the company must give you at least 2 days' notice of a board meeting. The meeting can be held as an audio conference, or as a teleconference, but not by separate telephone calls between pairs of directors at a time – the key is that all the directors can hear one another simultaneously.

Directors may appoint a chairperson. Unless the constitution provides otherwise, if the chairperson has not arrived at a meeting 5 minutes after starting time, the directors may appoint another to stand in.

The chairperson has a casting vote only if the company constitution provides for this. A casting vote is an additional vote used when normal votes are deadlocked for and against. It is not very common to provide for the chairperson to have a casting vote.

Be heard

Under the Act, if you are a director and oppose a resolution before the board, you should tell all other directors of this clearly either before or at the meeting. Otherwise, you are likely to be taken to agree. Expressing opposition can be important in limiting your exposure if the decision turns out to be a bad one. Ultimately if you are concerned about the consequences of a decision it may be safest to resign prior to the decision being made. Board responsibility is collective and membership can be enough to result in suffering a penalty imposed on the group.

All directors at the board meeting are presumed to agree unless they express their disagreement.

Board committees

Board committees to which certain matters have been delegated can decide their own meeting procedure. However, they should keep minutes (a record). Unless a company's constitution provides otherwise board votes require a simple majority.

Other companies

Exceptions: Some companies are registered under both the Companies Act and under the Co-operative Companies Act 1996, which provides special provisions such as allowing only suppliers to be shareholders. Similarly, port companies are covered by the Port Companies Act 1988 as well as by the Financial Reporting Act 1993.

Company records

Under the Companies Act, your company must keep at its registered office:

- the company's constitution (if it has one)
- minutes of all meetings and resolutions of all board meetings and board committees for the past 7 years
- present directors' names and addresses

- copies of the last 7 years' annual reports and all other documents given to shareholders, including those for classes of shares
- financial statements and group financial statements for the past 7 years
- copies of certificates given by directors over the past 7 years
- the share register
- the interests register.

Records must be written, or easily accessed and printed out. They must be in English or readily convertible to written English.

Accounting records

Directors must ensure accounting records are kept that:

- record and explain the company's transactions
- allow the financial position of the company to be determined with reasonable accuracy at any time
- comply with generally accepted accounting practices
- include necessary explanations and additional information to ensure the accounts give a true and fair view
- list details of money spent each day, and on what, and details of money received each day, and for what – invoices and the names of the other parties must be included
- record the assets and liabilities of the company
- record stock at the end of the financial year, and include details of stock-taking between balance dates
- are in English or can be readily translated into English.

Each director can be fined up to $10,000 when a company fails to comply.

Financial statements defined

Financial statements, under the Financial Reporting Act 1993, comprise in respect of entities trading for profit a statement of financial performance; and in the case of reporting entities a cashflow statement together with any notes or documents giving further information on these.

Breaches of the Act can lead to fines of up to $100,000 each for directors of companies, or $10,000 each for directors of smaller, exempt companies. These companies are explained on page 275.

Your company must also keep proper accounting records. These records may be kept away from the registered office and need not be kept in New Zealand. However, if the records are kept overseas, the company still has obligations under the Companies Act to send to, and keep at, a place in New Zealand accounts and returns that disclose the financial position of the company at 6-month intervals and will enable the financial statements to be completed. You must notify the Registrar of Companies of the places that your company's records are kept at.

Shareholders can apply to the courts to enforce the board's fulfilment of its accounting duties.

Annual report

The board is responsible for the company making the annual report available within 5 months of its balance date. Among items and information included in the annual report are:

- the financial statements
- a description, so far as the board believes is material for shareholders to appreciate the state of the company's affairs, or any change during the accounting period of the nature of the business of the company or the classes of business in which the company has an interest
- auditor's report
- value of pay and benefits received by each director
- the number of staff paid $100,000 or more, in climbing brackets of $10,000
- company donations during the financial year
- a list of directors at balance date, and any who ceased office during the year
- amounts paid to the auditor or audit firm, and amounts paid to the person or firm for other services.

The board must ensure each shareholder is sent a copy of the annual report at least 20 working days before the company's annual meeting. Each shareholder is entitled to a copy of the annual accounts, with the auditor's report. Most companies include these in one document with the annual report.

Generally accepted accounting practice

Financial statements must comply with generally accepted accounting practice. This means they must comply with applicable financial reporting standards as determined by the accounting profession and a Government-appointed board.

The financial statements must also give a true and fair view. This often requires notes and other information to be added.

Balance date

This is 31 March, unless directors choose another day. To change your company's balance date for accounting purposes you must get permission from the Registrar of Companies in advance and you will need to apply to the Inland Revenue Department if you also want to change your tax balance date from 31 March.

Share issues and dividends

As well as issuing shares for cash, your company can issue shares for other consideration such as property or services. The board's job is to set the terms so they are fair to existing shareholders.

A company may be able to give financial help, such as a loan, to help a person buy its shares. To do so, either all shareholders must agree in writing, or the board must follow a special procedure set out in the Companies Act. In either case, the board must have previously resolved to provide the assistance, that such assistance is in the best interests of the company, and the help given is fair and reasonable to the company. The board must give in full the grounds for these conclusions.

The board can decide to pay a dividend, but only if the company immediately afterwards meets the solvency test.

Minority rights

Shareholders can be divided into 'interest groups', or groups of shareholders whose rights to shares may be affected by an action or a proposal. Each interest group must approve any action by the company which affects the rights attached to shares. When this happens, the action can proceed.

There is protection for dissident members of an interest group. Where the dissident member of the interest group has voted shares against a resolution affecting the rights attached to those shares and the resolution is passed, then the minority shareholder can require the company to buy the shares, or arrange for someone else to buy them.

Similarly, minority buyout rights apply in relation to certain changes to a company's constitution, major transactions, and amalgamations.

Shareholders' meetings

Directors do not have a statutory right to attend shareholders' meetings. However, the company constitution may require them to be present. It is, of course, usual for directors to attend shareholders meetings and be available to answer questions.

The company should hold an annual meeting each calendar year. You get latitude in the first year – you have 18 months from registration to hold the first annual meeting. After that, the annual meeting must be held within 15 months of the previous one, and unless the company is an exempt company within 6 months of the balance date.

The Companies Act requires directors to call annual meetings, but sets no penalty if they don't. A company's constitution typically sets a quorum requirement for a meeting of shareholders. Unless the constitution provides otherwise, shareholders who between them can exercise a majority of the votes to be cast on the business to be transacted at the meeting are required to be present to constitute a quorum.

Where company constitutions do not provide rules for a chairperson to follow at an annual meeting, the Companies Act provides fallback provisions.

A company can, instead of holding an annual meeting, address matters required to be conducted at an annual meeting by a resolution in writing. The resolution needs to be passed by three-quarters of shareholders (unless the constitution requires a higher percentage for passing of the resolution). Many smaller companies use this provision.

Once the date of the annual meeting has been set, the board cannot change it, but once begun, the meeting can be adjourned in the normal way.

When an annual meeting takes place it has only one compulsory task: to appoint an auditor. The meeting can consider virtually anything else, provided notice has been given.

Typically it will deal with these matters, which will be listed in the agenda as ordinary business:

- consider financial reports from the year just ended
- elect directors
- appoint the auditor.

The chairperson should allow reasonable time to discuss management of the business. Shareholders can pass a resolution about management, but the board must only follow that if the constitution provides for this.

The Companies Act allows a company to do several things without the approval of a shareholder meeting. This is particularly useful for smaller firms. Provided the company is solvent, it can, with the written agreement of all shareholders:

- authorise dividends otherwise than in accordance with the provisions of the Companies Act, in respect of dividends
- approve a discount scheme (cheaper company goods or services for shareholders) otherwise than in accordance with the provisions of the Companies Act in respect of shareholder discounts
- buy its own shares otherwise than in accordance with the provisions of the Companies Act dealing with share buybacks by the company
- give financial help to a buyer of its shares otherwise than in accordance with the provisions of the Companies Act dealing with financial assistance
- approve fees and other benefits for directors otherwise than in accordance with the provisions of the Companies Act dealing with the remuneration and benefits for directors
- issue shares otherwise than in accordance with the provisions of the Companies Act dealing with the issue of shares
- approve a transaction in which a director is an interested party.

Special meetings

If a shareholders' meeting is not the annual meeting it is called a special meeting of shareholders. Shareholders with a total of 5% or more of voting rights can require the board to call a special meeting. In addition, any person authorised by a company's constitution may call a meeting.

A court may also order a meeting of shareholders to be held in such manner as it sees fit where it is satisfied that it is impracticable to call or conduct a meeting in the manner prescribed by the Companies Act or constitution or it is in the interests of the company that a meeting be held.

Meeting notice requirements

Unless a company's constitution deals with notice requirements, the provisions of the Companies Act in that regard apply. These require that notice of an annual meeting, with time and place, must go to every shareholder entitled to receive notice of the meeting, every director, and the auditor, at least 10 working days before the meeting. It must include the:

- nature of any business to be transacted – this must be detailed enough so that a shareholder can form a reasoned judgment in relation to it.
- text of any special resolution to be submitted to the meeting.

The notice needs to be detailed enough to give a shareholder a reasonable indication of proposals contained in it. If you send out a meeting notice, take care that the essence of the meeting's business is clear to shareholders. Subject to a company's constitution the accidental failure to comply with notice requirements will not invalidate a meeting.

As a rule, if all shareholders entitled to attend and vote at the meeting, attend the meeting without protest, an irregularity in the meeting notice can be waived.

If your company is closely held (owned by a small number of shareholders), meaning shareholders have a vital interest in company decisions, you should consider ensuring the constitution contains additional safeguards against the consequences of accidental irregularities in a notice of meeting.

Shareholders must be able to communicate with each other if the meeting is to be valid. If the meeting spills over into more than one room, and audio-visual links are deficient, the gathering cannot be regarded as a meeting, except to be adjourned.

A shareholders' meeting can invite or allow any person to attend for any purpose, provided the company constitution does not rule this out.

Who can vote

Generally, if your name is on the shareholders' register you can vote. A company constitution can give different or limited voting rights to different groups of shares.

Proxy vote

A proxy holder is a person to whom you delegate your voting right, in order for them to attend and vote at a meeting of shareholders. That person represents you as a shareholder. You can appoint a proxy in writing, and must sign an appointment form, which should specify whether the proxy is for the particular meeting or for a specified term. You must state the proxy's identity clearly.

If you tell the proxy which way to vote, your direction must be followed. The proxy can attend a shareholders' meeting and speak, and counts toward the numbers needed for a quorum.

Quorum

The company constitution can set a quorum for a shareholders' meeting. Otherwise, the default number under the Companies Act is sufficient shareholders to exercise a majority of votes, either in person, by post, or by proxy.

If a quorum of shareholders is not established within 30 minutes of the meeting beginning, then the Companies Act provides in certain circumstances for the meeting to be dissolved or in other circumstances that the meeting is adjourned. The shareholders' meeting must have a quorum for the whole meeting.

Voting rules at meetings

Subject to the constitution of the company the chairperson of the board (if one has been elected) controls the shareholders' meeting, but is subject to the wishes of the meeting. The wishes reveal themselves in voting. Unless a poll is called for, the meeting votes are by voice or a show of hands, the chairperson choosing between the two. Postal votes do not count in a voice vote. At an audio or audio-visual meeting, voting is by voice unless a poll is called for.

A company constitution cannot rule out the right of shareholders to demand a poll in which votes are taken in writing and counted. A poll can be called by:

- at least five shareholders with the right to vote
- shareholders holding at least 10% of the voting rights of shareholders who can vote at the meeting
- shareholders entitled to vote and with shares on which the aggregate amount paid up is not less than 10% of the total amount paid up on all shares that confer the right to vote, or
- the chairperson.

If you are a shareholder in a poll, you do not have to cast all of your voting rights the same way.

Either the company constitution or the meeting chairperson decides the method of conducting the poll.

Ordinary shareholder resolutions pass with a simple majority. Special resolutions (see below) need a 75% majority, or higher if the company constitution specifies.

Usually, the chairperson will put to the meeting a motion that the resolution be passed. Typically a seconder is sought but this is not a strict requirement unless a company constitution requires this. The chairperson can put resolutions to the vote as a block, if the meeting does not object. However, resolutions appointing directors must be voted on individually.

Special resolutions

Notice of any special resolution must be put to the meeting in advance, though if all shareholders agree, this requirement can be waived.

The Companies Act specifies that the following matters must be decided by special resolution, regardless of the company constitution. These include:

- adopting, altering, or revoking the company constitution
- approving a major transaction (see page 261)
- approving an amalgamation of the company
- putting the company into liquidation
- altering shareholder rights (in which case the action must be approved by a special resolution of each interest group).

Raising matters at meetings

As a shareholder, you can raise a matter for discussion at any shareholders' meeting at which you can vote. Just give written notice to the board, with the proposed resolution. If the board receives the notice 20 working days before the last day for giving notice to the meeting, the board must give notice of the proposal and text of the resolution at the company's expense.

The shareholder pays this cost where the notice is received between 5 and 20 days before the last date for giving notice of the meeting. The board can use its discretion on circulating the notice if it receives it less than 5 days before, with you paying the cost.

If the directors allow postal or proxy voting on the notice, they must allow you to include a statement for distribution of up to 1,000 words.

The chairperson

The company constitution can name a person as chairperson of shareholder meetings. If the chairperson does not arrive within 15 minutes of the advertised starting time, shareholders can choose one of themselves to chair the meeting.

The chairperson's two main roles are maintaining order at the meeting and establishing the consensus of the meeting on any question before it. If a chairperson makes a ruling in bad faith, or for an ulterior, unacceptable purpose, the ruling is invalid.

If you chair a shareholder meeting, identifying the meeting's consensus requires that the shareholders get a reasonable opportunity to air their views, and can express their vote. As with the majority, a minority group among the shareholders should be given an opportunity to be heard.

Minutes

The board should ensure that minutes of all shareholders' meetings are kept at the company's registered office for 7 years. Minutes of meetings give a brief summary of what happened at a meeting and record any resolutions passed.

Shareholders, or people they authorise, can check the minutes and certain other company records but must give a written notice of intention to inspect on the company. The company has to ensure the records are available for inspection at the place at which the company's records are kept between 9am and 5pm for 6 working days beginning on the third day after the notice has been given.

Auditor

As noted above, the only duty a company's annual meeting must perform is appoint its auditor – and set the auditor's fees. The job involves auditing the financial statements of the company for the accounting period after the meeting, and, if it is a holding company, auditing the group financial statements.

Small and medium companies can generally opt out of appointing an auditor. They do this by a resolution supported by every shareholder able to vote on it at an annual meeting. That is, they can opt out without holding an annual meeting.

Companies that cannot opt out include those that are issuers (a company which issues securities that are required to have a prospectus, or a prospectus and investment statement) and those 25% or more foreign-owned.

You cannot audit a company unless you are a chartered accountant, or are an Audit Department officer with written authorisation from the Controller and Auditor-General. A chartered accountant is a member of the Institute of Chartered Accountants of New Zealand, or an equivalent, approved, overseas institute. Those who cannot be a company's auditor include a:

- director or employee of the company
- partner of any of the company's directors or employees
- a body corporate
- anyone who, because of these reasons, cannot audit a related company.

Because of what might possibly underly a company changing its auditor, a company cannot replace an auditor qualified for reappointment, unless it gives that existing auditor 20 working days' written notice, and gives the auditor reasonable opportunity to address the shareholders on the appointment of another person, either in writing or at the annual meeting.

The same opportunity must be offered if the auditor does not want to be reappointed.

The company auditor has right of access at all times to company books and papers, and to information and explanations. A company officer who refuses an auditor access to books or papers or to provide information can face a fine of up to $10,000. A director who fails to make access available to an auditor can also be fined $10,000.

The auditor has access to the shareholders' meeting and is entitled to receive the same notice and communications as shareholders.

Solvency test

The solvency test protects creditors and shareholders. Before a company can pay dividends, buy back shares, or give financial assistance to itself, executives, staff, or shareholders, it must meet this test.

The company passes this test when it can pay its debts as they fall due in the normal course of business and when its assets are greater in value than its liabilities, including contingent liabilities (those it might have to pay, such as if the outcome of a pending court case is unfavourable).

Exempt companies

The Companies Act exempts a category of companies from many of its requirements. Exempt companies must have all of the following:

- assets of no more than $450,000
- annual turnover of no more than $1 million
- no subsidiaries and are not subsidiaries themselves
- no issued securities
- not an overseas company.

The financial statements of exempt companies do not have to comply with generally accepted accounting principles but must comply with the directions prescribed by the Governor-General by Order in Council.

If you are a director of an exempt company, you must ensure financial statements are completed within 5 months of the balance date, or, if all shareholders have approved, within 9 months. Your firm has 9 months after the company's balance date to prepare the annual report.

If you are a director of an exempt company and that company subsequently issues securities, such as shares or bonds, you will lose your exempt status.

Corporate governance principles

In the last 18 months or so, since high profile collapses like Enron in the US and HIH in Australia there as been a lot of discussion internationally on corporate governance.

This has resulted in some jurisdictions like the US, in new corporate governance rules being introduced for companies. In other jurisdictions like England and Australia, it has resulted in best practice codes being promulgated which, at least, listed companies must follow or explain why they are not.

In New Zealand, the New Zealand Exchange has finalised some new rules which companies listed on their markets must follow and a best practice code.

The Securities Commission is currently seeking input on what corporate governance principles New Zealand should adopt. It is intended that these principles will apply to a wider group of companies than listed companies. Similarly, it is intended that companies will either follow the principles or explain to their shareholders why they have chosen not to do so.

The sorts of corporate governance principles being debated include:

- the desirability of boards of directors and management engaging in constructive and rigorous debate
- the desirability of directors committing enough time to the role to complete it satisfactorily
- the desirability of the board focusing on the priorities of the business
- the need for the CEO to have the trust and confidence of the board
- the need for the board to be satisfied that the remuneration packages for directors and senior management are appropriate and in the company's best interests (in particular, the desirability to avoid packages for management that encourage short-termism)
- the desirability of boards adopting codes of ethics for themselves and all staff
- the importance of identifying and managing appropriately conflicts of interest
- the role of board subcommittees – most medium-large companies have separate audit committees, remuneration committees, and appointment committees however, this may not be necessary for smaller companies
- the desirability of having some independent directors on a board and, if so, the skills required of those people
- the importance of director evaluation
- the importance of succession planning at board level
- the desirability of boards meeting without management and executive directors from time to time
- the importance of clear delegations between the board and management
- the importance of companies identifying the risks to their business and having appropriate risk management programmes in place
- the appropriateness or not of a chief executive also being a board member

- the need to ensure auditors remain independent and do not become captured by the company or management
- the desirability of the CEO and CFO signing off on financial statements along with the auditor
- the desirability of boards reporting to shareholders on their corporate governance policies.

Many of these corporate governance issues are equally of importance to smaller companies as well as larger companies. It was anticipated that by early 2004 the Securities Commission will have reported to the Minister of Commerce on what principles it recommends New Zealand companies should adopt. However, companies should not wait for that to decide what principles they should be applying to endeavour to ensure their businesses have the right corporate governance focus for them.

CONTRACTS

Contracts can vary greatly in their form – they can be spoken agreements, a one-page document, an electronic message, or hundreds of pages complete with tables, graphs, plans, and other material. A contract is a legally binding arrangement between two parties that creates enforceable rights and obligations. If you are one of the parties, you and the other party each agree to give or promise something to the other. Contracts provide certainty on which businesses can act, and allocate risk.

Requirements of a contract

A contract can include written and unwritten agreements between parties, and agreements from custom. In a larger project, a contract might include documents such as invitation to tender, the supplying contractor's tender, post-tender correspondence, and a formal agreement. If other documents are included in the contract, to avoid later disputes, you need to specify which document prevails if there is a conflict.

There are five key elements to a contract:

- 'Offer' – one of you must make an offer to the other. The offer can be to do something, or a promise not to do something.
- 'Acceptance' – the other party must accept the offer. Acceptance must be unqualified, communicated to the offering party and in precisely the same terms as the offer. If an acceptance varies the offer terms, it becomes a counter-offer rather than an acceptance.
- 'Consideration' – if you seek to enforce the contract you must have done something or promised to do something in return for what you seek. Most often, you or the other party will have agreed to pay money in exchange for the goods or services covered by the contract.
- 'Certainty' – contract terms must be sufficiently certain or capable of being made certain to both of you.
- 'Intention' – both you and the other party must intend to create legal relations. An obvious example where this can be an issue is where work would normally be done free.

Consideration

No consideration, no contract. There must be an exchange of value. One party must promise to perform an act or refrain from acting in return for a promise from the other party. One of the promises will usually involve payment of money.

The amount of payment doesn't affect this requirement. If a contract is unfair to you or the other party, that is not enough to make it unenforceable.

However, past consideration is not consideration. For example, in a famous case sailors promised extra wages for completing a voyage they had already contracted to make were refused the payment when the ship docked. The courts rejected the sailors' claim because they had not performed any additional consideration.

Recent cases suggest a more liberal interpretation. If the promise of extra consideration for the same work provides some practical benefit to the other party the extra payment can be enforced.

Pre-contractual pointers

Groundwork

Before you negotiate a contract, do the groundwork. Identify what you need. If you can't explain what you want to a supplier, there's almost no chance of getting what you expected and it will be harder for you to take legal action if there are problems. Set out expected benefits and objectives at the outset. As each stage of the contract is completed, check these are being met.

Working out what you want should include an analysis of what you already have. For example, in purchasing a new computer system, ensure that:

- the new computer system is compatible with the software programs you need it to run
- Your staff are able to use it
- It fits in the room it will be installed in.

Be clear about your requirements from the start.

It's useful to do 'what-if' thinking. What if this happens? What if this changes? What if suddenly you need that? Use this questioning to establish what is relevant and important and include it in the contract. For example, for the new computer system, what happens if the suppliers don't deliver the system on time? What if the products don't conform to your requirements? What if the maker goes out of business?

As your ideas firm up, decide performance requirements and how you will measure them. Make sure your performance requirements are included in the contract.

Tendering

Once you have identified your needs, you must find a supplier. A request for information (RFI) from potential suppliers can be useful. An RFI generally seeks only business requirements, and requests minimum information on suppliers' financial and technical standard and products. This brings in better industry information without issuing your confidential information widely.

One of the most common ways of attracting contract offers is to call for tenders. For most small businesses, an open tender process, advertising for all those interested, will be too time-consuming when the responses come in.

You will probably find it more efficient to send out a request for tender (RFT) to two or three suppliers who have either provided you what you've required before, those who have good reputations in your industry, or to those you preferred from the results of the RFI.

As a purchaser, you have most negotiating strength at the beginning of the tender process, before the supplier locks you in. So prepare your tender documentation carefully. Similarly, as a supplier, you need to be careful with your response – make sure you set out your assumptions and any limitations on what you are able to provide. The information contained in these documents may have implications on each party's legal rights later on.

If you send out an RFT it should detail exactly what you want in business and technical terms. You should also deal with what legal terms are desired by either including a draft contract in the RFT or setting out the principles that are to apply in key legal areas. We'll look at what some of those key legal areas are later. Ensure the RFT makes it clear the party calling tenders is not bound to accept any of them, or the lowest one.

Specify the format for responses to your RFT – this will help you compare like with like. The RFT should also contain dates and criteria for meeting contract milestones.

When writing is right

Some contracts must be in writing. These include:

- contracts relating to land
- guarantees
- collective employment contracts
- Contracts that assign copyright.

While a contract does not have to be written, it is recommended for a couple of reasons. First, it clarifies obligations and focuses minds on the key issues. Secondly, unwanted implied terms may be specifically and clearly excluded. Thirdly, it provides evidence of what was agreed in the event of a dispute.

However, having a written contact is not always possible. Where you must rely on an oral contract, make written notes of what was said and agreed to. Make them as soon as possible after the conversation. If significant, always record the conversation and, if possible, confirm it in writing with the other party.

Types of contract

Exchange of letters

You can create a binding contract with an exchange of letters if the five essential elements of a contract (*see page X*) are present. Beware of inadvertently creating a contract this way where you have not yet decided if you want to proceed. If you do not want to create a binding contract at this time, make that clear in your letters.

Letters of intent

Letters of intent can create contractual obligations if the two parties want this. Again, take care you don't unintentionally create a contract if you do not want to.

In business you will also come across documents called a 'memorandum of understanding' or 'agreement in principle'. None of these terms have a certain legal meaning. You need to be clear about what the purpose of the document is and whether it is intended to be binding. In the rest of this section we refer to all of those document as letters of intent.

These documents are useful when you have reached agreement with the other party on a number of terms of a proposed contract, but the intention is that the contract will not become binding until some further condition has been met. They signal the start of a legal relationship and set the process for agreeing the full contract.

Some of the key requirements for a letter of intent are:

- state that the letter of intent doesn't contractually bind either party (provided that's what you want)
- record the intention of the parties to enter into a binding contract if they can agree on the final contract
- nominate a date by which the parties will reach final agreement
- outline the key terms of the relationship and indicate those that are agreed and those which require further negotiation
- refer to the documentation and correspondence between the parties which together records the details of the agreement reached so far between the parties
- consider disclaiming financial liability, or setting a cap on liability.

While a letter of intent can be used to enable services to start immediately, it is not ideal. It is better to use a short interim agreement to record the initial obligations to be performed while the full contract is being agreed.

Contractual content

What your contract should contain

You need to make sure your contract covers a description of the services or goods and the buyer's requirements, each party's obligations, price and payment, confidentiality, intellectual property, warranties, liabilities, indemnities, termination rights, and dispute resolution. Of course there are a multitude of other matters that can (or should) be included. However, from a practical perspective the number of contractual terms will depend on the value of the contract. The higher the value the more important it is to cover every angle.

Whether you are the buyer or seller you need to know what is being provided. If you are the buyer you need to know what you are getting. If you are the seller you need to know what is to be provided. Make sure all the buyer's requirements are specified so there can be no dispute later. If you are the party buying goods or services it is also a good idea to include remedy provisions so that, where goods have not been supplied by a deadline or the goods are unsatisfactory, you can require the supplier to meet the requirements immediately (if this is appropriate) and/or you can withhold payment until the requirements are met. For ongoing contracts, think about service levels and any monetary remedies for failure to meet those service levels.

Make sure the contract is clear as to all other obligations on a party. If you are the buyer, specify what else you want the supplier to be responsible for. This could include providing details to enable the buyer to get the site ready for the goods or providing reports on the progress of the project. If you are the seller, specify the buyer's obligations (ie your dependencies). This could be things like making personnel available or making timely decisions.

Price provisions can range from a fixed price to a price that is determined by a formula. Ideally, a fixed price should cover not only the fee for goods or services, but other costs of supply, such as freight and insurance. How the price is to be paid also needs to be dealt with. This could be monthly invoices or, where the contract is for a project, on successful completion of milestones.

To keep your company's information confidential, insert a confidentiality clause in the contract. It should provide that any information that you provide to the other party is confidential and limit use of that information to enabling the contract to be carried out. It is also prudent to insert a clause requiring the other party and its subcontractors to observe your security requirements when they are on your premises.

If the other party creates intellectual property for you, insert a clause reserving ownership of this property to you. The general rule is that, unless the parties have agreed otherwise, intellectual property belongs to the person that has commissioned the work. But be safe – spell it out. If you are the provider of the intellectual property you should try to retain ownership of intellectual property that you create (by only providing a licence to use the intellectual property).

As a buyer you want as many warranties as possible. These should include things like, that the goods/services meet your requirements, that the seller will use due care and skill in meeting its obligations and that it will use materials of high quality. As a supplier, consider any matters you depend on in performing the contract (eg other parties used by the buyer) and limit your warranties accordingly.

As a supplier you should try and limit your liability as far as possible. This can include things like a cap on total liability and an exclusions for consequential losses. As a buyer, you do not want liability limited so try and insert a clause in the contract under which the contractor indemnifies you against all costs as a result of a claim against you from negligent acts or breach of contract by the supplier, supplier's employees, or subcontractors. Of course, the extent of liability will always be a matter for negotiation between the parties and should reflect what is standard within the industry. Another way to deal with liability is to agree on 'liquidated' damages – this means that the party who is in breach of contract pays a specific sum (say, $1,000 a day) for that breach.

That said, a buyer should always seek an indemnity from the supplier for any breaches of third party intellectual property rights by goods or services supplied. The supplier should ensure that where it provides such an indemnity, it can take control of the defence of the infringement claim.

For both buyers and sellers it is important to set out clearly when each of them has the right to terminate the contract. A common provision is to allow termination 30 days after notifying the other party of the breach if the breach has not been cured. However, you need to think about other circumstances when you might want to be able to terminate the contract.

The contract should include procedures to be used if there is a dispute. Usually this follows the formula of discussions at the operational level and escalates up to the chief executive. If the dispute still cannot be resolved, mediation or arbitration should be provided for.

Another term you could think about is to require the supplier to have insurance cover to a specified level.

> **Key commercial issues in contracts**
>
> - goods/services – a description of what is to be provided
> - obligations – what other things is each party required to do
> - price – what it is and how is it to be paid
> - confidentiality – the contract should protect your information
> - intellectual property – set out who owns the intellectual property developed as part of the contract
> - warranties – these cover the things you relied on the supplier for
> - liability – set out the extent of the supplier's liability for breaches of the contract
> - indemnity – the supplier should indemnify you against breach of a third party's intellectual property rights
> - termination rights – the events that give a right to terminate the contract
> - dispute resolution – to provide a mechanism for disputes that cannot be settled amicably between the parties.

General damages

When a party breaches a contract, and the parties cannot come to an amicable arrangement, the injured party is usually left to seek redress itself. It is up to the injured party to prove its case and recover losses.

Liquidated damages

One way you can make this process easier is to have your contract provide for damages, credits, or rebates where the provider does not deliver on time, or deliver as required. However, if you are to enforce these clauses, the amount must be a genuine pre-estimate of the loss suffered. If it is not a genuine pre-estimate of the loss suffered for a breach, courts are likely to hold that it is a penalty and unenforceable.

Implied terms

Implied terms are not expressed in a contract, but are implied into a contract by law, in certain circumstances, to make the contract work effectively. An implied term must:

- be reasonable and equitable
- be necessary to make the contract work effectively
- be so obvious it 'goes without saying'
- be capable of being expressed clearly
- not contradict any of the contract's express terms.

Implied terms may also occur when there is an established custom in a certain industry or trade where the particular custom is so well known that anyone in the industry or trade would or should have known of the term.

The lesson (with implied terms of custom): if you do not want a specific term implied in the contract, specifically exclude it. You should note that some statutory implied terms cannot be excluded.

Third parties and subcontractors

Generally, only you and the other party to a contract can enforce it. This is called privity of contract. However, if you are a third party who obtains a benefit from a contract without being a party to it, you can enforce the contract if the parties to the contract intend you to be able to do so. The Contracts (Privity) Act 1982 creates this exception.

Accordingly, it is important to consider whether you want any aspect of your contract to be enforceable by third parties. If you do, you need to make it clear what provisions are enforceable by what third party. If you do not want any third party to be able to enforce provisions of the contract, it is prudent to exclude the application of the Contracts (Privity) Act.

One thing to watch if you do want a promise to benefit a third party is that, generally, you cannot alter that promise without the third party's agreement.

The rule that a person who is not a party to a contract cannot enforce the contract has implications where subcontractors are used. This means that the buyer cannot sue the subcontractor for breach of contract (only the seller can – the buyer has to sue the seller when the subcontractor's breach has caused the seller to breach the main contract). Similarly, if the seller goes broke without paying its subcontractor, the buyer does not have to pay that subcontractor. Of course, commercial reality means that if the seller goes broke the buyer and subcontractor often get together to recast the arrangements to enable the buyer to get what it requires.

Assignment

As a party to a contract you can assign your rights – what you receive under the contract – to a third party. However, you can only assign your obligations – with the consent of the other party to the contract. If that consent is given a new contract is created between the remaining party and the new party.

Many commercial contracts include clauses that either ban assignment completely, or allow it only with the other party's consent. This is an important matter to consider. For instance, if you are a seller and the contract provides for regular payments which you want to sell to a bank (ie cash up now) you need to make sure the contract does not prohibit you from assigning your right to the payments to that third party bank.

Boiler-plate clauses

These standard clauses cover minor, but important matters, common in nearly all contracts. Without these the court may impose a different rule on the parties. Typical examples of boiler-plate clauses are:

- the governing law – to determine which country's laws apply when the parties are located in different countries
- waiver – to preserve the rights of each party against delay or neglect in seeking to enforce its rights
- severability – to preserve fully as much of the contract as is not invalid, illegal, or unenforceable under the law
- notices – to establish certainty in the method of serving notices and demands under the contract.

Post contractual matters

Ending the contract

A contract can end in a variety of situations. For instance, it ends when you and the other party both fulfil the terms set out in the contract.

Termination is the most obvious example of the contract ending prematurely. Termination is only possible if the contract allows it (and you follow the requirements of the contract to exercise that right) or you have the right to cancel the contract under the Contractual Remedies Act 1979. Cancellation under that Act can only occur if:

- you were induced to enter the contract by a misrepresentation, a term of the contract is broken or it is clear a term will be broken by the other party; and
- the parties agreed that the truth of the representation or term is essential to that other party or its effect is to have a substantially adverse impact on the benefit or burden of the contract from the perspective of the cancelling party.

A contract can also end with repudiation – this is when you cancel it following the other party's refusal to comply with their obligations.

Or a contract can end by agreement. For example, if your circumstances change, you may want out of the contract. The other party must agree if you are not to breach the contract. Typically, one party agrees to termination only for something in return, such as a payment of money.

Frustration

Frustration occurs when a catastrophic event occurs, for which neither you nor the other party to the contract is responsible. One party suffering hardship, loss, or inconvenience is not enough to frustrate a contract. A fundamental change in circumstances is required. Examples are a concert hall burning down or an event having to be cancelled. Such an event 'frustrates' the contract. The contract terminates, and all future obligations cease.

The Frustrated Contracts Act 1944 then provides ways of addressing problems about contract obligations already performed and money already paid. It seeks to put each party in an equitable position based on what benefits have been paid and received.

Frustration only deals with extreme circumstances. Accordingly, it is important for a contract to deal with what happens when any event which is outside the control of the party affected impacts on the performance of that party's obligations. This is typically know as a *force majeure* event, such as an earthquake or flood which prevents fulfilment of the contract. It is wise to define the precise force majeure events you envisage – otherwise they may extend to those which you could reasonably expect the other party to control, minimise, or prevent altogether.

Mistakes

The Contractual Mistakes Act 1977 governs circumstances in which a court can help you when you enter a contract on the basis of a mistake.

This is a specific sort of mistake. It occurs if you enter into a contract with another party influenced by:

- a material mistaken belief by that party, which mistake was know by the other party
- a mistaken belief you and that party shared
- different mistaken beliefs about the same matter held by you and the other party.

To get relief under the Act:

- the mistake must result in a substantially unequal exchange of value or the provision of disproportionate benefits between the parties; and

- the contract must not provide for the party who was influenced by the mistake to assume the risk of a mistake. This is an important matter to consider where a contract is to put the risk of mistakes on a party.

This Act offers no help when the mistake, or mistakes, were made in interpretation of the contract.

If relief is available under this Act, the Court has wide powers to make such orders as it considers just, including validating the contract, cancelling the contract, varying the contract or ordering the payment of compensation.

Statutory considerations

With any contract there are numerous statutory provisions which affect or impact on the contract. It is important to bear these in mind in relation to the contract.

Capacity to sign

You need to ensure that those who sign for both contract parties can do so legally. If one party is a company, does the signatory have the company's express/implied authority to sign? If a party is an individual, are they of full age and have capacity to sign?

Contracts generally cannot be enforced against people under the age of 18. Exceptions include those who are married, and where a District Court has given approval to that person to enter a contract. However, under the Minors' Contracts Act 1969 a court can, in its discretion, enforce a contract against a minor. Before doing so it must take into consideration whether the contract was fair and reasonable when it was made.

Illegal contracts

Is any part of the contract illegal? Illegal contracts cannot be enforced. There are two types of illegal contract – those that are illegal on public policy grounds (eg agreements to commit crimes or to defeat the course of justice) and those that are illegal because they breach a statute. The Illegal Contracts Act 1970 gives courts wide powers to help parties caught, such as validating the contract or ordering compensation be paid. However, before doing so the court has regard to a wide range of matters, including the public interest.

The Illegal Contracts Act also provides wide powers to the court where a contract clause unreasonably restrains trade (which is unenforceable at law). These powers allow a court to delete the restraint, modify the restraint to make it reasonable or, in extreme cases, even refuse to enforce the contract.

Consumer guarantees

The Consumer Guarantees Act 1993 creates a number of statutory guarantees that apply to the supply of goods or services to consumers. These statutory guarantees include matters such as:

- a guarantee of acceptable quality and that the consumer will get good title in relation to the supply of goods
- the use of reasonable care and skill and fitness for purpose in relation to the supply of services.

Suppliers cannot generally contract out of the Consumer Guarantees Act (eg by providing that one or more of the statutory guarantees do not apply to the contract). However, where the contract is for business purposes, the Act does allow the parties to exclude the statutory guarantees.

A protection for you as a supplier is the requirement that consumers who want to reject goods under the Consumer Guarantees Act must do so within a reasonable time.

For further details on the Consumer Guarantees Act *see* Chapter 7 *Marketing and Sales*. It explains when your company may contract out of the Act's coverage when the transaction is business-to-business.

Hire purchases

The Hire Purchase Act 1971 covers what are technically hire agreements with a right to purchase. It also covers conditional sales agreements. In these agreements, buyers pay for goods by instalment, taking possession but not ownership before the final purchase. Hire purchase covers retail agreements only.

This Act states that, amongst other things, hire purchase agreements must be in writing and must contain certain information (eg description of the goods, the amount and number of instalments, certain financial details, and a set statement as to advice for purchasers). A number of terms are implied into hire purchase agreements by this Act (eg that the vendor has the right to sell the goods and that they are of merchantable quality).

Under this Act the purchaser also has a number of statutory rights. These include being able to pay the unpaid balance at any time.

Typically a hire purchase agreement will also be a credit contract. This means that the provisions of the Credit Contracts Act 1981 (or the Credit Contracts and Consumer Finance Act 2003, as the case may be) and the Credit (Repossession) Act 1997 will also apply.

Layby sales

Layby, in which a seller sets a good aside while a buyer completes payment, creates risk for consumers. The Layby Sales Act 1971 attempts to redress this by altering the general contract rule that risk passes to the buyer when a sale is made.

Instead risk passes when the goods are delivered (and paid for by the buyer). In addition, the seller of a layby good worth up to $7,500 is obliged to refund the buyer if the goods are sold to someone else or otherwise become unavailable.

Under this Act the buyer can cancel the contract at any time. However, if you are the layby seller, you will benefit from the Act's conditions covering non-completion of purchase by the buyer. Provisions in the Act help you recoup your costs. The Layby Sales Act is covered in more detail in the *Marketing and Sales* chapter.

Fair trading

The Fair Trading Act 1986, amongst other things, prohibits misleading and deceptive conduct in trade, false and misleading representations in trade, and other unfair practices. It is also an offence to breach most of these provisions.

Where a breach arises, the courts have wide powers to declare contracts or clauses in them invalid, order compensation, or vary the contract.

Sale of goods

While the Consumer Guarantees Act governs sales from retailer to consumer, the Sale of Goods Act 1908 governs sales of goods as well. However, where the Consumer Guarantees Act applies, its warranties apply instead of those in the Sale of Goods Act.

Provisions in the Sale of Goods Act govern:

- formation of a contract of sale
- effect of the contract
- performance of the contract
- rights to the goods of an unpaid seller
- remedies available to the seller and buyer if the contract is breached.

Under this Act the following points need to be kept in mind:

- where the goods perish before risk in them transfers to the buyer (see below on when this is), the contract can be avoided by the buyer
- if the price (or a mechanism for determining the price) is not set out in the contract, the buyer is only required to pay a reasonable price
- unless negated, there are implied warranties that the seller has the right to sell the goods and they are free from all encumbrances
- there are implied warranties that the goods will correspond with their description, will be fit for any purpose made known to the seller and, where the goods are bought by description from a dealer of those goods, a warranty of merchantable quality is implied.

This Act also regulates when title and risk in the goods passes. Title passes when the parties intend it to pass and there are detailed rules to work this out. Generally the rules mean title passes when the contract is made, unless the parties agree to some other time. Risk in the goods passes when title passes, also unless otherwise

COMPLIANCE AND YOUR BUSINESS

agreed by the parties. Accordingly, it is important for your contract to make it clear when both title and risk pass where the default rules are not appropriate to the arrangement.

This Act also regulates what matters as to delivery and sets out what is required for acceptance of goods. Delivery itself is to be determined by the contract, but if the wrong quantity is delivered the buyer can reject it all, reject the excess, or pay for what is delivered at the contract rate. Acceptance occurs once the buyer indicates acceptance or a reasonable time has passed after delivery.

Where you, as the seller, are not paid for the goods, this Act grants you certain rights. Essentially these rights allow the seller to retain the goods and resell them (after notice to the buyer and the price is not paid) in order to recover the price.

This Act also regulates the buyer's and seller's remedies. If the price is unpaid, the seller can enforce payment. If the claim is for losses suffered, the amount recoverable is determined by reference to that loss directly and naturally resulting, in the ordinary course of events, from the breach.

Under the Act, rights, duties, or liabilities that arise by implication of law may be negated or varied by express agreement between the parties. In this regard, the parties can make sure the contract sets out all applicable terms. Accordingly, it is important to make sure that you understand the contract and are not giving up rights without getting something in return.

If your business involves off-shore sales bear in mind that the Sales of Goods (United Nations Convention) Act 1994 applies. Generally it applies rules similar to those applying to domestic contracts, but not always. It can be contracted out of if the parties agree. Often agreeing that it does not apply is the better approach so that all applicable terms are contained in the contract.

Your rights under the Sale of Goods Act 1908

Haven't been paid for your goods? In certain situations you can:
- take a 'lien' on the goods – that is, retain possession of someone's goods pending payment
- sue for the price of unpaid goods (where title has passed to the buyer)
- sue for damages if a buyer wrongfully refuses to accept goods
- stop goods in transit to an insolvent buyer
- resell goods where notice of resale is given to the buyer (and the buyer does not pay the price within a reasonable time).

Haven't received the goods? If you are a buyer, in certain circumstances, you can:
- sue for damages for non-delivery of goods
- compel a seller to complete the sale – perform the sales contract.

CONTRACTS

The PPSA

If your business provides credit for someone to buy personal property and you take a security interest in that personal property, the Personal Property Securities Act 1999 (the PPSA) applies to the contract. An example is where your business lends a buyer money to buy a boat (which is less than 24 metres registered length) using the boat at collateral for the loan. In return, the buyer undertakes to repay the loan over a specific period at a particular interest rate. Your business then has a security interest in the boat until the buyer pays it off. In such a situation, provided you register your security interest in the boat on the Personal Property Securities Register ('PPSR') and you have a security agreement with the buyer you should have priority over any other creditor that may subsequently take a security interest in the boat.

Exceptions to PPSA title

Under the PPSA, the person who buys a good, say a boat, from the person you sold it to does not get clear title if you still have a security interest in the boat registered on the PPSR.

But note three important exceptions to this rule for goods, where buyers get the goods free of the security interest:

- motor-vehicles – if you as a consumer buy a car from a registered trader and the registered trader does not disclose the security interest to you under the Motor Vehicle Sales Act 2003 (or if that Act does not apply, in writing) before you buy
- trade purchases – if you buy the goods from a seller in the ordinary course of their business and do not know that the sale breaches a security interest
- consumer goods – if you buy consumer goods (as defined) valued at less than $2,000 and do not know of the security interest.

The PPSA applies to 'security interests' in personal property. A 'security interest' generally secures the payment of money as in the case of the boat discussed above.

As a seller, you register security interests in the PPSR. The PPSR is the online register that holds the details of New Zealand security interests in personal property. It contains information about the debtor (the person who owes the money), the secured party (your firm, if it lent the money), a description of the personal property, which the PPSR calls the collateral, and a description of the security interest created. Run by the Ministry of Economic Development, the register can be accessed at *www.ppsr.govt.nz*.

If you fail to register a security interest when you sell goods on credit you will slip down the queue to sit with other unsecured creditors if the buyer goes into bankruptcy or liquidation. A PPSA-registered security interest takes priority over an unregistered one. And if an unregistered good is sold on, you may lose priority to a subsequent buyer, or that buyer's creditors.

Non-compliance with the PPSA can negate the Sale of Goods Act provision that allows you to insert a Romalpa clause into a sales contract. A Romalpa clause, named for the company in the legal case in which the principle was established, tries to allow you as a trader to retain title to goods until the purchase price has been paid. Thus, if you want to retain title after delivery but until payment, make sure you comply with the PPSA.

Watch these Acts

Other Acts you cannot contract out of include:

- The Credit (Repossession) Act 1997 which sets rules for repossession of consumer goods.
- The Door to Door Sales Act 1967 which regulates contracts related to the sale and hire of goods and the provision of service at places other than the trader's normal place of business. This Act requires contracts to be in writing and contain the particulars prescribed by the Act. The buyer also has the right to cancel the contract within 7 days.
- The Credit Contracts Act 1981 which gives the court power to 're-open' oppressive credit contracts (to be repealed from 1 April 2005 by the Credit Contracts and Consumer Finance Act 2003, which contains a similar, but revamped regime).
- The Sale of Liquor Act 1989 which makes it illegal to sell liquor to persons under the age of 18, to sell liquor on certain days (Good Friday, Easter Sunday, Christmas Day, and before 1pm on Anzac Day, except in certain limited cases), and requires anyone wanting to sell liquor to have a licence to do so.
- Tobacco legislation.

Electronic contracts

Electronic rather than written

We have earlier emphasised the wisdom of putting contracts on paper rather than relying on oral arrangements. However, there is another possibility, the electronic contract.

The Electronic Transactions Act 2002 which recently came into force confirms the legal status of electronic messages and contracts – they are as valid as they would be if on paper.

The Act does not apply to the myriad of day-to-day contracts that don't have to be in writing or signed, such as buying or selling inventory. In this case its up to the parties to decide on the form of the contract. Of course the validity of the contract will still depend on the usual rules of contract, most of which have been outlined earlier in this chapter.

Where this Act will be useful is where legislation currently requires the contract to be in writing (eg guarantees and hire purchase agreements). What it provides is that legislation which requires a written contract can be satisfied by an electronic contract if:

- the parties consent (including by conduct) to using an electronic contract; and
- the information (ie content of the contract) is readily accessible so as to be usable for subsequent reference.

Electronic signatures

If a statute requires a signature on a contract (eg a guarantee), this Act provides a mechanism to use an electronic signature instead, provided that the parties consent. To do so, the electronic signature must:

- adequately identify the signatory and adequately indicate the signatory's approval of the information to which the signature relates; and
- be as reliable as is appropriate given the purpose for which, and the circumstances in which, the signature is required.

At its simplest level an electronic signature could be a scanned-in image of a written signature. However, this is fairly insecure and may not meet the reliability test. The Act goes on to outline the circumstances in which reliability is presumed. These are where:

- the means of creating the electronic signature is linked to, and under the control of, the signatory and no other person
- any alteration to the electronic signature made after the time of signing is detectable
- where the purpose of the legal requirement for a signature is to provide assurance as to the integrity of the information to which it relates, any alteration made to that information after the time of signing is detectable.

While this is not the only way to satisfy the reliability test (and of course the presumption can be rebutted by other evidence), it provides a bias towards using digital signatures so that the presumption is met.

Of course there are some exceptions to application of the writing and signature provisions of this Act (ie where it cannot be used), eg wills and documents that need a high level of authenticity.

COMPLIANCE AND YOUR BUSINESS

> ### Risks and what to do about them
>
> Risks from the evolving nature of ecommerce law can be reduced by thinking about all the practical issues of doing business online and designing a strategy for dealing with them before you start.
>
> In considering those practical issues, bear in mind the following key points for website contracts:
>
> - Specify your contract process. A website should spell out that it is making an advertisement (in technical terms, an invitation to treat), not making an offer to the world.
> - Make it clear who the website applies to and what the governing law is.
> - Spell out that the customer is making the offer, which the seller is free to accept or reject. Otherwise, the site owner may end up contracting to supply quantities well beyond ability to supply or it may be contracted to supply to countries where it is illegal for the seller to do so.
> - As an extra precaution, state on the site that the online contract will be binding if and when the seller accepts the buyer's offer.
> - Set out all the terms of the contract and require the buyer to accept them before making the offer.

Other considerations for electronic commerce

In most respects, doing business electronically is no different to doing business in a paper-based environment. All the same considerations must be taken into account. The most important analysis is the practical implications of those considerations from an electronic perspective. For instance, if your business allows sales over the internet, consider the audience. If it is just New Zealand you need to make it clear that sales are only to New Zealanders.

One aspect of electronic commerce does, however, require special mention. That is the timing of notices or messages, where your contract allows these to be done electronically. The Electronic Transactions Act defines time of dispatch as the moment when the electronic message first enters an information system outside the control of the originator – when it leaves your stand-alone computer, or the mail server that links your network to the Internet.

The time of receipt, for a recipient with a designated information system for receiving electronic communications, is when the communication enters that system. Otherwise, the time of receipt is when the communication comes to the attention of the recipient. Determining the time of receipt can be particularly important if the contract provides particular timeframes for sending notices.

Designating an information system can be done by just stating that replies are to be sent to a particular email address. Accordingly, it is important to be very careful in designating an information system. For instance, what if the recipient was away or your information system is operated by a third party? Receipt could happen without your knowledge.

You can also contract out of this provision in the Act. Again, this may be sensible, so when entering into a contract set out your own rules to permit electronic notices or messages and when they are to be considered received.

INDEX

A

abandonment of employment, 59
abatement notices, 216
ACC, 112
access by unions, 26-27
accident compensation
    claims process, 116
    earner levy, 172-173
    employer claims reports, 117
    employer levies, 114-115, 171-172
    rehabilitation, 116-117
    self-employed people, 115, 173
    tax deductible levies, 174
    weekly compensation, 116
accidents
    duties if someone seriously harmed, 84
    first aid, 81-83
    notification of OSH, 84, 85-87
    procedure where no serious harm, 88
    register, 83-84
    who must record and report accidents, 88
advertising
    Advertising Standards Codes, 239
    Direct Marketing Association, 241
    Fair Trading Act
        claims about products or services, 234-237
        comparative advertising, 237-238
        free credit, 238-239
        free delivery, 239
        free gifts, 238
        puffery, 238
        small print and long words, 238
advertising for staff, 3
agricultural workers, 110
alcohol policy, 25-26
"all practicable steps", definition of, 70-71
allowances and PAYE, 166
annual leave, 31-33
anti-competitive behaviour, 248-251
Antiquities Act 1975, 227
appeals against resource consent decisions, 214
apprentice employees, 12
archaeological sites, 226-227
armed forces volunteers, leave entitlements, 40-41
arrest warrants, 136
artefacts, discovery of, 227
asbestos regulations, 108
assignment
    contracts, 287
    lease, 190
auditor, appointment of, 274-275
audits, tax, 182

B

bargaining
    break down of, 17-18
unfair bargaining, 16-17
bereavement leave, 34-36
board of directors see companies
boiler-plate clauses, 287
brand protection see intellectual property
building work
    BIA rulings re compliance with code, 186
    Building Act 1991
        proposed law changes, 184, 185
        summary of requirements, 184
    building approval, 185-186
    building consent, 185-186
    code compliance certificate, 186
    fixing illegal work, 186
    project information memorandum, 185
buildings
    energy efficiency, 189
    fire safety, 188, 189
    occupier's liability, 188
    warrants of fitness, 187
    workplace obligations, 187-189
buying commercial property see property

C

casual employees
    holiday pay, 31
    nature of employment relationship, 10, 13
child support deductions
    employers' responsibilities, 174-175
    filing requirements, 169, 170
    wage records, 164
clothing, labelling of, 233
collective agreements *see also* **employment agreements**
    mandatory requirements, 15-16, 19
    unfair bargaining, 17
Commerce Act 1986, 248-251
Commerce Commission, 233, 250
commercial property *see* **property**
companies
    annual report, 268
    approval of major transactions, 261
    balance date, 268
    Board committees, 266
    board of directors, 262
    board quorum, 262
    calculation of income tax, 154
    CEO's terms of engagement, 263

299

COMPLIANCE AND YOUR BUSINESS

confidential information, 265
constitution, 261
defined, 145
delegation of board power, 262
directors
    disclosure of interests, 264-265
    good faith, 263
    remuneration, 262
    standard of care, 263-264
    withholding taxes, 170-171
directors' meetings, 265-266
exempt companies, 275
financial statements, 267-268
generally accepted accounting practice, 268
indemnification of directors and employees, 263
reckless trading, 263
record-keeping, 266-267
registration under Acts other than Companies Act, 266
share issues and dividends, 268-269
shareholders' meetings *see* **shareholders' meetings**
shareholders' rights *see* **shareholders**
solvency test, 275

comparative advertising, 237-238
compensation for hurt and humiliation, 58
complaints
    consumer complaints, 245-246
    privacy, 124
compliance orders
    HSE Act, 103
    HSNO Act, 222
confidential information
    company information, 265
    disclosure by police, 136
    legal privilege, 138-139
conflicts of interest, policy on, 25
constructive dismissal, 57-58
Consumer Affairs, Ministry of, 243
Consumer Guarantees Act 1993
    complaints, 245-246
    contracts and, 290
    obligations under, 244-245
    refunds, 246-247
contamination of site, evidence of, 201
contractors
    duties under HSE Act, 98-99
    nature of employment relationship, 13-14
    withholding taxes, 170-171
contracts
    assignment, 287
    boiler-plate clauses, 287
    cancellation, 287

capacity to sign, 289
consideration, 280
Consumer Guarantees Act, 290
contents of, 283-285
Credit Contracts Act, 290
Credit Contracts Act 1981, 294
Credit (Repossession) Act 1997, 294
Door to Door Sales Act 1967, 294
electronic contracts, 294-297
ending the contract, 287-288
exchange of letters, 282
Fair Trading Act, 291
frustration, 288
general damages, 285
groundwork to negotiations, 281
Hire Purchase Act, 290
illegal contracts, 289
implied terms, 286
key commercial issues, 285
key elements, 280
Layby Sales Act, 290-291
letters of intent, 282-283
liquidated damages, 285
mistakes, 288-289
Personal Property Securities Act, 293-294
repudiation, 288
requirement for writing, 282
Sale of Goods Act, 291-292
Sale of Liquor Act 1989, 294
subcontractors, 286
tendering, 281-282
third parties, enforcement by, 286

Contracts (Privity) Act 1982, 286
Contractual Mistakes Act 1977, 288-289
Contractual Remedies Act 1979
    cancellation under, 287
    property sales and, 199
copyright, 252
corporate governance *see also* **companies; shareholders' meetings**
    key legislation, 260
    principles, 276-277
council officers, powers of entry and inquiry, 137-138
counterfeit goods, 255-256
Credit Contracts Act 1981, 290, 294
Credit (Repossession) Act 1997, 294
criminal investigations, 59
cross-leasing, 196-197
customer databases, privacy and, 251
Customs, lodging protection notices with, 256
cybersquatting, 255

INDEX

D

damages, 285
dangerous goods, 221
dangerous work
   regulations, 109-110
   right to refuse, 97
deductions from wages see wages
defence force volunteers, leave entitlements, 40-41
Direct Marketing Association, 241
directors see **companies**
discipline and dismissal process see also
personal grievances
   abandonment of employment, 59
   compensation for hurt and humiliation, 58
   constructive dismissal, 57-58
   expectations of Authority and Court, 41-42
   failure to perform, 43-48
   final pay, 61
   justified dismissal, 42
   misconduct, 48-53
   misconduct/serious misconduct distinction, 55-56
   notice periods, 61
   police investigations, 59
   problems leading to dismissal, 43
   serious misconduct, 53-55
   sick employee, 59-60
   suspension, 56-57
   warnings, 47-48
disclosure
   directors' interests, 264-265
   Government departments and agencies, requirements of, 137
   police disclosure of confidential information, 136
   protected disclosures, 130-134
discrimination
   grounds for raising personal grievance, 42
   hiring staff, 3-7
   prohibited grounds, 3
dismissal see also **discipline and dismissal process**
   abandonment of employment, 59
   failure to perform, 47-48
   misconduct, 52
   misrepresentation by employee, 8-9
   serious misconduct, 53-55
   sick employee, 59-60
dispute resolution procedures, explanation of, in employment agreement, 21
Disputes Tribunal, 248
district plans, 207
domain names, cybersquatting and, 255
Door to Door Sales Act 1967, 241, 294

drug testing policy, 25-26
duress, 42
duty free goods, zero-rating of, 158

E

electronic contracts, 294-297
email use
   monitoring, 128
   policy, 25
emergencies, plans and procedures for, 81
employee participation systems, 91-95
employees
   duties under HSE Act, 96-97
   earner levy, 172-173
   types of employment relationship, 9-13, 14
employers
   accident compensation obligations see **accident compensation**
   accidents register, 88
   duties under Health and Safety Regulations, 108-109
   duties under HSE see **Health and Safety in Employment Act 1992**
   tax responsibilities see **tax**
employment agreements
   alcohol and drug testing policy, 25-26
   conflicts of interest, policy on, 25
   explanation of dispute resolution procedures, 21
   internet and email policy, 25
   key points to cover, 19-22
   mandatory requirements
      collective agreements, 15-16, 19
      individual employment agreements, 14-15, 19
   optional clauses, 22-24
   preparation tips, 18-19
   purpose, 14
   restraint of trade clauses, 24
   unfair bargaining, 16-17
Employment Court
   expectations in dismissal process, 41-42
   jurisdiction, 66
   procedure, 66
employment law obligations
   discipline and dismissal see **discipline and dismissal process**
   employment agreements see **employment agreements**
   hiring staff see **hiring staff**
   leave entitlements see **leave**
   main obligations, 2
   reasons for compliance, 1-2
   redundancy, 61-62

COMPLIANCE AND YOUR BUSINESS

retirement, 63
sale of business, 63
union rights, 26-27
wages *see* **wages**
Employment Relations Act 2000, guide to, 9-11
Employment Relations Authority
compliance orders, 103
expectations in dismissal process, 41-42
procedure, 65
role of, 65
employment relations education leave, 40
Employment Relations Service, 63-65
energy efficiency of buildings, 189
enforcement order under RMA, 216
entry powers, 136-138
environment
Antiquities Act, 227
historic heritage, 224-227
HSNO Act *see* **Hazardous Substances and New Organisms Act 1996**
key legislation, 204
ozone layer protection, 223-224
risk management, 228-229
RMA *see* **Resource Management Act 1991**
exchange of letters, 282
exempt companies, 275
exported goods, zero-rating of, 158

F

failure to perform, 43-48
Fair Trading Act 1986
advertising *see* **advertising**
Commerce Commission, role of, 233
contracts and, 291
fake goods, 256
guide to, 232-233
harassment and coercion, 241-242
labelling of clothing, 233
product safety standards, 233
property sales and, 199
therapeutic products, 233-234
faulty goods, 245-247
final pay where dismissal, 61
fire safety obligations, 188, 189
first aid, 81-83
fixed-term employees, 11
fringe benefit tax (FBT)
accounting for and payment, 178-179
calculation of, 177-178
defined, 177
filing requirements, 170
record-keeping, 178

frustration of contract, 288

G

general damages, 285
Government departments and agencies, disclosure requirements of, 137
GST (goods and services tax)
accounting for, 159-160
defined, 157
exempt activities and supplies, 158
exports and imports, 158
filing returns, 161
payments, 162
prices to include, 241
registration, 157
return dates, 161
tax invoices, 158-159
taxable periods, 160

H

hazard management
dealing with significant hazards, 75-76
employers' responsibilities, 69
hazard, definition of, 71
hazard identification form, 77
identification of hazards, 73-75
monitoring exposure to hazards, 77
OOS, 88-90
protective clothing, 77
stress, 90-91
hazard notices, 102
Hazardous Substances and New Organisms Act 1996
advice agencies, 222
enforcement, 221-222
hazardous substances
application for approval, 218
control regime, 218-219
dangerous goods, 221
defined, 217-218
employers' responsibilities, 108, 219-220
pesticides, 220-221
toxic substances, 220
transition arrangements, 220-221
new organisms
application for approval, 218
defined, 218
offences, 222
penalties, 216
purpose, 217
strict liability, 222
test certificates, 222
health and safety *see also* **Hazardous Substances and**

New Organisms Act 1996; Health and Safety in Employment Act 1992; Health and Safety in Employment Regulations
    accident compensation *see* **accident compensation**
    advice agencies, 112
    asbestos regulations, 108
    checklist, 112-114
    key legislation, 67

Health and Safety in Employment Act 1992
    accidents *see* **accidents**
    administration of, 101-106
    duties under
        contractors, 98-99
        employee's duties, 96-97
        employers, 69-70
        people selling or supplying plant, 100-101
        people who control a workplace, 99-100
        principals, 97-98
        self-employed people, 99
    emergencies, plans and procedures for, 81
    employee participation systems, 91-95
    enforcement
        compliance orders, 103
        hazard notices, 102
        improvement notices, 102
        infringement notices, 103
        insurance against fines, 106
        prohibition notices, 102
        prosecutions, 103-104
    first aid, 81-83
    hazard management *see* **hazard management**
    health and safety inspectors, 101
    health and safety representatives, 94
    informing and training employees, 69-70, 78-80
    key terms
        all practicable steps, 70-71
        hazard, 71
        serious harm, 72
    offences and penalties, 104-105
    OOS, 88-90
    people on work experience/on-the-job training, 96
    reasons for compliance with, 68
    right to refuse to do dangerous work, 97
    smoking in workplace, 106-107
    social events, 107
    stress, 90-91
    volunteers, protection of, 95-96
    where the Act applies, 68-69
    who the Act applies to, 68

Health and Safety in Employment Regulations
    agricultural workers, 110
    designers of plant, 111
    designers of protective clothing, 111
    employers' duties, 108-109
    manufacturers and suppliers of plant, 111
    noise, 109
    other specific hazards, 109-110
    overcrowding, 109
    penalties, 111
    young people, 110

health and safety inspectors
    powers of entry, 137
    role of, 101

health and safety representatives, 94

hearing of resource consent applications, 213

Hire Purchase Act 1971, 290

hiring staff
    advertising, 3
    apprentice employees, 12
    casual employees, 10
    fixed-term employees, 11
    job offers, 8
    key legislation, 2
    misrepresentation by employee, 8-9
    part-time work, 14
    privacy
        collection and use of personal information, 7
        reference checks, 127-128
    probationary periods, 12
    questioning candidates, 3-6
    seasonal employees, 12
    types of employment relationship, 9-14

historic heritage, 224-227

Historic Places Trust, 225-226

holiday entitlements
    annual leave, 31-33
    recent law changes, 35-36
    statutory holidays, 33-34

holiday pay, 31-33

Human Rights Act 1993
    guide to, 4-6
    hiring staff and, 3-7

hurt and humiliation, compensation for, 58

I

illegal contracts, 289

imported goods, GST levies on, 158

improvement notices, 102

imputation credits, 155

income tax
    calculation of, 153-154
    expenses, deductibility of, 152
    filing tax returns, 152-153
    imputation credits, 155

income, definition of, 151
payments, 155
provisional tax, 156-157
tax credits, 154-155
tax rates, 153
independent contractors see contractors
individual employment agreements
alcohol and drug testing policy, 25-26
conflicts of interest, policy on, 25
explanation of dispute resolution procedures, 21
internet and email policy, 25
key points to cover, 19-22
mandatory requirements, 14-15, 19
optional clauses, 22-24
preparation tips, 18
restraint of trade clauses, 24
unfair bargaining, 16-17
inertia selling, 241
INFOexpress, 147
information
legal privilege, 138-139
privacy see **privacy**
protected disclosures, 130-134
informing employees, for HSE Act compliance, 69-70, 78-80
infringement notices
HSE Act, 103
HSNO Act, 222
RMA, 215
Inland Revenue Department, 146-147
insurance against fines under HSE Act, 106
intellectual property
brand protection, 251, 257
copyright, 252
cybersquatting, 255
fakes, forgeries, counterfeits and piracy, 255-256
parallel importing, 255
patents, 252-253
protection of ideas, 252
trade marks, 253-255
interest on under- or over-payments of tax, 180-181
internet
cybersquatting, 255
monitoring use, 128
policy, 25
interviewing job applicants, 3-7
IRD numbers, 146
iwi consultation, 212

J
job advertisements, 3
job application forms, 3-7
job offers, 8
jury leave, 41

L
labelling of clothing, 233
Layby Sales Act 1971, 290-291
leasing
assignment of lease, 190
body corporate rules, 192
checklist, 191-192
contracts, 189
director guarantees, 190
outgoings and maintenance obligations, 191
rent, 190-191
rights of use, 192
signage, 193
sinking fund, 192
sub-letting, 190
leave
annual leave, 31-33
defence force volunteers, 40-41
employment relations education leave, 40
jury leave, 41
no contracting out, 30
parental leave, 36-40
recent law changes, 35-36
public holidays, 33-34
special leave, 34-35
voting leave, 41
legal privilege, 138-139
letters of intent, 282-283
lien, 292
liquidated damages, 285
lockouts, 17-18
lump sum payments and PAYE, 167

M
Maritime Safety Authority, 112
market research, privacy and, 125
marketing see **also intellectual property**
advertising see **advertising**
customer databases, privacy and, 251
key legislation, 232
mediation, 63-65
minimum wages, 30
Ministry of Consumer Affairs, 243
misconduct
discipline and dismissal process, 48-53
serious misconduct, comparison with, 55-56

misrepresentation by employee, 8-9
mistakes, contractual, 288-289
motor vehicles, calculation of FBT on, 178

N

national policy statement, 207
new employees, collective agreements and, 16
new organisms, 218
New Zealand Bill of Rights Act 1990, 136
New Zealand Coastal Policy Statement, 207
noise, 109
non-resident withholding tax (NRWT), 163
notice periods for dismissal, 61

O

occupational overuse syndrome (OOS), 88-90
Occupier's Liability Act, 187, 188
offences
    health and safety, 104-105
    HSNO Act, 216, 222
    tax, 181
OSH (Occupational Safety and Health Service)
    administration of HSE Act, 101
    health and safety inspectors
    powers of entry, 137
    role of, 101
    reporting of accidents, 84, 85-87
overcrowding, 109
Overseas Investment Commission, approval by, 197-198
Ozone Layer Protection Act 1996, 223-224

P

parallel importing, 255
parental leave, 36-40
partnership
    calculation of income tax, 153
    defined, 145
part-time work, 14
patents, 252-253
pay slips, 28-29
PAYE
    accounting for and payment, 168
    allowances and, 166
    calculation of, 166-167
    defined, 165
    employer deduction forms, 169
    employer monthly schedule, 168
    filing requirements, 169, 170
    lump sum payments and, 167
    tax codes, 166
penalties
    health and safety, 104-105, 111

HSNO Act, 216
    tax, 179-180
people controlling a workplace, duties under HSE Act, 99-100
personal grievances *see also* discipline and dismissal process
    grounds for raising, 42
    remedies, 43
personal injury compensation *see* accident compensation
Personal Property Securities Act 1999, 293-294
pesticides, 220-221
phone calls, taping of, 126-127
pirated goods, 255-256
plant, duties of sellers, manufacturers, or suppliers of, 100-101, 111
police
    investigations, 59
    powers of entry and inquiry, 136
poor performance, 43-48
port companies, 266
powers of entry and inquiry, 136-138
price fixing, 249, 250
principals
    accidents register, 88
    duties under HSE Act, 97-98
privacy
    appointing a privacy officer, 121-122
    complaints, 124
    customer databases, 251
    dealing with personal information, 120-121
    emails and internet, 128
    hiring staff
        collection and use of personal information, 7
        reference checks, 127-128
    market research and, 125
    Privacy Act 1993
        checklist for compliance, 130
        scope, 120
        who the Act applies to, 120
    requests to see personal information, 122-124
    security cameras, 126
    taping of phone calls, 126-127
    tax and, 148
    unique identifiers, 121
Privacy Commissioner, 129
probationary periods, 12
product safety standards, 233
pro-forma invoicing, 242
prohibition notices, 102
project information memorandum (PIM), 185
property

building work *see* **building work**
buying a company with existing properties
    due diligence checklist, 202
    site contamination, 201
    title information, 200
    transfer of consents, 200
buying and selling
    buyer beware, 199
    forms of title, 196-197
    Overseas Investment Commission approval, 197-198
    title searches, 194-195
    Treaty of Waitangi claims, 197
    zoning and property use, 195-196
leasing, 189-193
liability of building owners *see* **buildings**
prosecutions under HSE Act, 103-104
Protected Disclosures Act 2000, 130-134
protection notices, 256
protective clothing
    duties of designers of, 111
    hazard management, 77
provisional tax, 156-157
public holidays, 33-34
pyramid selling, 242, 243

R

racial harassment, 42
reckless trading, 263
recording of phone calls, 126-127
record-keeping
    checklist for wage records, 164
    companies, 266-267
    FBT, 178
    tax records, 148-151
recovery of overpaid wages, 28
recovery of wages by employee, 28-30
recruitment *see* hiring staff
redundancy, 61-62
referral selling, 242
refunds, 246-247
regional plans, 207
regional policy statements, 207
register of accidents *see* **accidents**
repudiation of contract, 288
request for information (RFI), 281-282
resale price maintenance, 249
resident withholding tax (RWT), 163
Resource Management Act 1991
    advice, 210
    consultation, 210-212

enforcement
    abatement notice, 216
    enforcement order, 216
    infringement notice, 215
historic heritage, 224
iwi consultation, 212
obligations, 205
overview, 206
powers of entry, 138
regional and district plans, 207
resource consents
    appeals against decisions, 214
    application for, 208-210
    assessment of environmental effects, 209-210
    breaching conditions, 215-216
    compliance with, 214, 215
    lodging applications, 212-213
    public hearings, 213
    renewal, 215
    transfer of, 200
    when required, 204-205, 207-208
types of activities, 204-205
restraint of trade clauses, 24
restrictive trade practices, 248
retirement, 63

S

sale of business, 63
Sale of Goods Act 1908, 247, 291-292
Sale of Liquor Act 1989, 294
sales
    Consumer Guarantees Act
        complaints, 245-246
        obligations under, 244-245
        refunds, 246-247
    customer databases, privacy and, 251
    disclosure of cost, 241
    Disputes Tribunal, 248
    inclusion of GST, 241
    inertia selling, 241
    pro-forma invoicing, 242
    pyramid selling, 242, 243
    referral selling, 242
    responsibility for staff, 241
    Sale of Goods Act, 247
    standing behind products or services, 244
search warrants, 136
seasonal employees, 12
security cameras, 126
security interests, 293-294
self-employed people

INDEX

accident compensation, 115, 173
accidents register, 88
duties under HSE Act, 99
student loan repayment, 176
selling commercial property *see* **property**
serious harm, definition of, 72
serious misconduct
    discipline and dismissal process, 53-55
    misconduct, comparison with, 55-56
sexual harassment, 42
shareholders
    meetings *see* **shareholders' meetings**
    minority rights, 269
    resolutions in writing, 270
    rights, 260-261
    written agreements authorising certain acts, 270
shareholders' meetings
    appointment of auditor, 274-275
    chairperson, 273-274
    minutes, 274
    notice requirements, 271
    obligation to hold, 269
    proxy votes, 272
    quorum, 272
    raising matters, 273
    special meetings, 271
    special resolutions, 273
    voting rights, 272
    voting rules, 272-273
sick employee, dismissal of, 59-60
sick leave, 34-36
sickness during annual leave, 32
site contamination, evidence of, 201
smoking in workplace, 106-107
social events, employers' obligations re, 107
sole trader
    calculation of income tax, 153
    defined, 145
specified superannuation contributions withholding tax (SSCWT)
    employers' responsibilities, 176
    filing requirements, 169, 170
    proposed law changes, 176
    wage records, 164
statutory holidays, 33-34
stress, 90-91
strikes
    lawfulness, 17-18
    suspension of workers, 18
student loan deductions
    employers' responsibilities, 175-176
    filing requirements, 169, 170
    self-employed people, 176
wage records, 164
subcontractors, breach of contract, 286
sub-letting, 190
suspension
    justification for, 56
    striking workers, 18

T

taping of phone calls, 126-127
tax
    audits, 182
    criminal offences, 181
    employers' responsibilities, 163-164
        ACC levies, 171-173, 174
        checklist for wage records, 164
        deductions, 174-176
        employee/self-employed distinction, 164
        employer deduction forms, 169
        employer monthly schedule, 168
        FBT, 177-179
        filing requirements, 169-170
        PAYE, 165-168
        summary of, 165
        withholding taxes, 170-171
    FBT *see* **fringe benefit tax (FBT)**
    GST *see* **GST (goods and services tax)**
    income tax *see* **income tax**
    Inland Revenue Department, 146-147
    interest, 180-181
    IRD numbers, 146
    key legislation, 145
    non-resident withholding tax, 163
    penalties
        avoiding, 143
        filing late returns, 179
        late payments, 180
        shortfall penalties, 180
    privacy and, 148
    professional help, 142
    proposed law changes, 151
    reasons for compliance, 143
    record-keeping, 148-151
    resident withholding tax, 163
    summary of obligations, 147
    tax agents, 143
    tax year, 146
    types, 143-144
    types of business, 145
    voluntary disclosures, 181
tax invoices, 158-159
tendering, 281-282

test certificates, 222
therapeutic products, 233-234
title, forms of, 196-197
title searches, 194-195
toxic substances, 220
trade marks, 253-255
training, for HSE Act compliance, 69-70, 78-80
Treaty of Waitangi claims, property purchase and, 197
Trespass Act 1980, 134-135
trusts
    calculation of income tax, 154
    defined, 145

U

unfair bargaining, 16-17
union involvement and duress, 42
union rights, 26-27
unit titles, 196
unjustifiable action disadvantaging employee, 42
unjustified dismissal, 42
unsolicited goods, 241

V

video surveillance, 126
volunteers
    health and safety, 95-96
    leave entitlements, 40-41
voting leave, 41

W

wages
    deductions
        child support payments, 174-175
        lawful deductions, 28
        payment to IRD, 174
        SSCWT, 176
        student loan repayments, 175-176
    how to pay, 27
    minimum wages, 30
    pay slips, 28-29
    PAYE *see* **PAYE**
    recovery of, 28-30
    recovery of overpayments, 28
    wage and time records, 29
    when to pay, 28
    who to pay, 27
warnings, 47-48
whistleblowing, 130-134
withholding taxes, 170-171
WorkPlace Cover levy, 114-115
workplace safety, participation in, 91-95
workplace stress, 90-91

Y

young people, duties in relation to, 110

Z

zoning and property use, 195-196